Let's learn Japanese together 1!

みんなで学ぼう日本語 1

Min'na de manaboo Nihongo 1
Basic Japanese 1

Shin`ichi Okamoto
Christian Flack

Easy Japanese Learning

Foreword

This book is the English translation of "Lass uns zusammen Japanisch lernen 1!".
After many years of teaching the Japanese language, we would like to offer you once again
the completely updated, revised and improved "Let's Learn Japanese Together 1" (Japanese
Basic Level 1) with various optional additions in its sixth new edition. The follow-up volume
"Let's learn Japanese together 2" (Japanese Basic Level 2) is also available to continue
learning Japanese.

This book is the first volume of two. The first volume here is aimed at beginners with no
previous knowledge of Japanese who want to acquire a basic knowledge of the language for
everyday use, while the second volume is intended for advanced beginners who want to
reach the intermediate level. Both volumes contain 15 lessons each, each consisting of an
introductory conversation text for reading and language practice, followed by questions on the
text, a vocabulary list, a kanji list (Chinese characters), a grammar section with explanations
and exercises and a final lesson test. In terms of scope, the textbook "Let's learn Japanese
together 1" corresponds to the volume that you should have mastered when taking the
Japanese Proficiency Test Level 5 of the "Japan Foundation" and is therefore ideally suited as
preparation.

To make it easier for beginners, a Roomaji version (Latin transcription) has been created up to
lesson 3 of this book instead of a Japanese text version. However, for good learning success,
it is important that you have a good command of the Japanese alphabets (hiragana, katakana,
46 characters each) and kanji (Chinese characters), because character practice is an
unavoidable part of learning Japanese and all texts from lesson 4 onwards are written in
Japanese characters only. With the help of this textbook, you can learn Japanese easily,
systematically and effectively. The grammar is explained simply and comprehensibly and
reinforced with exercises. In the appendix you will find all the answers to the questions on the
text, the exercises and the lesson test, a conjugation table of verbs, common idioms and the
Japanese-English and English-Japanese basic vocabulary list with approx. 1,000 words. This
can be useful as a learning aid.

When learning a new language, it is important to develop the four elements of speaking,
listening, reading, and writing together. To effectively promote these elements, we have
prepared a learning support program and two practice books for grammar and composition.
This learning support program (YouTube) includes various audio and video files related to
textbook text, vocabulary, kanji, and grammar questions, and is available free of charge. You
can find the link on the Manabi Language School website (www.sprachschule-manabi.de).
Please use this service in conjunction with this textbook.

Finally, as people who have been involved in teaching and learning Japanese for many years, we would like to encourage you to never give up when learning Japanese. Learning Japanese takes a lot of time and honest effort, but perseverance makes perfect!

June 2025   Shin'ichi Okamoto Christian Flack

Biographical information from the German National Library

The German National Library lists this publication in the German National Bibliography;

detailed bibliographic data is available on the Internet at http://dnb.d-nb.de.

Legal notice :

© 2025 Shin`ichi Okamoto, Christian Flack

Publisher: BoD · Books on Demand GmbH, Überseering 33,

22297 Hamburg, bod@bod.de

Print: Libri Plureos GmbH, Friedensallee 273, 22763 Hamburg

ISBN: 978-3-8192-0968-0

Contents

Shortcuts

1-st. V: one-step verb	IW: interrogative word	PS present tense
5-st. V: five-steps verb	Intr. V: Intransitive verb	PT: preterite tense
A: action	MC: main clause	PV: positive
AP: auxiliary particle	MF: masu form	S: subject
AV: adverb	N: noun	SC: sub clause
BF: basic form	NA: na-adjective	SCK: stroke count of Kanji
CF: colloquial form	NPF: nonpolite form	SoMF: stem of the masu form
e.g.: for example	NV: negative	Ta-F: ta-form
HF: honorific form	Nai-F: nai form	Te-F: te-form
IA: I-adjective	O: object	Tr. V: transitive verb
IV: irregular verb	P: predicate	V: verb

phonetic characters

ひらがなとカタカナ

Hiragana and Katakana

Syllable table: **Hiragana** (left) and **Katakana** (right) 104 Syllables

Basic sounds (46 syllables)

1	a	あ	ア	i	い	イ	u	う	ウ	e	え	エ	o	お	オ
2	ka	か	カ	ki	き	キ	ku	く	ク	ke	け	ケ	ko	こ	コ
3	sa	さ	サ	shi	し	シ	su	す	ス	se	せ	セ	so	そ	ソ
4	ta	た	タ	chi	ち	チ	tsu	つ	ツ	te	て	テ	to	と	ト
5	na	な	ナ	ni	に	ニ	nu	ぬ	ヌ	ne	ね	ネ	no	の	ノ
6	ha	は	ハ	hi	ひ	ヒ	fu	ふ	フ	he	へ	ヘ	ho	ほ	ホ
7	ma	ま	マ	mi	み	ミ	mu	む	ム	me	め	メ	mo	も	モ
8	ya	や	ヤ				yu	ゆ	ユ				yo	よ	ヨ
9	ra	ら	ラ	ri	り	リ	ru	る	ル	re	れ	レ	ro	ろ	ロ
10	wa	わ	ワ										(w)o	を	ヲ
11	n	ん	ン												

Voiced sounds (25 syllables)

12	ga	が	ガ	gi	ぎ	ギ	gu	ぐ	グ	ge	げ	ゲ	go	ご	ゴ
13	za	ざ	ザ	ji	じ	ジ	zu	ず	ズ	ze	ぜ	ゼ	zo	ぞ	ゾ
14	da	だ	ダ	ji	ぢ	ヂ	zu	づ	ヅ	de	で	デ	do	ど	ド
15	ba	ば	バ	bi	び	ビ	bu	ぶ	ブ	be	べ	ベ	bo	ぼ	ボ
16	pa	ぱ	パ	pi	ぴ	ピ	pu	ぷ	プ	pe	ぺ	ペ	po	ぽ	ポ

Palatalised sounds (33 syllables)

17	kya	きゃ	キャ	kyu	きゅ	キュ	kyo	きょ	キョ
18	gya	ぎゃ	ギャ	gyu	ぎゅ	ギュ	gyo	ぎょ	ギョ
19	sha	しゃ	シャ	shu	しゅ	シュ	sho	しょ	ショ
20	ja	じゃ	ジャ	ju	じゅ	ジュ	jo	じょ	ジョ
21	cha	ちゃ	チャ	chu	ちゅ	チュ	cho	ちょ	チョ
22	nya	にゃ	ニャ	nyu	にゅ	ニュ	nyo	にょ	ニョ
23	hya	ひゃ	ヒャ	hyu	ひゅ	ヒュ	hyo	ひょ	ヒョ
24	bya	びゃ	ビャ	byu	びゅ	ビュ	byo	びょ	ビョ
25	pya	ぴゃ	ピャ	pyu	ぴゅ	ピュ	pyo	ぴょ	ピョ
26	mya	みゃ	ミャ	myu	みゅ	ミュ	myo	みょ	ミョ
27	rya	りゃ	リャ	ryu	りゅ	リュ	ryo	りょ	リョ

Japanese sentences and texts are normally written using a mixture of hiragana, katakana and kanji (Chinese characters). Hiragana is used for auxiliary particles, adverbs, endings of verbs or adjectives and conjunctions etc. The katakana are used almost exclusively for foreign words and onomatopoeia. These two syllabic characters were derived from kanji in the Heian period (794-1192) in order to be able to write one's own language freely with hiragana or read Chinese terms easily with katakana. You can therefore initially write everything in hiragana and katakana.

Stroke order of the hiragana

あ	い	う	え	お
か	き	く	け	こ
さ	し	す	せ	そ
た	ち	つ	て	と
な	に	ぬ	ね	の
は	ひ	ふ	へ	ほ
ま	み	む	め	も
や		ゆ		よ
ら	り	る	れ	ろ
わ		を		ん

· き (ki) and さ (sa) are drawn in the other font "Gothic" き and さ. See p.10.

Stroke order of the Katakana

ア	イ	ウ	エ	オ
カ	キ	ク	ケ	コ
サ	シ	ス	セ	ソ
タ	チ	ツ	テ	ト
ナ	ニ	ヌ	ネ	ノ
ハ	ヒ	フ	ヘ	ホ
マ	ミ	ム	メ	モ
ヤ		ユ		ヨ
ラ	リ	ル	レ	ロ
ワ		ヲ		ン

Hiragana reading exercise 1

Basic sounds

* See Hiragana rules.on page14

あいうえお	**あ**い * 3 love	**あ**おい blue	う**え** on, over	い**え** house	**お**おい * 1 many
かきくけこ	か**お** face	**か**く * 4 write	**き**く hear	い**け** pond	ここ here
さしすせそ	**あ**さ morning	う**し** cow	**す**し sushi	**せ**かい world	そこ there
たちつてと	**き**た north	**ち**かい near	**つ**くえ desk	**て**つ iron	**と**けい clock
なにぬねの	**な**に what	**に**し west	い**ぬ** dog	**ね**こ cat	**き**のう yesterday
はひふへほ	は**な** flower/nose	**ひ**と human	**ふ**ね ship	**へ**そ navel	**ほ**し star
まみむめも	な**まえ** name	**み**な**み** south	**む**ね chest	あ**め**・あ**め** rain / candy	**く**も cloud
や　ゆ　よ	**や**ま mountain	**め** snow	**よ**む read	**ゆ**き snow	**や**さい vegetable
らりるれろ	**そ**ら sky	**り**ゆう reason	**よ**る night	**れ**い example/zero	**い**ろ colour
わ　　　を	**わ**たし I	か**わ** river	に**わ** garden	ほ**ん**をよむ * 6 read a book	
ん	**て**んき weather	**も**ん gate	**き**ん gold	**に**ほん Japan	**お**んな woman

Voiced sounds

がぎぐげご	**ひ**がし east	**ぎ**んこう bank	**お**よぐ swim	**げ**んき healthy	**に**ほんご Japanese
ざじずぜぞ	**ざ**っし * 2 magazine	**じ**かん time	み**ず** water	**し**ぜん nature	**ぞ**う elephant
だぢづでど	**だ**いがく university	**ち**ぢむ * 5 shrink	**つ**づく continue	**で**んわ telephone	**ど**こ where
ばびぶべぼ	た**ば**こ cigarette	**び**ん bottle	**し**んぶん newspaper	**べ**んり convenient	**ぼ**うし hat
ぱぴぷぺぽ	**い**っぱん general	**え**んぴつ pencil	**き**っぷ ticket	**か**んぺき perfect	**さ**んぽ walk

It is enough to add two small strokes or a small squiggle to the basic sounds (k, s, t, h rows) to write voiced sounds, such as か→が, さ→ざ, は→ば and ぱ.

Palatalised sounds

きゃきゅきょ	**きゃ**く customer	**きゅ**うか vacation	**きょ**ねん last year	**とう**きょう Tokyo
ぎゃぎゅぎょ	**ぎゃ**く reverse	**ぎゅ**うにく beef	**とう**ぎゅう bullfighting	**さん**ぎょう industry
しゃしゅしょ	**しゃ**かい society	**しゅ**るい variety	**とし**ょかん library	**しゃ**しん photo

じゃじゅじょ	にんじゃ ninja	じゅぎょう lesson	たんじょうび birthday	じゃがいも potato
ちゃちゅちょ	おちゃ tea	ちゅうごく China	ちょっと a little	おもちゃ toy
にゃにゅにょ	にゃあにゃあ meow	しゅうにゅう income	にょう urination	ぎゅうにゅう milk
ひゃひゅひょ	ひゃく hundred	にゃく two hundred	ひょう table	ひょうげん expression
びゃびゅびょ	さんびゃく three hundred	びゅうびゅう sound of the wind	びょうき disease	びょういん hospital
ぴゃぴゅぴょ	ろっぴゃく six hundred	はっぴゃく eight hundred	ぴゅうぴゅう sound of the wind	はっぴょう publication
みゃみゅみょ	みゃく pulse	さんみゃく mountain range	みょうじ surname	きみょう strange
りゃりゅりょ	しょうりゃく abbreviation	いちりゅう first class	りょこう travel	りょうり cooking

For broken sounds, ya, yu and yo (y-series) are added to ki, gi, shi, ji, chi, ni, hi, bi, pi, mi and ri (i-ending syllable series from the basic sounds). The first character (ki, gi, shi, ji, chi, ni, hi, bi, pi, mi and ri) is capitalised and the second character (ya, yu and yo) is lower case, and they are not pronounced as two syllables, but as one syllable short (kya, kyu, kyo).

Hiragana-Rules

1. Long vowels: They are pronounced twice as long as single vowels.

ああ [aa] おかあさん mother, おばあさん grandmother
いい [ii] いいえ no, おじいさん grandfather, おにいさん older brother
うう [uu] くうき air, ゆうめい famous, こうつう traffic
ええ [ee] ええ yes, ねえ hey, おねえさん older sister
えい [ee] えいが movies, えいご English, せんせい teacher
おお [oo] おおきい big, こおり ice, とおり street
おう [oo] おとうさん father, おとうと younger brother, いもうと younger sister

Attention!: おばさん aunt, おじさん uncle, いえ house, とり bird, ゆめ dream

2. Double consonants:
A short pause (one beat) must be made when a small つ (tsu) is placed before the consonants. おっと (husband), for example, therefore has three bars [1 お 2 __ 3 と / otto], but if there is no pause in the place of the small つ, there are only two bars おと [1 お 2 と / oto] and this is called "noise". The small つ is not pronounced.

がっこう school, にっぽん Japan, きっと sure, ざっし magazine
きっぷ ticket, はっきり clear, ゆっくり slowly, やっと finally

3. Accent
The Japanese accent is not a stress accent (strong or weak) as in many European languages, but a pitch accent (high or low). The syllables of the vocabulary that are printed in bold on the hiragana and katakana table have an accent and are therefore pronounced higher than other syllables.

4 . De-vocalisation:
The vowels 'i' and 'u' become voiceless when these vowels are placed after voiceless consonants (ch, f, k, p, s, shi, t, ts) at the end of a word, or when they are placed between two voiceless consonants.

かく ka_k_u,   です de_s_u,   すし su_shi_,   えんぴつ en_p_i_ts_u,   つくえ _ts_u_k_ue

5 . The use of じ／ち (ji) and ず／づ (zu):
In most cases じ and ず are used, but in the next few cases ち and づ are used.

1. if you have to write "ji" or "zu" directly after ち or つ:
   ちぢむ shrink,   つづく continue,   つづり letters

2. if the second part of the compound word is originally written ち or つ:
   はなぢ Nosebleed   =   はな Nose + ち bleed
   みかづき Crescent   =   みっか the third day + つき moon
   こづれ with the child   =   こ child + つれる take along

6 . The spelling for the three auxiliary particles (HP) : „wa", „o" and „e"

1. "wa" is an HP for the subject or topic and is written with は.
   わたしはにほんじんです。   I am Japanese.
2. "o" is an HP for the object and is written with を.
   わたしはほんをよみます。   I read the book.
3. "e" is an HP for the direction and is written with へ.
   わたしはにほんへいきます。   I will go to Japan.

* A small circle (maru) "。" is placed at the end of the sentence instead of a dot as it is generally used in Europe or America".".
In addition, a comma (ten) "、" can be used to make sentences easier to understand.

Hiragana reading exercise 2

おはようございます。	Good morning!
こんにちは。	Good afternoon! / Good day!
こんばんは。	Good evening!
さようなら。	Goodbye!
おやすみなさい。	Good night!
A：ありがとうございます。	Thank you!
B：どういたしまして。	You are welcome!
K：はじめまして、きむらです。	Nice to meet you, I am Kimura.
どうぞ、よろしく。	I am very pleased to make your acquaintance!
M：はじめまして、まちだです。	Nice to meet you, I'm Machida.
こちらこそ、どうぞよろしく。	I am also very pleased to make your acquaintance!
Y：こんにちは、なかむらさん。	Good afternoon, Mr Nakamura!
N：あ、やまださん、こんにちは。	Oh, Mrs Yamada, Good afternoon!
Y：おげんきですか。	How are you?
N：はい、おかげさまでげんきです。	Yes, thanks to you, I am fine.
やまださんは。	And you, Mrs Yamada?

Y：ええ、わたしもげんきです。	Yes, I'm fine too.
A：これはなんですか。	What is this?
B：それはにほんごのほんです。	It is a Japanese book.
A：これもにほんごのほんですか。	Is this also a Japanese book?
B：はい、そうです。	Yes, it is.
A：では、あれもにほんごのほんですか。	Well, is that a Japanese book too?
B：いいえ、そうではありません。	No, it is not.
あれはえいごのほんです。	That is an English book.

A：あのひとはささきさんですか。	Is he Mr. Sasaki?
B：いいえ、そうではありません。	No, he is not.
A：だれですか。	Who is he?
B：あのひとはたなかさんですよ。	He is Mr. Tanaka.
A：ああ、そうですか。	I see.
たなかさんはなんですか。	What is Mr. Tanaka?
B：たなかさんはにほんごのせんせいです。	He is a Japanese teacher.

K：これはいくらですか。	How much is this?
V：それはいちまん（10000）えんです。	It's 10000-Yen.
K：ちょっとたかいですね。	It is a little bit expensive.
では、これはいくらですか。	Then, how much is this?
V：それはごせん（5000）えんです。	It's 5000-Yen.
K：ああ、そうですか。	Okay!
じゃあ、これをください。	Please give me this then.
V：はい、どうもありがとうございました。	Gladly, thank you very much

A：すみません。えきはどこですか。	Excuse me! Where is the train station?
B：えきはあそこですよ。	The train station is over there.
A：ぎんこうはどこですか。	Where is the bank?
B：ぎんこうはそこです。	The bank is there.
A：では、ゆうびんきょくはどこですか。	Well, where is the post office?
B：ゆうびんきょくはえきのとなりです。	The post office is next to the train station.
A：そうですか。どうもありがとう。	I see. Thank you very much.

M：きたのさん、しゅうまつなにを	Mr. Kitano, what will you do this weekend?
しますか。	
K：えいがをみます。まえださんは。	I'll watch a movie. What about you?
M：わたしはとくになにもしません。	I won't do anything in particular.
K：じゃあ、まえださんもえいがを	Then, why don't you also watch a movie,
みませんか。	Mr. Maeda?
M：はい、よろこんで。	Yes, with pleasure.

Katakana- Reading Exercise 1

Basic sounds

アイウエオ	アエイオウ	ウエアオイ	オエウイア	**ア**イ eye	**エ**アー *1 air
カキクケコ	**カ**ー car	**キ**ー key	**ケ**ーキ cake	**ク**ッキー *2 cookie	ココア hot chocolate
サシスセソ	**サ**ッカー soccer	**シ**ーソー seesaw	キ**オ**スク kiosk	**エ**ッセイ essay	**ソ**ース sauce
タチツテト	**タ**クシー taxi	**エ**チケット etiquette	**ツ**アー tour	**テ**スト test	ス**ケ**ート skate
ナニヌネノ	**ナ**ッツ nuts	**テ**ニス tennis	**カ**ヌー canoe	**ネ**クタイ necktie	**ノ**ート notebook
ハヒフヘホ	**ハ**ート heart	**ヒ**ット hit	**ナ**イフ knife	**ヘ**アー hear	**ホ**ット hot
マミムメモ	**マ**ッチ match	**ミ**ニスカート miniskirt	**ム**ード mood	**メ**モ notes	**モ**ード mode
ヤ　ユ　ヨ	**タ**イヤ tyre	**ユ**ニーク unique	**ヨ**ット yacht	**ヤ**ッケ jacket	**ユ**ーモア humour
ラリルレロ	**ク**ラス class	リ**サ**イクル recycle	**フ**ルーツ fruit	**レ**ター letter	**ロ**ケット rocket
ワ　　ヲ	**ワ**ルツ waltz	**ワ**ースト worst	**ワ**イフ wife	ワルツヲオ**ド**ル dance a waltz	
ン	**ラ**イオン lion	**メ**イン main	**ワ**イン wine	**ラ**イン line / Rhine	**テ**ント tent

Voiced sounds

ガギグゲゴ	**ガソ**リン gasoline	エネ**ル**ギー energy	**グ**ッド good	**ゲ**ーム game	**ゴ**ム gum
ザジズゼゾ	**ユ**ーザー user	**ジ**ーンズ jeans	**ゼ**ロ zero	**ラ**ジオ radio	**ゾ**ーン zone
ダヂヅデド	**ダ**メージ damage	**ダ**イヤモンド diamond	**デ**ート dating	**デ**ータ data	**ド**ラマ drama
バビブベボ	**バ**ナナ banana	**ビ**ール beer	**ブ**ック book	**ベ**スト best	**ボ**ート boat
パピプペポ	**パ**ン bread	**ピ**アノ piano	**プ**ール (swimming) pool	**ペ**ン pen	ス**ポ**ーツ sports

Palatalised sounds

キャキュキョ	**キャ**ット vat	**キャ**ラメル caramel	**キャ**プテン captain	**キャ**リア career
ギャギュギョ	**ギャ**ング gangster	**ギャ**ンブル gambling	ギャップ gap	**ギャ**グ gag
シャシュショ	**シャ**ワー shower	**シャ**ツ shirt	**シュ**ーズ shoes	**ショ**ッピング shopping
ジャジュジョ	**ジャ**ズ jazz	**ジュ**ース juice	ジョ**ギ**ング jogging	**ジョ**ーク joke

チャチュチョ	**チャ**ンス chance	チューインガム chewing gum	**チョ**ーク chalk	**チャ**ンピオン champion
ニャニュニョ	**ニャー**ニャー meow meow	ニューイヤー new year's	**ニュ**ース news	ニュ**ア**ンス nuance
ヒャヒュヒョ	ヒュー**マ**ニズム humanism	**ヒュ**ッテ Hütte	**ヒュ**ーズ fuse	**ヒュ**ーストン Houston
ビャビュビョ	**ビュ**ーティフル beautiful	ビュフェー buffet	**ビュ**レット bullet	ビュー**ティ**ーサロン Beauty salon
ピャピュピョ	**ピュ**ーマ puma	**ピュ**ーレ puree	**ピュ**ーリタン puritan	コン**ピュ**ータ computer
ミャミュミョ	**ミュ**ージック music	**ミュ**ージカル musical	**ミュ**ーズ muse	**ミュ**ージアム museum
リャリュリョ	リュッ**ク**サック rucksack/backpack	リュー**マチ** rheumatism	ス**ク**リュー screw	**リュ**ーベック Lubeck

* 1 An elongation mark "ー" is used for long vowels.
* 2 A small ツ (tsu) is used for double consonants in the same way as in Hiragana.

Additional katakana syllables

In addition to the 104 original Japanese syllables, new, additional Katakana syllables have been introduced to make it easier to pronounce and write foreign words.

ウィ wi	**ウィ**ークエンド weekend	**ウィ**ーン Vienna	**ウィ**スキー whisky	**ウィ**ンター winter
ウェ we	**ウェ**ディング wedding	**ウェ**スタン western	ウェイト weight	**ウェ**ルカム welcome
ウォ wo	**ウォ**ーター water	**ウォ**ッチ watch	**ウォ**ッカ vodka	**ウォ**ークマン Walkman
シェ she	**シェ**フ chef	**シェ**リー sherry	シェパード Shepherd	**シェ**ーマ schema
ジェ je	**ジェ**ット jet	**ジェ**ントルマン gentleman	**ジェ**ラシー jealousy	ジェイアール JR (Japan Railway)
ティ ti	**ティ**ー tea	パー**ティ**ー party	**ティ**ーチャー teacher	ハイ**ティ**ーン high-teen
チェ che	**チェ**アー chair	**チェ**リー cherry	**チェ**ス chess	**チェ**ーン chain
ツァ tsa	モー**ツァ**ルト Mozart	**ピッ**ツァ pizza	**ツァ**ー Zar	**ツァ**ラ**ツ**ストラ Zarathustra
ディ di	**ディ**ナー dinner	**ディ**スコ disco	ディレクター director	**ディ**ーゼル diesel
デュ dyu	デュッ**セ**ルド**ルフ** Düsseldorf	**デュ**ースブルク Duisburg	**デュ**エット duet	**デュ**ーク duke
ファ fa	**ファ**ッション fashion	**ファ**ン fan	**ファ**ンタジー fantasy	**ファ**ミリー family
フィ fi	**フィ**ットネス fitness	**フィ**ッシュ fish	**フィ**ルム film	**フィ**ンガー finger

フェ fe	フェイス face	フェンシング fencing	フェアー fair	フェリー ferry
フォ fo	テレフォン telephone	フォーク fork	フォーム form	フォト photo

· In principle, the B series (バビブベボ) is used for the syllables **va, vi, ve, vo**.
バリエーション (variation), ビデオ(video), レベル (level), ボーカル (vocal)

Katakana-Reading Exercise 2

わたしのなまえはシュミットです。	My name is Schmidt.
ドイツのデュッセルドルフからきま	I come from Düsseldorf in Germany.
した。コンピュータ・エンジニアで	I am a computer engineer.
す。しゅみはジャズとスキーです。	My hobby is jazz and skiing.
あさごはんにパンとチーズをたべま	I eat bread and cheese for breakfast.
す。そしてコーヒーをのみます。	And I drink coffee.
ウィークエンドにともだちとテニス	At the weekend I play tennis with friends.
をします。ともだちはきたのさんと	They are Mr. Kitano, Stefan, Michael and Julia.
シュテファンとミヒャエルとユリア	
です。わたしたちはスポーツのあと	We drink beer or wine after doing sports.
でビールやワインをのみます。	

K : ドイツにはどんなまちがありますか。	What cities are there in Germany?
S : ベルリン、ハンブルグ、ミュンヘン、	Berlin, Hamburg, Munich,
ケルン、デュッセルドルフ、	Cologne, Dusseldorf,
エッセン、フランクフルト、	Essen, Frankfurt,
ハノーファー、ライプツィヒ	Hannover, Leipzig etc.
などがおおきいです。	are large.
K : どんなまちがきれいですか。	Which city is beautiful?
S : ハイデルベルクがきれいです。	Heidelberg is beautiful.

S : きょうデパートでかいものをします。	Today I will buy something at a department store.
K : なにをかいますか。	What do you want to buy?
S : カメラとボールペンとシーディーと	I want to buy a camera, a ballpoint pen, a CD,
ネクタイとポロシャツをかいます。	a tie, and a polo shirt.
K : たくさんかいますね。	You want to buy a lot of things.
S : はい、それからバナナやオレンジや	Yes, and I also buy bananas, oranges, pizza,
ピッツァ、バターもかいますよ。	and butter.

これがわたしのマンションです。	This is my apartment.
へやはみっつあります。	There are three rooms.
ここはリビングルームです。	This is the living room.
そこはキッチンです。	There is the kitchen.
トイレとバスルームはあそこです。	Toilet and bathroom are over there.
ベランダもありますよ。	There is also a balcony.

K : あしたはユリアのたんじょうびで	Tomorrow is Julia's birthday.
すね。なにをプレゼントしますか。	What will you give her?
S : グラスをプレゼントします。	I'll give her a set of drinking glasses.
K : ぼくはアルバムをプレゼントします。	I'm giving her an album.

S：パーティーがありますね。
K：ええ、シャンペンでかんぱい
　　します。そしてみんなでハッピー
バースデーをうたいます。

シュミットさんのかいしゃはコンピュ
ータのスペシャリストです。たくさん
ノウハウやテクニックがあります。
シュミットさんはソフトウェアをプロ
グラミングします。いろいろなデータ
やメディアをつかいます。
そしてファイルにバックアップします。
ストレスもおおいです。でもシュミット
さんはいつもあたらしいプロジェクトに
チャレンジします。

There's a party, isn't there?
Yes, we're toasting with champagne.
And we'll sing "Happy Birthday"
together.

Mr. Schmidt's company is a computer
specialist.
It has a lot of know-how and technology.
Mr. Schmidt programs software.
He uses many files and media.

And he saves them in folders.
He may have a lot of stress, but he
always challenges himself with
new projects.

第１課　だいいっか　Dai I-kka

あいさつ　ー　しりあう
Aisatsu - Shiriau

Lesson 1　あいさつ　－　しりあう

マイヤー　：はじめまして、マイヤーです。　どうぞ よろしく。
きたの　　：はじめまして、きたの です。
　　　　　　こちらこそ どうぞ よろしく。
マイヤー　：わたしの めいし です。どうぞ。
きたの　　：あ、どうも。わたしのも どうぞ。
マイヤー　：どうも ありがとうございます。
きたの　　：ドイツの がくせいさん ですか。
マイヤー　：はい、そうです。きたのさんも がくせいさんですか。
きたの　　：いいえ、そうでは ありません。　かいしゃいんです。
マイヤー　：かいしゃは どちら ですか。
きたの　　：ゾミーです。

Aisatsu – Shiriau
Mayer: Hajimemashite, Mayer desu. Doozo yoroshiku!
Kitano: Hajimemashite, Kitano desu. Kochirakoso doozo yoroshiku!
Mayer: Watashi no meishi desu. Doozo!
Kitano: A, doomo! Watashi no mo, doozo!
Mayer: Doomo arigatoo gozaimasu.
Kitano: Doitsu no gakusei-san desu ka.
Mayer: Hai, soo desu. Kitano-san mo gakusei-san desu ka.
Kitano: Iie, soo dewa arimasen. Kaishain desu.
Mayer: Kaisha wa dochira desu ka.
Kitano: Zomy desu.

Translation of the text

Greeting - getting to know each other

Mayer: How do you do! My name is Mayer. Very nice to meet you!
Kitano: How do you do! I'm Kitano. It's very nice to meet you, too!
Mayer: This is my business card.
Kitano: Oh, thank you! Here's mine!
Mayer: Thank you very much!
Kitano: Are you a student from Germany?
Mayer: Yes, that's right. Are you also a student?
Kitano: No, I'm not. I am a company employee.
Mayer: Which company do you work for?
Kitano: Zomy.

Questions about the text

1. Kono on'na no hito no namae wa nan desu ka.
2. Kono otoko no hito no namae wa nan desu ka.
3. Mayer-san wa doitsu no gakuse desu ka.
4. Kitano-san mo gakusei desu ka.
5. Kitano-san no kaisha no namae wa nan desu ka.

Vocabulary and idioms

Vocabulary	Reading	English
あちら	achira	the person over there, see page 28.
あいさつ	aisatsu	greeting
アメリカ人　じん	amerika-jin	American
あなた	anata	you
あの〜	ano ~	that ~
あれ	are	that
ありがとうございます	arigatoo gozaimasu	Thank you.
あそこ	asoko	there
ばら	bara	rose
ビデオ	bideo	video
ボールペン	boorupen	ballpoint pen
中国人　ちゅうごくじん	chuugoku-jin	Chinese person
大学　だいがく	daigaku	University
だれ	dare	who
だれの	dare no	whose
電車　でんしゃ	densha	train
どちら	dochira	who, what and where, see page 28.
ドイツ（人）	doitsu(jin)	Germany (German)
どこ	doko	where
どなた	donata	who = dare
どの	dono	which (-r, -s) ＋noun
どうも	doomo	very, Thanks!
どうぞよろしく	doozo yoroshiku	pleased to meet you
どれ	dore	which
英語　えいご	eigo	English
鉛筆　えんぴつ	enpitsu	pencil
ファックス	fakkusu	fax
富士山　ふじさん	Fujisan	Mt. Fuji
学生　がくせい	gakusei	student
はじめまして	hajimemashite	How do you do?
はい	hai	yes
花　はな	hana	flower
林　はやし	hayashi	grove, here: family name
人　ひと	hito	human
本　ほん	hon	book
イギリス人　じん	igirisu-jin	Englishman
いいえ	iie	no
会社　かいしゃ	kaisha	company
会社員　かいしゃいん	kaishain	employee(s)
カメラ	kamera	camera
彼女　かのじょ	kanojo	she
彼　かれ	kare	he
川　かわ	kawa	river
木　き	ki	tree
こちら	kochira	here, this person, see page 28.
こちらこそ	kochira koso	My pleasure, please do.

ここ	koko	here
この〜	kono ~	the＋noun with me
コンピュータ	konpyuuta	computer
これ	kore	this with me
車　くるま	kuruma	car, wagon
名刺　めいし	meishi	business card
も	mo	too
森　もり	mori	forest, here: family name
名前　なまえ	namae	name
何　なん・なに	nan / nani	what: 何 is read "nan" if it is followed by the syllable "de", "no", "to" or the number word. otherwise it is read as "nani".
何の　なんの	nan no	what kind of
日本語　にほんご	nihongo	Japanese
日本人　にほんじん	nihon-jin	japanese people
女の人　おんなのひと	on'na no hito	woman
男の人　おとこのひと	otoko no hito	man
練習（する）　れんしゅう	renshuu(suru)	exercise, practise
桜　さくら	sakura	cherry tree, cherry blossom
〜さん	san	Mr. ~ Mrs. ~ (name suffix)
生徒　せいと	seito	pupils
先生　せんせい	sensei	teacher
新聞　しんぶん	shinbun	newspaper
知り合う　しりあう	shiriau	get to know
そちら	sochira	the person with you, see page 28.
そこ	soko	there (at your place)
そう	soo	so
その〜	sono ~	the＋noun with you
それ	sore	that with you
ステレオ	sutereo	stereo
田　た	ta	rice field
テレビ	terebi	television
時計　とけい	tokei	clock
私　わたし	watashi	I
山　やま	yama	mountain

Personal pronouns

	Singular	Plural
1. Person	watashi (I)	watashi-tachi / wareware (we)
2. Person	anata (you)	anata-tachi / anata-gata (you)
3. Person	kare (he)	kare-tachi / kare-ra (they)
	kanojo (she)	kanojo-tachi / kanojo-ra (they)

Kanji: Chinese characters

Ideograph: A kanji itself has one or more meanings, e.g. "日" means the day and the sun.

Two readings: **On-yomi** (Sino-Japanese reading) und **Kun-yomi** (Japanese reading).
In Japanese, each kanji (Chinese character) basically has two ways of reading, namely "On-yomi" and "Kun-yomi". "On-yomi" is a Sino-Japanese reading that was previously introduced with the Chinese terms directly from China, and "Kun-yomi" is the Japanese reading that was later produced by applying the kanji introduced from China to originally Japanese words. For example, the kanji "人" (human) is read "jin" and "nin" in Japanese by On-yomi, but "hito" by Kun-yomi. "Hito" is originally a Japanese term that the Japanese understand and use in everyday life as a person, but 'jin' and 'nin' are not. However, there are many composites (more kanji combined written terms), mostly introduced from China. This is usually done using "On-yomi", such as "人間" (ningen: human), "人口" (jinkoo: population), etc. In China, of course, there is only one reading for a kanji, but in Japan there are several readings because these Chinese characters have been adapted by Japan to a different vocabulary system.
常用漢字 (**Jooyoo-Kanji**): 2136 kanji were selected by the Japanese government in 2010 and are used in everyday Japanese life. Nouns, verbs and adjectives are usually written in kanji except for vocabulary endings.

Kanji

Kanji	SCK	English	On-yomi *Kun-yomi*	Usage / Composites
日	4	day, sun	nichi / ni / jitsu *hi*	日本　nihon / Japan 日本人　nihonjin / Japanese (person)
本	5	origin, book	hon / pon *moto*	日本語　nihongo / Japanese 本屋　hon'ya / bookstore
人	2	man	jin / nin *hito*	人間　ningen / human 人口　jinkoo / population
木	4	tree	moku / boku *ki*	木星　mokusei / Jupiter 木曜日 mokuyoobi / Thursday
林	8	grove	rin *hayashi*	山林 sanrin / mountains and forest 竹林 chikurin / bamboo grove
森	12	forest	shin *mori*	森林 shinrin / woods 黒い森 kuroi mori / Black Forest
山	3	mountain	san *yama*	富士山　Fuji-san / Mt. Fuji 火山* kazan / volcano
川	3	river	sen *kawa*	ライン川* rain-**gawa** / (river) Rhine ドナウ川* donau-**gawa** / (river) Donau
田	5	rice field	den *ta*	田んぼ　tanbo / rice field 田畑　tahata / fields

・SCK: stroke count of Kanji ・stroke order of Kanji: See also page 211.

* The first syllable of the kanji character, which begins with K, S, T and H, sometimes changes to a voiced sound (G, Z, D and B) when it is added to another kanji (word)
and forms a compound. 川 (**kawa**) → ライン川 (Rhine-**gawa**), 山(**san**) →火山 (**ka**zan),
寺(**tera**) → 山寺(yama**dera**), 花(**hana**) → 草花 (kusa**bana**)

Grammar and exercises

Be verb: Present tense

(1) **S** (subject) **wa P** (predicate) desu.   (S is P.)

Question: Sore wa boorupen desu ka.
           Is that a ballpoint pen?
Answer: Hai, soo desu. Boorupen desu.
           Yes, it is. This is a ballpoint pen.
Question: Sore mo boorupen desu ka.
           Is that also a ballpoint pen?
Answer: Iie, soo dewa (yes) arimasen. Enpitsu desu.
           No, that's not right. It's a pencil.

"wa" is an auxiliary particle (AP) for a topic (subject). "desu" corresponds to 'to be' in English. "ka" is an interrogative particle (?). "mo" is an AP that corresponds to 'also' in English. The AP "wa" is omitted when "mo" is used. The short form "soo desu" or "soo dewa arimasen" is often used in the answer. "ja" can be used colloquially in the negative answer instead of 'dewa'.

[Renshuu = Exercise]
1 . kuruma → hai → iie / densha   2 . kamera → hai → iie / video
3 . sutereo → hai → iie / terebi   4 . konpyuuta → hai → iie / fakkusu

(2) **Interrogative**: "nan" (what)

Question: Sore wa nan desu ka.
          What is that?
Answer 1: Kore wa video desu.
          This is a video camera.
Answer 2: Kore wa Zomy no video desu.
          The one I have is a Zomy video camera.

"no" is an auxiliary particle (AP) for the genitive, the possessive or for prepositions (of, from and in). The demonstrative pronoun "kore" refers to an object on the speaker's side, "sore" refers to an object on the interlocutor's side and "are" refers to an object that is distant from both. "kore" and 'sore' must be exchanged in questions and answers. This is not the case with "are".

[Renshuu]
1 . terebi   2 . fakkusu   3 . tokei   4 . nihongo no hon

(3) **Interrogative**: "donata"* (who)

Question: (Anata wa) donata desu ka.
           Who are you?
Answer: Watashi wa Mayer desu.
           I am Mr. Mayer.

"Dare" can also be used, but 'donata' is more polite than 'dare'.

"Anata wa" is often omitted in everyday conversation as it sounds strict or harsh.

However, the name, profession and position of the interlocutor can be used instead.

Question : (Anata wa) doitsu-jin desu ka.

           Are you German?

Answer 1: Hai, soo desu.

           Yes, I am.

Answer 2: Iie, soo dewa arimasen. Igirisu-jin desu.

           No, that's not right. I am English.

[Renshuu]

1 . nihon-jin → hai   2 . chuugoku-jin → iie / amerika-jin   3 . sensei → hai

4 . seito → iie / gakusei   5 . kaishain → hai   6 . Kitano-san → iie / Kawata

(4) **Introduction**

Instead of "kore", "sore" and "are", "kochira", "sochira" and "achira" must be used for people.
When used politely, these can be used not only for people, but also for objects or places.

K: Mayer-san, **sochira** wa donata desu ka.

    Ms. Mayer, who is the man / woman with you?

M: **Kochira** wa Tanaka-san desu.

    This is Mr. / Mrs. Tanaka.

T: Tanaka desu. Hajimemashite!

    How do you do? My name is Tanaka.

K: Hajimemashite! Kitano desu.

    How do you do? My name is Kitano.

(5) interrogative: "**nan no**" (what for): Question about the variety

Question: Are wa nan no ki desu ka.

    What kind of tree is that over there?

Answer: Are wa sakura no ki desu.

    This is a cherry tree.

[Renshuu]

1 . hana / bara   2 . hon / nihongo

3 . shinbun / eigo   4 . kaisha / konpyuuta

(6) **interrogative:** "**dare no**" (whose)

Question: Kore wa dare no hon desu ka.

    Whose book is this?

Answer: Sore wa watashi no (hon) desu.

    It is my book.

[Renshuu]

1. kamera / kare
2. kuruma / kanojo
3. terebi / Kawada-san
4. tokei / Yamada-san

(7) Attributive form of demonstrative pronouns: kono N, sono N, ano N

They are always used with the **noun**.

Question: Kono **hon** wa dare no desu ka.

   Whose book is this?

Answer: (Sono **hon** wa) Mayer-san no (hon) desu.

   The book belongs to Mrs. Mayer.

Question: Kono **hon** wa nan no hon desu ka.

   What kind of book is this?

Answer: (Sono **hon** wa) nihongo no hon desu.

   It's a Japanese book.

[Renshuu]

1. hana / Mori-san / bara
2. shinbun / Kitano-san / eigo
3. hon / Hayashi-san / konpyuuta
4. kuruma / kaisha / sutereo

paraphrasing into the attributive form 1. Kore wa Kitano-san no kuruma desu. →
Kono ________________________________.

2. Sore wa kamera no kaisha desu. → Sono ________________________________.
3. Kochira wa Mayer-san desu. → Kono ________________________________.
4. Are wa Fuji-san desu.. → Ano ________________________________.

Ko-so-a-do- Table (demonstrative pronouns)

		object	person	attributive form	place see L.3.
ko	with the speaker	**kore** this with me	**kochira** the human with me	**kono+Noun** the Noun with me	**koko** here
so	with the conversation partner	**Sore** it with you	**sochira** the human with you	**sono+Noun** the Noun with you	**soko** there with you
a	away from both	**are** that over there	**achira** the human over there	**ano+Noun** the Noun over there	**asoko** over there
do	Question	**dore** which	**dochira** which	**dono+Nomen** which Noun	**doko** where

<u>More information</u>

"Kochira", "sochira", "achira" and "dochira" can be used in polite conversation not only for people for people, but also for objects, places and directions.

Kochira wa Yamashita-Sensei desu. (human)

This is the teacher, Mr. Yamashita

Sochira wa Kitano-san no kuruma desu. (object)

This is Mr. Kitano's car.

Kaisha wa **dochira** desu ka. (This is an ambiguous question.)

Where is your company? (place) / In which company do you work? (name)

Kaisha wa **achira** desu. / **Zomy** desu.

The company is over there. (Place) / I work at Zomy. (name)

Daigaku wa **dochira** desu ka. (direction: not visible)

Where is the university?

Daigaku wa **achira** desu. (direction: not visible)

The university is in this direction.

Lesson test Dai-1-ka

（1）Insert a correct auxiliary particle or the correct vocabulary in (   ).

1. Hans-san (   ) doitsu-jin desu ka. →   Hai, (   ) desu.

2. John-san (   ) doitsu-jin desu ka. →   Iie, (   ) arimasen. Igirisu-jin desu.

3. Sore wa nan desu ka. →   (   ) wa shinbun desu.

4. (   ) shinbun (   ) dare (   ) desu ka. →   Watashi (   ) shinbun desu.

5. (   ) shinbun desu ka. →   Nihongo (   ) shinbun desu.

（2）Answer the questions.

1. Kore wa pen desu ka.   (hai)

2. Sore wa eigo no hon desu ka. (iie)

3. Sore wa nan no hon desu ka.   (nihongo)

4. Are wa nan desu ka.   (kamera)

5. Sore wa dare no kamera desu ka   (Mayer-san)

6. Kare wa dare desu ka.   (Kitano-san)

7. Kitano-san wa gakusei desu ka.   (kaishain)

8. Anata wa donata desu ka.

9. Anata wa nan desu ka.

10. Anata wa nani-jin desu ka.

（3）Translate the following sentences into Japanese.

1. How do you do? My name is Yamada. It's nice to meet you!

2. The pleasure is all mine!

3. This is my business card.

4. Are you a student from Germany? Yes, I am.

5. I'm an employee at the Nihon newspaper.

Hajimemashite, Yamada desu.
Doozo yoroshiku!

第２課　だいにか　Dai Ni-ka

お元気ですか。

O-genki desu ka.

Lesson 2　お元気ですか

きたの　　　：マイヤーさん、こんにちは。
マイヤー　　：あ、きたのさん、こんにちは。
きたの　　　：お元気ですか。
マイヤー　　：はい、ありがとう。元気です。
　　　　　　　きたのさんも お元気ですか。
きたの　　　：ええ、ぼくも 元気ですよ。マイヤーさんの 新しいアパートは いかがですか。
マイヤー　　：ええ、とても いいですよ。大きくない ですが、きれいなアパートです。
きたの　　　：しずかですか。
マイヤー　　：いいえ、あまりしずか ではありません。
きたの　　　：そうですか。べんりですか。
マイヤー　　：はい、たいへん べんりです。えきも スーパーも 近いです。

O-genki desu ka.
Kitano: Mayer-san, kon'nichiwa.
Mayer: Ah, Kitano-san, kon'nichiwa.
Kitano: O-genki desu ka.
Mayer: Hai, arigatoo. Genki desu. Kitano-san mo o-genki desu ka.
Kitano: Ee, boku mo genki desu yo. Mayer-san no atarashii apaato wa ikaga desu ka.
Mayer: Ee, totemo ii desu yo. Ookikunai desu ga, kirei-na apaato desu.
Kitano: Shizuka desu ka?
Mayer: Iie, amari shizuka dewa arimasen.
Kitano: Soo desu ka. Benri desu ka.
Mayer: Hai, taihen benri desu. Eki mo suupaa mo chikai desu.

Translation of the text

How are you?
Kitano: Good afternoon, Mrs. Mayer!
Mayer: Oh, good afternoon, Mr. Kitano!
Kitano: How are you?
Mayer: Thank you, I'm fine! And you?
Kitano: Thank you, I'm fine too. How is your new apartment?
Mayer: Yes, I quite like it. It's not big, but it's nice.
Kitano: Is it quiet there?
Mayer: No, it's not very quiet.
Kitano: Oh, really? Is it conveniently located?
Mayer: Yes, very. Both the train station and the supermarket are nearby.

Questions about the text
1．Mayer-san wa genki desu ka.
2．Kitano-san mo genki desu ka.
3．Mayer-san no apaato wa don'na apaato desu ka.
4．Mayer-san no apaato wa shizuka desu ka.
5．Mayer-san no apaato wa fuben desu ka.
6．Mayer-san no apaato wa eki ni chikai desu ka.

Vocabulary and idioms

Vocabulary	reading	English
ああ	aa	alas
あまり～ません	amari ~ masen	not so
アパート	apaato	apartment
新しい　あたらしい	atarashii	new
便利（な）　べんり（な）	benri-na	practical
ぼく	boku	I (male)
小さい　ちいさい	chiisai	small
近い　ちかい	chikai	close
でも	demo	but (for two sentences)
どんな	don'na	what for (question after A and N)
どう	doo	how
ええ	ee	yes
駅　えき	eki	station
不便（な）　ふべん（な）	fuben(na)	impractical
古い　ふるい	furui	old
～が	~ ga	but
学校　がっこう	gakkoo	school
元気（な）　げんき（な）	genki(na)	healthy
速い　はやい	hayai	fast
いい	ii	good
いかが	ikaga	how (more polite than　どう)
自動車　じどうしゃ	jidoosha	car = 車　くるま　kuruma
きれい（な）	kirei(na)	beautiful, clean
こんにちは	Kon'nich wa!	Good afternoon!
町　まち	machi	city
ね	ne	AP for confirmation: isn't it?
お	o-	polite prefix for nouns
大きい　おおきい	ookii	big
静か（な）　しずか（な）	shizuka(na)	quiet, silent
小学校　しょうがっこう	shoogakkoo	elementary school
そして	soshite	and (for two sets)
スーパー	suupaa	supermarket
大変　たいへん	taihen	very
高い　たかい	takai	expensive, high
遠い　とおい	tooi	far
図書館　としょかん	toshokan	library
とても	totemo	very
若い　わかい	wakai	young
安い　やすい	yasui	cheap
よ	yo	ending particle for emphasis
有名（な）　ゆうめい（な）	yuumei(na)	famous

Kanji

Kanji	SCK	English	On-yomi *Kun-yomi*	usage / composites
大	3	big	dai *oo-kii*	大きい　ookii / big 大学　daigaku / university
小	3	small	shoo *chii-sai*	小さい　chiisai / small 小学校　shoogakkoo / elementary school
高	10	high expensive	koo *taka-i*	高い　takai / high, expensive 高校　kookoo / high school
新	13	new	shin *atara-shii*	新しい　atarashii / new 新聞　shinbun / newspaper
古	5	old	ko *furu-i*	古い　furui / old 古典　koten / classic
近	7	close	kin *chika-i*	近い　chikai / close 近所　kinjo / neighborhood
元	4	origin	gen / gan *moto*	元気　genki / healthy 元日　ganjitsu / first day of the new year
気	6	feeling, desire	ki	天気　tenki / weather 電気　denki / electricity
有	6	There is ~	yuu / u *a-ru*	有名　yuumei / famous 有料　yuuryoo / charges apply
名	6	name	mei, myoo *na*	名前　namae / name 名刺　meishi / business card
前	9	in front (of) before	zen *mae*	前方　zenpoo / forward 以前　izen / before
町	7	city	choo *machi*	大きい町　oo-kii machi / big town 新しい町　atara-shii machi / new town
学	8	learn	gaku *mana-bu*	学校　gakkoo / school 大学　daigaku / university
校	10	school	koo	中学校　chuugakkoo / junior high school 校長　koochoo / school headmaster
花	7	flower	ka *hana*	桜の花　sakura no hana / cherry blossom 菊の花　kiku no hana / chrysanthemum

· The stem of most verbs and adjectives is written in kanji, but the ending, the so-called
conjugated part (the part of the word after the stroke in Kun-yomi) such as oo-kii 大きい
is written in hiragana.
· SCK: stroke number of the kanji　· stroke order of the kanji: See page 211.

Grammar and exercises

Adjectives (present tense)

(1) **I-adjective** ending with "**i**" : ookii (big), chiisai (small), atarashii (new), furui (old) etc.

① Predicative use: S wa adjecive cesu. (S is P.)

Question: Mayer-san no apaato wa ookii desu ka.

  Is your flat big, Mrs Meyer?

Answer 1: Hai, ookii desu.

  Yes, it is big.

Answer 2: Iie, ooki-ku-nai desu (ooki-ku arimasen). Chiisai desu.

  No, it is not big. It is small.

In the negative form, the ending "**I**" is omitted and **"ku-nai"** is inserted. Instead of **"ku-nai desu"**, **"ku-arimasen"** can be used.

Exception: ii (good) ⇒ yokunai (not good)

"Hai, soo desu" and "Iie, soo dewa arimasen" (Lesson 1) can't be used for the answer.
You have to answer the question with the same adjective.

[Renshuu]

1. shoogakoo / atarashii / furui   2. toshokan / chikai / tooi

3. jidoosha / takai / yasui   4. machi / ookii / chiisai

② Attributive use: S wa adjective + noun desu. (S is P.)

Question: Sore wa hayai kuruma desu ka.

  Is this a fast car?

Answer1: Hai, hayai kuruma desu.

  Yes, it is a fast car.

Answer 2: Iie, hayai kuruma dewa arimasen. / Iie, hayakunai kuruma desu.

  No, it's not a fast car.

[Renshuu]

1. atarashii / gakkoo   2. furui / hon

3. takai / konpyuuta   4. yasui / apaato

<u>Exception:</u>

"Ookii" (big) and "chiisai" (small) can also be used with "na" when used attributively, such as **ooki-na** hito (a big person), **chiisa-na** ie (a small house). "Chikai" (near), however, must be used with "no", such as chikaku **no** eki (a railway station nearby).

Connecting words (conjunction): **soshite** (and), **demo** (but)
They are used for two sentences and are placed at the beginning of the second sentence.

Sono gakusei wa wakai desu. Soshite genki desu.

The student is young. And he is healthy.

Sono machi wa ookiku nai desu / arimasen. Demo kirei desu.

The city is not big. But it is beautiful.

The AP "ga" is also used as "but" by inserting "ga" at the end of the first sentence and continuing the second sentence directly after the comma ",".

Sono machi wa ookiku nai desu / arimasen **ga,** kirei desu.
The city is not big, but it is beautiful.

The <u>Te-form</u> must be used to list adjectives or nouns one after the other in a sentence. (see L.7)

(2) **Na-adjective** ending in "na": genki-na (healthy), kirei-na (beautiful), benri-na (practical)

① Predicative use: "na" is not appended.

Question: Sono kamera wa benri desu ka.
            Is the camera practical?

Answer 1: Hai, benri desu.
            Yes, it is practical.
Answer 2: Iie, benri dewa arimasen. (Fuben desu.)
            No, it is not practical. (It's impractical.)

Hai, soo desu" and "Iie, soo dewa arimasen" cannot be used here either.

[Renshuu]
1．sono hana / kirei   2．sono machi / shizuka
3．sono hito / genki   4．sono hito / yuumei

② Attributive use: "na" is added.

Question: Sore wa benri-na kuruma desu ka.
            Is it a practical car?
Answer 1: Hai, benri-na kuruma desu.
            Yes, it's a practical car.
Answer 2: Iie, benri-na kuruma dewa arimasen.
            No, it is not a practical car.

[Renshuu]
1．kirei-na machi   2．shizuka-na machi   3．genki-na hito   4．yuumei-na hito

(3) **Adverbs:** "**totemo**", "**taihen**" (very) and "**amari ~ nai**" (not so)

① Question about characteristics with "**ikaga**"/ "**doo**" (how ~?: predicative)
   "ikaga" is a more polite form of "doo".

Question: Kono apaato wa ikaga desu ka.
            What is this flat like?
Answer 1: Totemo atarashii desu.
            It is very new.
Answer 2: Amari atarashikunai desu.
            It is not so new.
Question: Sono apaato wa ikaga desu ka.
            How is the flat?

Answer 1: Totemo kirei desu.

    It is very beautiful.

Answer 2: Amari kirei dewa arimasen.

    It is not so beautiful.

"amari" is always used in the negative form (-nai desu / -masen).

[Renshuu]

1．machi / furui   2．kamera / benri   3．kuruma / hayai   4．hana / kirei

② Question about the property with "**don'na**" (what for~ ?: attributive)

Question: Sore wa don'na kuruma desu ka.

    What kind of car is this?

Answer 1: Totemo benrina kuruma desu.

    This is a very practical car.

Answer 2: Amari benrina kuruma dewa arimasen.

    This is not a practical car.

[Renshuu]

1．hana / kirei   2．apaato / shizuka   3．gakkoo / furui   4．kamera / yasui

(4) **Auxiliary particles** (AP) "ne" and "yo"

The two auxiliary particles are used at the end of the sentence to add different nuances. With "ne", the speaker confirms the content of the sentence to the interlocutor like "isn't it?" in English and demands agreement from them. In contrast to "ne", "yo" is used to draw the interlocutor's attention to what they do not know. In English, "You know?" is used at the beginning of a sentence.

The speaker assumes that the interlocutor also knows this.

A :Kyoo wa ii tenki desu **ne**. The weather is nice today, isn't it?

B: Ee, soo desu ne. Yes, it really is.

The speaker tells the interlocutor in a slightly emphasized tone.

A: Kyoo wa ii tenki desu **yo**. Do you know? The weather is nice today.

B: Aa, soo desu ka. (with a lowering intonation) Oh, really?

[Renshuu]

1．kono jidoosha / hayai / ne   2．sono machi / amari / kirei / yo

3．ano toshokan / atarashii / ne   4．kono apaato / totemo / benri / yo

Lesson test Dai 2-ka

（1）Use the adjectives according to the instructions.
1．Kare no apaato wa _________________. (new)
2．Sono machi wa ____________ ga, totemo ___________. (not new / beautiful)
3．Kanojo wa ________________ hito desu. (quiet)
4．Sono kuruma wa _________________. (not so expensive)
5．Sono kamera wa ga, totemo _________________. (small / practical)

（2）Answer the questions with "amari".
1．Eki wa chikai desu ka.
2．Anata (-san) no machi wa yuumei desu ka.
3．Sono sutereo wa ii desu ka.
4．Kanojo wa genki desu ka.
5．Sono tokei wa atarashii desu ka.

（3）Rewrite the sentences in the attributive use of the adjectives.
1．Sono machi wa ookii desu.
2．Kono hana wa kirei desu.
3．Mori-san wa wakai desu.
4．Kyoto wa totemo furui desu.
5．Kono konpyuuta wa amari benri dewa arimasen.

（4）Ask the appropriate questions.
1．Hai, kono shinbun wa atarashii desu.
2．Iie, watashi no konpyuuta wa benri dewa arimasen.
3．Sono terebi wa taihen ii desu yo.
4．Kore wa totemo hayai kuruma desu yo.

第３課 だいさんか Dai San-ka

いくつありますか。

Ikutsu arimasu ka.

Lesson 3　いくつ ありますか。

きたの　　　：マイヤーさんの アパートに へやが いくつ ありますか。

マイヤー　　：三_{みっ}つ あります。 ようしつと わしつと だいどころです。

きたの　　　：ふろも ありますか。

マイヤー　　：いいえ、ふろは ありませんが、シャワーが あります。

きたの　　　：そうですか。でんわは ありますか。

マイヤー　　：はい、ありますよ。

きたの　　　：でんわばんごうは 何_{なん}ばんですか。

マイヤー　　：３４５の７８９０です。

きたの　　　：マイヤーさんは 何人_{なんにん}かぞくですか。

マイヤー　　：５人_{にん}かぞくです。 ちちとはは、あにとあねが います。きたのさんの ところは？

きたの　　　：６人_{にん}かぞくです。 ちちとはは、それから いもうとが 一人_{ひとり} と

　　　　　　　おとうとが 二人_{ふたり} います。ねこも 一_{いっ}ぴき いますよ。

マイヤー　　：そうですか。大_{だい}かぞく ですね。

Ikutsu arimasu ka.
Kitano: Mayer-san no apaato ni heya ga ikutsu arimasu ka.
Mayer: Mittsu arimasu. Yooshitsu to washitsu to daidokoro desu.
Kitano: Furo mo arimasu ka.
Mayer: Iie, furo wa arimasen ga, shawaa ga arimasu.
Kitano: Soo desu ka. Denwa wa arimasu ka.
Mayer: Hai, arimasu yo.
Kitano: Denwa-bangoo wa nanban desu ka.
Mayer: 345 no 7890 desu.
Kitano: Mayer-san wa nan'nin kazoku desu ka.
Mayer: Go-nin kazoku desu. Chichi to haha, ani to ane ga imasu. Kitano-san no tokoro wa?
Kitano: Roku-nin kazoku desu. Chichi to haha sorekara imooto ga hitori to otooto ga futari
　　　　imasu. Neko mo ippiki imasu yo.
Mayer: Soo desu ka. Dai-kazoku desu ne.

Translation of the text
How many are there?
Kitano: How many rooms are there in your flat?
Mayer: Three. A western room, a Japanese room and a kitchen.
Kitano: Is there also a bathroom?
Mayer: No, there's no bathroom, but there is a shower.
Kitano: Oh, really? Do you have a telephone?
Mayer: Yes.
Kitano: What is your telephone number?
Mayer: It's 345/7890.
Kitano: How big is your family?
Mayer: We are a family of five. My father, my mother, an older brother and an older sister.
　　　　And how big is your family?
Kitano: It's a family of six people. My father, my mother, a younger sister and two younger
　　　　brothers. We also have a cat.
Mayer: Oh? That's a big family, isn't it?

Questions about the text

1. Mayer-san no apaato ni heya ga ikutsu arimasu ka.
2. Don'na heya ga arimasu ka.
3. Furo ga arimasu ka.
4. Mayer-san no denwa-bangoo wa nanban desu ka.
5. Mayer-san wa nan'nin-kazoku desu ka.
6. Don'na hito ga imasu ka.
7. Kitano-san wa nan'nin-kazoku desu ka.
8. Don'na hito ga imasu ka.

Vocabulary and idioms

Vocabulary	reading	English
間　あいだ	aida	between
姉　あね	ane	older sister (own)
兄　あに	ani	older brother (own)
ある	aru	are located (for objects)
病院　びょういん	byooin	hospital, doctor's office
父　ちち	chichi	own father
近くに～　ちかくに～	chikaku ni	nearby (with a verb)
中学校　ちゅうがっこう	chuugakkoo	middle school
大家族　だいかぞく	dai-kazoku	large family
台所　だいどころ	daidokoro	kitchen
～だけ	dake	only (used in the positive form)
だれ	dare	who
だれもいません	dare mo imasen	Nobody is there.
電話　でんわ	denwa	telephone
電話番号　でんわばんごう	denwa-bangoo	telephone number
デパート	depaato	department store
土曜日　どようび	doyoobi	Saturday
ふろ	furo	bathroom
が	ga	AP for the subject
月曜日　げつようび	getsuyoobi	Monday
母　はは	haha	own mother
部屋　へや	heya	room
左　ひだり	hidari	left
本棚　ほんだな	hondana	bookshelf
いくつ	ikutsu	how many, how many pieces (countable)
妹　いもうと	imooto	younger sister
今　いま	ima	now
犬　いぬ	inu	dog
いる	iru	are located (for humans and animals)
いす	isu	chair
辞書　じしょ	jisho	dictionary
かばん	kaban	bag
～か月（間）かげつ（かん）	ka-getsu (kan)	month(s)
紙　かみ	kami	paper
火曜日　かようび	kayoobi	Tuesday
家族　かぞく	kazoku	family

金曜日 きんようび	kin'yoobi	Friday
子供 こども	kodomo	child
公園 こうえん	kooen	park
今日 きょう	kyoo	today
教室 きょうしつ	kyooshitsu	classroom
前 まえ	mae	in front
右 みぎ	migi	right
三つ みっつ	mittsu	three, three pieces
木曜日 もくようび	mokuyoobi	Thursday
向かい むかい	mukai	opposite
長い ながい	nagai	long
中 なか	naka	in, inside
何もありません なに	nani mo arimasen	Nothing is there.
猫 ねこ	neko	cat
～年（間） ねん（かん）	nen (kan)	year(s)
に	ni	AP for location, time and destination
日曜日 にちようび	nichiyoobi	Sunday
庭 にわ	niwa	garden
ノート	nooto	notebook, booklet
お母さん おかあさん	okaasan	mother of others, call name
奥 おく	oku	in the back of a room
お兄さん おにいさん	oniisan	older brother of others, call name
お姉さん おねえさん	oneesan	older sister of others, call name
お父さん おとうさん	otoosan	father of others, call name
弟 おとうと	otooto	younger brother
シャワー	shawaa	shower
～しか	shika	only (used in the negative form)
下 した	shita	under, below
～週（間） しゅう（かん）	shuu (kan)	week(s)
ソファー	sofaa	sofa
そうですか。	soo desu ka.	That's how it is!
それから	sorekara	and, the
水曜日 すいようび	suiyoobi	Wednesday
と	to	and (for nomina, complete)
ところ	tokoro	place
となり	tonari	next to
机 つくえ	tsukue	table, desk
上 うえ	ue	on, above, over
馬 うま	uma	horse
後ろ うしろ	ushiro	behind
和室 わしつ	washitsu	Japanese room
や	ya	and (for nouns, incomplete)
横 よこ	yoko	next to, horizontal
洋室 ようしつ	yooshitsu	European room
郵便局 ゆうびんきょく	yuubinkyoku	post office

Kanji

Kanji	SCK	English	On-yomi *Kun-yomi*	Usage / Composites
一	1	one	ichi *hito-tsu*	一人　hitori / one person 一つ　hitotsu / one, a piece
二	2	two	ni *futa-tsu*	二人　futari / two people 二つ　futatsu / two, two pieces
三	3	three	san *mi-ttsu*	三台　san'dai / three machines 三つ　mittsu / three, three pieces
四	5	four	shi yon, *yo-ttsu*	四台　yon-dai / four machines 四つ　yottsu / four, four pieces
五	4	five	go *itsu-tsu*	五枚　go-mai / five flat things 五つ　itsutsu / five, five pieces
六	4	six	roku *mu-ttsu*	六枚　roku-mai / six flat things 六つ　muttsu / six, six pieces
七	2	seven	shichi nana, *nana-tsu*	七本　nana-hon / seven long things 七つ　nanatsu / seven, seven pieces
八	2	eight	hachi *ya-ttsu*	八本　hachi-hon / eight long things 八つ　yattsu / eight, eight pieces
九	2	nine	kyuu / ku *kokono-tsu*	九冊　kyuu-satsu / nine books 九つ　kokonotsu / nine, nine pieces
十	2	ten	juu *too*	十冊　ju-ssatsu / ten books 十　too / ten, ten pieces
百	6	one hundred	hyaku	百円　hyaku-en / one hundred yen 百年　hyaku-nen / one hundred years
千	3	thousand	sen	千円　sen-en / one thousand yen 千年　sen-nen / one thousand years
万	3	ten thousand	man	一万円　ichiman-en / ten thousand yen 十万円　juuman-en / one hundred thousand yen
上	3	up, above	joo *ue*	上級　jookyuu / upper grade 上等　jootoo / high quality
下	3	under	ge, ka *shita*	下級　kakyuu / lower grade 下等　katoo / low quality
中	4	in	chuu *naka*	中級　chuukyuu / intermediate level 中学校　chuugakkoo / middle school
犬	4	dog	ken *inu*	子犬　koinu / puppy 番犬　banken / guard dog

・ SC: stroke count of the kanji　・ stroke sequence of the kanji: see page 211.

Numbers

0	1	2	3	4	5	6	7	8	9
rei/zero	ichi	ni	san	shi / yon	go	roku	nana / shichi	hachi	kyuu
10	11	12	13	14	15	16	17	18	19
juu	juu-ichi	juu-ni	juu-san	juu-shi juu-yon	juu-go	juu-roku	juu-nana juu-shichi	juu-hachi	juu-kyuu
20	21	22	23	24	25	26	27	28	29
ni-juu	nijuu-ichi	nijuu-ni	nijuu-san	nijuu-shi nijuu-yon	nijuu-go	nijuu-roku	nijuu-nana nijuu-shichi	nijuu-hachi	nijuu-kyuu
30	40	50	60	70	80	90	97	98	99
san-juu	yon-juu	go-juu	roku-juu	nana-juu shichi-juu	hachi-juu	kyuu-juu	kyuu-juu-nana kyuu-juu-shichi	kyuu-juu-hachi	kyuu-juu-kyuu
100	200	300	400	500	600	700	800	900	1000
hyaku	ni-hyaku	san-byaku	yon-hyaku	go-hyaku	ro-ppyaku	nana-hyaku shichi-hyaku	ha-ppyaku	kyuu-hyaku	sen
2000	3000	4000	5000	6000	7000	8000	9000	9500	10000
ni-sen	san-zen	yon-sen	go-sen	roku-sen	nana-sen shichi-sen	ha-ssen	kyuu-sen	kyuu-sen-go-hyaku	ichi-man

Number words

	-tsu *1	-nin 人	-ko 個	-dai 台	-mai 枚	-satsu 冊
	general except animals & humans	humans	small piece ball, apple, stone...	machine, car, television...	flat things paper, card stamp	stapled things book, notebook
1	hitotsu	hitori	i-kko	ichi-dai	ichi-mai	i-ssatsu
2	futatsu	futari	ni-ko	ni-dai	ni-mai	ni-satsu
3	mittsu	san-nin	san-ko	san-dai	san-mai	san-satsu
4	yottsu	yo-nin	yon-ko	yon-dai	yon-mai	yon-satsu
5	itsutsu	go-nin	go-ko	go-dai	go-mai	go-satsu
6	muttsu	roku-nin	ro-kko	roku-dai	roku-mai	roku-satsu
7	nanatsu	nana-nin shichi-nin	nana-ko shichi-ko	nana-dai shichi-dai	nana-mai shichi-mai	nana-satsu shichi-satsu
8	yattsu	hachi-nin	ha-kko	hachi-dai	hachi-mai	ha-ssatsu
9	kokonotsu	kyuu-nin	kyuu-ko	kyuu-dai	kyuu-mai	kyuu-satsu
10	too	juu-nin	ju/ji-kko	juu-dai	juu-mai	ju/ji-ssatsu
?	ikutsu	nan-nin	nan-ko	nan-dai	nan-mai	nan-satsu

	-hon 本	-hai 杯	-hiki 匹	-wa 羽	-kai 回*2・階	-sai 才（歳）
	long things pen, tree ...	mug with contents	animal	bird	frequency floor	age
1	i-ppon	i-ppai	i-ppiki	ichi-wa	i-kkai	i-ssai
2	ni-hon	ni-hai	ni-hiki	ni-wa	ni-kai	ni-sai
3	san-bon	san-bai	san-biki	san-wa	san-kai	san-sai
4	yon-hon	yon-hai	yon-hiki	yon-wa	yon-kai	yon-sai
5	go-hon	go-hai	go-hiki	go-wa	go-kai	go-sai
6	ro-ppon	ro-ppai	ro-ppiki	roku-wa	ro-kkai	roku-sai
7	nana-hon shichi-hon	nana-hai shichi-hai	nana-hiki shichi-hiki	nana-wa shichi-wa	nana-kai shichi-kai	nana-sai shichi-sai
8	ha-ppon	ha-ppai	ha-ppiki	hachi-wa	hachi-kai	ha-ssai
9	kyuu-hon	kyuu-hai	kyuu-hiki	kyuu-wa	kyuu-kai	kyuu-sai
10	ju-ppon	ju-/ji-ppai	ju/ji-ppiki	juu-wa	ju/ji-kkai	ju/ji-ssai
?	nan-bon	nan-bai	nan-biki	nan-wa	nan-kai	nan-sai

* 1   With "tsu" you can only count up to ten. Normal numbers are used for more than ten.

* 2   For frequencies, do (度) can also be used. ?: Question words (how many?)

Date
calendar days: -ka/-nichi (Duration: mikka-kan = three days)

1	tsuitachi (ichinichi kan)	11	juu-ichi-nichi (-kan)	21	ni-juu-ichi-nichi (-kan)
2	futsu-ka (-kan)	12	juu-ni-nichi (-kan)	22	ni-juu-ni-nichi (-kan)
3	mik-ka (-kan)	13	juu-san-nichi (-kan)	23	ni-juu-san-nichi (-kan)
4	yok-ka (-kan)	14	juu-yokka (-kan)	24	ni-juu-yokka (-kan)
5	itsu-ka (-kan)	15	juu-go-nichi (-kan)	25	ni-juu-go-nichi (-kan)
6	mui-ka (-kan)	16	juu-roku-nichi (-kan)	26	ni-juu-roku-nichi (-kan)
7	nano-ka (-kan)	17	juu-shichi-nichi (-kan)	27	ni-juu-shichi-nichi (-kan)
8	yoo-ka (-kan)	18	juu-hachi-nichi (-kan)	28	ni-juu-hachi-nichi (-kan)
9	kokono-ka (-kan)	19	juu-ku-nichi (-kan)	29	ni-juu-ku-nichi (-kan)
10	too-ka (-kan)	20	hatsu-ka (-kan)	30	san-juu-nichi (-kan)
				31	san-juu-ichi-nichi (-kan)
Kyoo wa nan nichi desu ka. (What day is it today?)					
Nan-nichi-kan desu ka. (How many days?)					

Weekdays: -yoobi

getsu-yoobi	Monday	kin-yoobi	Friday
ka-yoobi	Tuesday	do-yoobi	Saturday
sui-yoobi	Wednesday	nichi-yoobi	Sunday
moku-yoobi	Thursday		
Kyoo wa nan-yoobi desu ka. (What day of the week do we have today?)			

Weeks (duration)

i-sshuukan	one week	roku-shuukan	six weeks
ni-shuukan	two weeks	nana-shuukan	seven weeks
san-shuukan	three weeks	ha-sshuukan	eight weeks
yon-shuukan	four weeks	kyuu-shuukan	nine weeks
go-shuukan	five weeks	ju-sshuukan	ten weeks

Month names: -gatsu

ichi-gatsu	January	shichi-gatsu	July
ni-gatsu	February	hachi-gatsu	August
san-gatsu	March	ku-gatsu	September
shi-gatsu	April	juu-gatsu	October
go-gatsu	May	juuichi-gatsu	November
roku-gatsu	June	juuni-gatsu	December
Ima nan-gatsu desu ka. (What month do we have right now?)			

Months (duration)

i-kkagetsu (kan)	one month	ro-kkagetsu (kan)	six months
ni-kagetsu (kan)	two months	shichi-kagetsu (kan)	seven months
san-kagetsu (kan)	three months	ha-kkagetsu (kan)	eight months
yon-kagetsu (kan)	four months	kyuu-kagetsu (kan)	nine months
go-kagetsu (kan)	five months	ju-kkagetsu (kan)	ten months

Years (duration)

ichi-nen (kan)	one year	roku-nen (kan)	six years
ni-nen (kan)	two years	shichi-nen (kan)	seven years
san-nen (kan)	three years	hachi-nen (kan)	eight years
yo-nen (kan)	four years	kyuu-nen (kan)	nine years
go-nen (kan)	five years	juu-nen (kan)	ten years

Grammar and exercises

Being there (to be)

"**imasu**" is used for people and animals.
"**arimasu**" is used for other objects.

(1) **P ni S ga imasu / arimasu.**   (P = place, S = subject)

Question: Heya ni **dare ga** imasu ka?
Who is in the room?
Answer 1: Yamada-san to Tanaka-san **ga** imasu.
Mrs. Yamada and Mr. Tanaka are there.
Answer 2: Dare mo imasen.
No one is there.

The AP "**ga**" is used for the subject when the subject refers to new information
and when the focus of the sentence is on it. "**ni**" is an auxiliary particle,
which comes after the place of the feeling. "**to**" is an auxiliary particle for complete
enumerations (and).

[Renshuu]

1．apaato, Schmidt-san to Maria-san   2．ie, Tanaka-san to Kimura-san
3．kyooshitsu, sensei to gakusei   4．niwa, inu to neko to uma

Question: Heya ni **nani ga** arimasu ka.
What is in the room?
Answer 1: Terebi ya rajio ga arimasu.
There is a television and a radio.
Answer 2: Nani mo arimasen.
Nothing is there.
"**ya**" is an auxiliary particle for incomplete enumerations (and ~ etc.)

[Renshuu]

1．kono heya, sutereo ya konpyuuta   2．sono heya, hondana ya sofaa
3．ano heya, tsukue ya isu   4．anata no machi, byooin ya yuubinkyoku ya kooen

(2) **Numeral + imasu / arimasu**

Question: Soko ni hito ga **nan-nin*** imasu ka.
How many people are there?
Answer: 5(Go)-nin* imasu.
There are five people.
Question: Soko ni heya ga **ikutsu*** arimasu ka?
How many rooms are there?
Answer: Mittsu* arimasu.
There are three rooms.

* Depending on the object, different numerals must be used, e.g. "-nin" for
people, "-tsu" for objects in general, "-dai" for machines or devices,
"-mai" for flat things like paper, "-hon" for long things like a pencil
"-satsu" for books. (See the table of number words on the vocabulary page!)

[Renshuu]

1. koko / nihon-jin / 1 (hitori)
2. soko / doitsu-jin / 2 (futari)
3. asoko / gakusei / 3 (san)-nin
4. soko / sofaa / 1 (hitotsu)
5. asoko / kami / 5 (go)-mai
6. koko / kuruma / 6 (roku)-dai
7. soko / hon / 7 (nana)-satsu
8. asoko / pen / 4 (yon)-hon

"**dake**" and "**shika**" (only):

Both mean "only" and are used after a number word. "**dake**" is used with <u>positive</u> verb forms, but "**shika**" is only used with <u>negative</u> verb forms and emphasizes a small number or small amounts. "**shika**" is used when you actually want more.

Kaban ga hitotsu **dake arimasu**. / Kaban ga hitotsu **shika arimasen**.
There is only one bag.
Soko ni kodomo ga hitori **dake imasu**. */* Soko ni kodomo ga hitori **shika imasen**.
There is only one child there.

(3) **Location information : S wa O ni imasu / arimasu.**

Question: Tanaka-san **wa doko ni** imasu ka.
       Where is Mr. Tanaka?
Answer: (Tanaka-san **wa)** heya ni imasu.
       He is in the room.

"**wa**" is an auxiliary particle for the subject of the sentence and is used when the predicate (the back part of the sentence) has new information and the focus of the sentence.

[Renshuu]

1. Minami-san / kaisha
2. Machida-san / daigaku
3. inu to neko / niwa
4. sensei / kyooshitsu
5. okaasan / daidokoro
6. kodomo / chuugakkoo

Question: Jisho wa **doko ni** arimasu ka.
       Where is the dictionary?
Answer: Tsukue no **ue** ni arimasu
       On the table.

[Exact location information]

~ no **ue** ni (on ~)	~ no **shita** ni (under ~)	~ no **naka** ni (in ~)
~ no **mae** ni (in front of ~)	~ no **ushiro** ni (behind ~)	~ no **tonari** ni (next to ~)
~ no **yoko** ni (next to ~)	~ no **hidari** ni (left of ~)	~ no **migi** ni (right of ~)
~ no **chikaku** ni (near ~)	~ no **mukai** ni (opposite ~)	
~ no **oku** ni (back of the house)	~ to ~ no **aida** ni (between ~ and ~)	

- Pay attention to the order in which places are mentioned.
  "Tsukue no ue (ni)" means "on the table", but "ue no tsukue" means "the table on top".
- "being close" is "chikai desu", but it conjugates into the form "chikaku ni" when used with "arimasu" and "imasu".
- oku" means "at the back of a room" and "interior" or "depth"

[Renshuu]

1．kaban / tsukue / shita
2．konpyuuta / tsukue / tonari
3．depaato / eki / mae
4．toshokan / yuubinkyoku / ushiro
5．terebi / sutereo / denwa / aida
6．furo / heya / oku
7．gakkoo / kooen / mukai
8．byooin / eki / chikaku

Lesson test Dai 3-ka

（1）Complete the sentences with the words given.
1．koko／nihon-jin／3-nin／doitsu-jin／5-nin
2．heya／nani → tsukue／futatsu／terebi／1-dai
3．tsukue／ue／hon／3-satsu／nooto／2-satsu／tokei／hitotsu
4．jisho／doko → jisho／kaban／naka
5．Tanaka-san／doko → Tanaka-san／kaisha
6．niwa／ki／5-hon／soshite／inu／2-hiki／neko／3-biki

（2）Answer the questions.
1．～san (Anata) no apaato ni sutereo ga arimasu ka.
2．～san (Anata) no machi ni depaato ga ikutsu arimasu ka.
3．～san (Anata) no kaisha ni nihon-jin ya chuugoku-jin ga imasu ka.
4．Doitsu ni takai yama ga arimasu ka.
5．Doitsu ni nagai kawa ga arimasu ka.
6．～san (Anata) no heya ni hon ga nan-satsu arimasu ka.

（3）Translate the English sentences into Japanese

1．What is in the room?
2．There is a table, a bookshelf and a TV in the room
3．Where is Mr. Tanaka?
4．He is in front of the station
5．How many books are on the table
6．In this town there is a supermarket, a nice park, a train station, etc

Tanaka-san wa doko ni imasu ka?

Tanaka-san wa Okuda-san to Sasaki-san no aida ni imasu yo.

47

第４課 だいよんか Dai Yon-ka

きたのさんの朝
Kitano-san no asa

Lesson 4　きたのさんの朝

マイヤー　：きたのさんは あさ何時に おきますか。

きたの　　：ぼくは あさ6時に おきます。

マイヤー　：あさごはんは 何を 食べますか。

きたの　　：ごはんを 食べます。 そして みそしるを 飲みます。 マイヤーさんは？

マイヤー　：わたしは いつも パンとコーヒーです。 ときどき りんごや みかんも 食べます。
　　　　　　きたのさんは 何時に いえを 出ますか。

きたの　　：7時ごろ 出ます。

マイヤー　：何で 会社に 行きますか。

きたの　　：バスと 電車で 行きます。

マイヤー　：会社まで どのぐらい かかりますか。

きたの　　：1時間半 ぐらい かかります。

マイヤー　：ああ、それは ちょっとながい ですね。

きたの　　：ええ、ですから 電車の中で 新聞や ざっしを 読みます。

マイヤー　：そうですか。 わたしは 電車の中で よく おんがくを 聞きます。

Translation of the text

Mr. Kitano's morning
Mayer: Mr. Kitano, what time do you usually get up in the morning?
Kitano: I get up at 6 o'clock.
Mayer: What do you eat for breakfast?
Kitano: I eat rice. And I also eat miso soup. And you, Mrs. Mayer?
Mayer: A slice of bread and a cup of coffee. Sometimes I also eat an apple
　　　　or a tangerine. When do you leave home?
Kitano: I leave around 7 o'clock.
Mayer: How do you get to work?
Kitano: I take the bus and the train.
Mayer: How long does it take to get to the company?
Kitano: It takes about an hour and a half.
Mayer: Oh, it takes quite a long time, doesn't it?
Kitano: Yes, that's why I read newspapers or magazines on the train.
Mayer: Is that so? I often listen to music on the train.

Questions about the text
1．きたのさんは朝何時におきますか。
2．あさごはんは何を食べますか。
3．マイヤーさんは何を食べますか。
4．きたのさんは何時にいえを出ますか。
5．会社に何で行きますか。

6．会社までどのくらいかかりますか。

7．きたのさんは電車の中で何をしますか。

8．マイヤーさんは電車の中で何をしますか。

Vocabulary and idioms

Vocabulary	reading	English
歩いて　あるいて	aruite	walking
歩く　あるく	aruku	walking on foot
朝　あさ	asa	morning
朝ご飯　あさごはん	asagohan	breakfast
晩　ばん	ban	evening
晩ご飯　ばんごはん	bangohan	dinner
バス	basu	bus
勉強（する）　べんきょう	benkyoo(suru)	learning, study
ビール	biiru	beer
ちょっと	chotto	a little
で	de	AP for the means, AP for the place of action
出る　でる	deru	go out, leave
ですから	desukara	therefore
どのぐらい	donogurai	how much, how many
分　ふん	fun	minute
午後　ごご	gogo	afternoon
ご飯　ごはん	gohan	food, rice
ごろ	goro	approximate (only for the time)
午前　ごぜん	gozen	morning, forenoon
ぐらい、くらい	gurai, kurai	approximately (generally usable)
半　はん	han	half
働く　はたらく	hataraku	work
へ	e	AP for the direction
昼　ひる	hiru	midday, noon
昼ご飯　ひるごはん	hirugohan	lunch
本　ほん	hon	book
家　いえ・うち	ie, uchi	house, flat
行く　いく・ゆく	iku, yuku	go, drive
いつも	itsumo	always
～時　じ	ji	~ o'clock
時間　じかん	jikan	hour
自転車　じてんしゃ	jitensha	bicycle
ジュース	juusu	juice
帰る、家に～　かえる	kaeru, ie ni kaeru	return, go home
会議　かいぎ	kaigi	conference, meeting
買い物（する）　かいもの	kaimono(suru)	shopping, shopping
かかる	kakaru	it takes ~
から	kara	from
買う　かう	kau	buy
聞く　きく	kiku	hear, ask

紅茶　こうちゃ	koocha	black tea
コーヒー	koohii	coffee
果物　くだもの	kudamono	fruit
来る　くる	kuru	come
まで	made	until
みかん	mikan	tangerine
みんな	min'na	all, everything
見る　みる	miru	see
ミルク	miruku	milk
味噌汁　みそしる	miso-shiru	Miso soup
水　みず	mizu	water
何時　なんじ	nan-ji	what time
寝る　ねる	neru	sleep, go to bed
に	ni	AP for time, AP for destination
日本語　にほんご	nihongo	Japanese
飲み物　のみもの	nomimono	drinks
飲む　のむ	nomu	drink
を	o	AP for the direct object
お茶　おちゃ	ocha	tea
お菓子　おかし	okashi	sweets
起きる　おきる	okiru	get up (out of bed)
音楽　おんがく	ongaku	music
お酒　おさけ	osake	Sake, rice wine
パン	pan	bread
りんご	ringo	apple
新聞　しんぶん	shinbun	newspaper
～過ぎ　すぎ	sugi	shortly after ~ (time)
する	suru	do
食べる　たべる	taberu	eat
卵　たまご	tamago	egg
テレビを見る　みる	terebi o miru	watch television
時々　ときどき	tokidoki	sometimes
(～が)続く　つづく	tsuzuku	continue
野菜　やさい	yasai	vegetables
よく	yoku	often, a lot
読む　よむ	yomu	read
雑誌　ざっし	zasshi	Journal, magazine

Kanji

Kanji	SC	English	On-yomi *Kun-yomi*	Usage / Composites
何	7	what	ka, nan *nani*	何人　nan'nin / how many people 何円　nan'en / how many yen
時	10	time, date	ji *toki*	時間　jikan / time 時計　tokei / clock

間	12	between	kan, ken *aida, ma*	人間 ningen / human 中間 chuukan / middle, between
半	5	half	han *naka*	半分 hanbun / half 半年 hantoshi / half a year
分	4	minute divide	fun *wa-keru*	部分 bubun / part 自分 jibun / yourself
食	9	eat	shoku *ta-beru*	食事 shokuji / food 日本食 nihonshoku / Japanese food
出	5	go out	shutsu *de-ru*	出発 shuppatsu / departure 出口 deguchi / exit
会	6	meet	kai *a-u*	会社 kaisha / company 会議 kaigi / meeting
社	7	shrine	sha *yashiro*	社会 shakai / company 神社 jinja / shrine
電	13	electricity	den	電車 densha / train 電気 denki / electricity, stream
車	7	car	sha *kuruma*	自動車 jidoosha / car 電車 densha / train, railroad
行	6	walk	koo, gyoo *i-ku, yu-ku*	旅行 ryokoo / journey 行動 koodoo / action
来	7	drive	rai *ku-ru*	来週 raishuu / next week 来月 raigetsu / next month
読	14	come	doku *yo-mu*	読書 dokusho / reading 読者 dokusha / reader
聞	14	hear ask	bun *ki-ku*	新聞 shinbun / newspaper 見聞 kenbun / experience

· SC: stroke count of the kanji · stroke sequence of the kanji: see page 212.

Grammar and exercises

Verbs (present tense)

1-step verbs / 5-step verbs / two irregular verbs

	Basic form	Masu form	English	Features
1-step verbs	**oki-ru** **ne-ru** **tabe-ru**	oki-masu ne-masu tabe-masu	get up sleep eat	The ending of the basic form is always "**ru**". The vowel before the ending is always either "**e**" or "**i**". *
5-step verbs	no-mu i-ku kaka-ru	no-**mi**-masu i-**ki**-masu kaka-**ri**-masu	drink walk take	Five vowel endings depending on the verb forms: a, i, u, e, o Basic form: "**u**", Masu form: "**i**"
irregular verbs	ku-ru su-ru	ki-masu shi-masu	come do	The vowel of the verb stem changes.

Basic form (BF) = infinitive = the form that appears in the dictionary and is used as a familiar (polite-empty) form. See L.9.
Masu form = a polite form normally used in everyday conversation.
To negate the masu form, you only need to replace masu with **masen**.
oki-masu → oki-masen,　nomi-masu → nomi-masen,　ki-masu → ki-masen
* However, there are some 5-step verbs that have the ending "-**iru**" or "-**eru**", such as **kae**ru (to return), **hai**ru (to go in), **hashi**ru (to run), **shi**ru (to know), **ki**ru (to cut), etc.

(1) Time indication

A：朝何時におきますか
　　What time do you get up in the morning?

B: ６時におきます。
　　I get up at 6 o'clock.

A：ばん何時にねますか。
　　What time do you go to bed at night?

B: 11時にねます。
　　I go to bed at 11 o'clock.

・ "に" is used as an auxiliary particle (AP) here to indicate the time (6-ji ni = at 6 o'clock).
・ The subject is often omitted if it is clearly recognizable from the situation.
・ The verb in the present tense can be used both for actions and facts in the present and for those in the future, as well as for those in the future.

「れんしゅう」
1．７時／10時半　　　　　　2．７時半／11時半ごろ (without に)
3．8時10分前／11時45分　　4．6時15分／12時すぎ

(2) Object + verb

A: 何を食べますか。
　　What do you eat?

B: ごはんを食べます。
　　I eat rice.

A: 何を飲みますか。
　　What do you drink?

B: コーヒーを飲みます。
　　I drink coffee.

A: 水も飲みますか。
　　Do you also drink water?

B: はい、水も飲みます。
　　Yes, I also drink water.

B: いいえ、水は飲みません。
　　No, I don't drink water.

・ The AP "を (o)" is used after a direct object.
・ The AP "を" is omitted if the AP "**も**" is (also) used.
・ The AP "**は** (wa)" can also be used for the object if it is thematized and contrasted with the other.

「れんしゅう」
1．パン／ジュース／コーヒー　　2．たまご／おさけ／ビール
3．やさい／おちゃ／こうちゃ　　4．くだもの／みず／牛乳（ミルク）

(3) With what?

A: 何時に家を出ますか。
　　What time do you leave home?
B: 朝8時に出ます。
　　I leave at 8 o'clock in the morning.
A: 何で会社に行きますか。
　　How do you go to the office?
B: 電車で行きます。
　　I go to the office by train.
A: 何時に家に帰りますか。
　　What time do you go home?
B: 晩6時ごろ帰ります。
　　I go home around 6:00 p.m.

・The AP "で" is used according to the means (transportation, tools or languages).
　Exception: on foot: **あるいて** (but without で)
・The AP "に" is also used for the destination (kaisha ni = to the company).
　Instead of "に", the directional AP "へ (e)" (to) can also be used.

「れんしゅう」
1．7時半／バス／5時　　　　　2．7時／車／6時半
3．8時15分／自転車／7時　　4．8時20分／あるいて／9時10分

(4) Duration

A: 家から会社までどのぐらいかかりますか。
　　How long does it take from home to the company?
B: 電車で1時間ぐらいかかります。
　　It takes about 1 hour by train.

「れんしゅう」
1．家／駅／バス／10分　　　　　2．家／学校／自転車／15分
3．家／公園／あるいて／5分　　　4．家／郵便局／車／20分
5．家／ベルリン／電車／4時間　　6．家／町／自動車／1時間半

"かかる" is used for the length of time it takes to reach a place or complete a task,
whereas the verb "つづく" is used to express the duration of events / circumstances.

会議は晩10時までつづきました。The conference continued until 10 o'clock in the evening.
"から" and "まで" (from ~ to ~) can also be used to specify the time.
9時から晩6時まではたらきます。　　I work from 9 to 6 o'clock in the evening.

(5) Indication of the place of action

A: そこで何_{なに}をしますか。

What do you do there?

B: 本_{ほん}を読_よみます。

I read books.

"で" is the AP for the place where an action takes place. (AP of the place of action)
This is not to be confused with the AP for the place of being there "に". (see L.3!)

「れんしゅう」

1．台所_{だいどころ}／ごはん／食_たべる　　2．会社_{かいしゃ}／はたらく

3．学校_{がっこう}／日本語_{にほんご}／勉強_{べんきょう}する　　4．へや／テレビ／見_みる

5．図書館_{としょかん}／本_{ほん}／読_よむ　　6．スーパー／おかしとのみもの／買_かう

みんなの一日_{いちにち}、何_{なに}をしますか。　　(Be careful when reading 4 and 9 o'clock.)

	Time	マイヤーさん	きたのさん	あなた
	6時_じ		おきる	
	7時	おきる	いえを出る	
	8時	いえを出_でる		
午前_{ごぜん}	9時_く		会社_{かいしゃ}で働_{はたら}く*	
	10時	大学_{だいがく}でべんきょうする*		
	11時			
	12時		ひるごはんを食_たべる	
	1時	ひるごはんを食_たべる	しんぶんを読_よむ	
	2時			
	3時			
	4時_よ			
	5時	いえにかえる		
午後_{ごご}	6時	買_かい物_{もの}する	いえにかえる	
	7時	ばんごはんを食_たべる	ばんごはんを食_たべる	
	8時	日本語_{にほんご}をべんきょうする	ビールをのむ	
	9時_く	おんがくを聞_きく	テレビを見_みる	
	10時	本_{ほん}を読_よむ		
	11時		ねる	
	12時	ねる		

* The AP から is used here after the time because work or learning takes a long time.

minutes: 分^{ふん}

1分	2分	3分	4分	5分	6分
いっぷん	にふん	さんぷん	よんぷん	ごふん	ろっぷん
7分	8分	9分	10分	11分	12分
ななふん	はっぷん	きゅうふん	じゅっぷん	じゅういっぷん	じゅうにふん
20分	35分	48分	59分	60分	何分
にじゅっぷん	さんじゅうごふん	よんじゅうはっぷん	ごじゅうきゅうふん	ろくじゅっぷん	なんぷん

いま何時、何分ですか。 ⇒ いま 11時11分です。

Lesson test

（1）Use the correct auxiliary particle.

1．わたしは朝7時＿＿おきます。

2．そしてあさごはん＿＿食べます。

3．8時＿＿いえ＿＿出ます。

4．わたし＿＿電車＿＿会社＿＿行きます。

5．電車＿＿中＿＿本＿＿ざっし＿＿読みます。

6．いえ＿＿＿＿会社＿＿＿＿＿1時間ぐらいかかります。

7．9時＿＿＿＿5時＿＿＿＿はたらきます。

8．6時＿＿＿＿いえ＿＿＿かえります。

（2）Answer the questions.

1．あさごはんは何を食べますか。

2．コーヒーを飲みますか、お茶を飲みますか。

3．何で会社に行きますか。

4．どのくらいはたらきますか。

5．どこで買い物しますか。

6．晩に何をしますか。

（3）Translate the sentences into Japanese.

1．How long does it take to walk from your home to the station?

2．I eat a slice of bread and an apple in the evening.

3．I don't drink coffee.

4．I watch TV and listen to music at home.

5．I go to bed around 11 o'clock.

第５課 だいごか Dai Go-ka

何をしましたか。
Nani o shimashita ka.

Lesson 5　何<ruby>なに</ruby>をしましたか。

北野<ruby>きたの</ruby>　　　：マイヤーさんは　しゅうまつ　どこかに　行<ruby>い</ruby>きましたか。

マイヤー　：いいえ、どこにも　行<ruby>い</ruby>きませんでした。　家<ruby>いえ</ruby>で　日本語<ruby>にほんご</ruby>のしゅくだいを　しました。

北野<ruby>きたの</ruby>　　　：そうですか。　ぼくは　友<ruby>とも</ruby>だちと　買<ruby>か</ruby>いものを　しました。

マイヤー　：何<ruby>なに</ruby>を　買<ruby>か</ruby>いましたか。

北野<ruby>きたの</ruby>　　　：デパートで　くつと　ＣＤを　買<ruby>か</ruby>いました。

マイヤー　：そうですか。　それから　何<ruby>なに</ruby>を　しましたか。

北野<ruby>きたの</ruby>　　　：公園<ruby>こうえん</ruby>を　さんぽしました。　そして　ごはんを　食<ruby>た</ruby>べに行<ruby>い</ruby>きました。

マイヤー　：何<ruby>なに</ruby>を　食<ruby>た</ruby>べましたか。

北野<ruby>きたの</ruby>　　　：すしを　食<ruby>た</ruby>べました。　マイヤーさんは　もう　日本料理<ruby>にほんりょうり</ruby>を　食<ruby>た</ruby>べましたか。

マイヤー　：いいえ、まだです。

北野<ruby>きたの</ruby>　　　：じゃあ、こんど　いっしょに　食<ruby>た</ruby>べに　行<ruby>い</ruby>きませんか。

マイヤー　：はい、ぜひ！　よろこんで。

Translation of the text

What did you do?
Kitano : Ms. Mayer, did you go out at the weekend?
Mayer : No, I didn't go out.
　　　　　I was at home doing my Japanese homework.
Kitano : I see! I went shopping with a friend.
Mayer : What did you buy?
Kitano : I bought some shoes and a CD at the department store.
Mayer : Nice! And what else did you do?
Kitano : We went for a walk in the park and then went out to eat.
Mayer : What did you eat?
Kitano : We ate sushi. Have you ever eaten Japanese food before?
Mayer : No, never.
Kitano : Then let's go out for Japanese food together?
Mayer : Yes, I would love to!

Questions about the text

1．マイヤーさんはしゅうまつ何<ruby>なに</ruby>をしましたか。
2．北野<ruby>きたの</ruby>さんは何<ruby>なに</ruby>をしましたか。
3．北野<ruby>きたの</ruby>さんはどこでＣＤとくつを買<ruby>か</ruby>いましたか。
4．それから何<ruby>なに</ruby>をしましたか。
5．北野<ruby>きたの</ruby>さんは何<ruby>なに</ruby>を食<ruby>た</ruby>べましたか。
6．マイヤーさんはもう日本料理<ruby>にほんりょうり</ruby>を食<ruby>た</ruby>べましたか。
7．マイヤーさんと北野<ruby>きたの</ruby>さんは何<ruby>なに</ruby>をしますか。

Vocabulary and idioms

vocabulary	reading	English
明日　あした	ashita	tomorrow
～に会う　あう	au	meet
出かける　でかける	dekakeru	go out, go away
だれか	dareka	someone
どこか	dokoka	nowhere
どこにも～ない	doko nimo ~nai	nowhere
映画　えいが	eiga	movie
駅前　えきまえ	ekimae	in front of the station
船　ふね	fune	ship
外国　がいこく	gaikoku	foreign country
橋　はし	hashi	bridge
話す　はなす	hanasu	speak
走る　はしる	hashiru	run, drive
飛行機　ひこうき	hikooki	airplane
一人で　ひとりで	hitori de	alone
本屋　ほんや	hon'ya	bookshop
いいえ、まだです	Iie, mada desu	No, not yet
いっしょに	issho ni	together
いつ	itsu	when
じゃあ	jaa	then
書く　かく	kaku	write
かな	kana	hiragana and katakana
借りる　かりる	kariru	borrow
漢字　かんじ		kanji, Chinese characters
昨日　きのう	kinoo	yesterday
喫茶店　きっさてん	kissaten	coffee shop
切手　きって	kitte	stamp
今日　きょう	kyoo	today
今度　こんど	kondo	this time, in the near future
コンサート	konsaato	concert
公園　こうえん	kooen	park
交差点　こうさてん	koosaten	crossing
靴　くつ	kutsu	shoes
靴下　くつした	kutsushita	socks
教科書　きょうかしょ	kyookasho	textbook
まだ	mada	still
道　みち	michi	street, road
もう	moo	already
日本料理　にほんりょうり	nihon-ryoori	Japanese food
踊る　おどる	odoru	dance
泳ぐ　およぐ	oyogu	swim
料理（する）　りょうり	ryoori(suru)	cooking, dish, food, cook
散歩（する）　さんぽ	sanpo(suru)	walk, go for a walk
仕事（する）　しごと	shigoto	working, work
CD	shii-dii	CD
宿題　しゅくだい	shukudai	homework
週末　しゅうまつ	shuumatsu	weekend

空 そら	sora	sky
寿司 すし	sushi	sushi
～と	~ to	with ~
飛ぶ とぶ	tobu	fly, jump
友達 ともだち	tomodachi	friend(s)
通る とおる	tooru	pass by
海 うみ	umi	sea
渡る わたる	wataru	cross
喜んで よろこんで	yorokonde	gladly
ぜひ	zehi	without fail

Kanji

Kanji	SC	English	On-yomi *Kun-yomi*	Usage / Composites
外	5	outside	gai *soto*	外国 gaikoku / foreigner 外国人 gaikokujin / foreigner
国	8	state, country	koku *kuni*	国家 kokka / State 国歌 kokka / national anthem
語	14	language, word	go *kata-ru*	日本語 nihon-go / Japanese 言語 gengo / language
友	4	friend(s)	yuu *tomo*	友達 tomodachi / friend(s) 友人 yuujin / friend(s)
買	12	buy	bai *ka-u*	売買 baibai / to buy and sell 買い物 kaimono / shopping
公	4	public	koo *ooyake*	公園 kooen / park 公立 kooritsu / public
園	13	garden, park	en *sono*	庭園 teien / large garden 花園 hanazono / flower garden
私	7	I, private	shi *watashi*	私立 shiritsu / privately founded 私用 shiyoo / private matter
見	7	see	ken *mi-ru*	見物 kenbutsu / visit 見学 kengaku / visit
起	10	get up, stand up	ki *o-kiru*	起きる okiru / get up 起床 kishoo / to get up
飲	12	drink	in *no-mu*	飲食 inshoku / to eat and drink 飲料水 inryoosui / drinking water
話	13	speak	wa *hana-su*	電話 denwa / telephone 話題 wadai / topic of conversation
書	10	write	sho *ka-ku*	書道 shodoo / calligraphy 書き方 kakikata / way of writing
走	7	run, drive	soo *hashi-ru*	走る hashi-ru / run, drive 競走 kyoosoo / race
空	8	sky	kuu *sora*	空気 kuuki / air 空間 kuukan / space
海	9	sea	kai *umi*	海外 kaigai / overseas 海岸 kaigan / coast

・SC: stroke count of the kanji ・stroke sequence of the kanji: see page 212.

Grammar and exercises

Verbs - past tense

	Basic form	Positive (-mashita)	Negative (-masen deshita)
1-step verbs	起きる 食べる	起きました 食べました	起きませんでした 食べませんでした
5-step verbs	飲む 買う	飲みました 買いました	飲みませんでした 買いませんでした
irregular verbs	来る する	来ました しました	来ませんでした しませんでした

(1) Question about an activity in the past

A: 今日*どこへ行きましたか。
  Where did you go today?
B: 町へ行きました。
  I went to the city.
A: だれと*行きましたか。
  With whom did you go?
B: 友だちと*行きました。
  I went with a friend.
A: 町で何をしましたか。
  What did you do in the city?
B: 買い物をしました。
  I shopped.

* AP"に" for time is omitted except in the case of the time and the specific date.

* AP"と" here means "**with someone**". However, "**alone**" means "一人で".

「れんしゅう」
1．町／友だち／映画／見る　　2．大学／一人／日本語／べんきょうする
3．外国／一人／仕事／する　　4．海／父／およぐ
5．デパート／母／くつ下／買う　6．きっ茶店／友だち／コーヒー／飲む

(2) Question word + も + V (negative) = absolute negation (not at all)

A: 何を買いましたか。
  What did you buy?
B: 何も買いませんでした。
  I didn't buy anything.

「れんしゅう」
1．食べる　　2．飲む　　3．見る　　4．聞く
5．読む　　6．書く　　7．話す　　8．する

Other question words (だれ, どこ) can also be used.

今日だれか来ましたか。　→　いいえ、**だれも**来ませんでした。
Did anyone come today?　　　No, no one came.

どこかに行きましたか。　→　いいえ、**どこにも**行きませんでした。
Did you go anywhere?　　　　No, I didn't go anywhere.

(3) Spatial movements

私は公園**を**さんぽしました。
I went for a walk in the park.

"**を**" is an AP for the place where a spatial movement takes place.

「れんしゅう」

1．かのじょ／道／あるく　　2．かれ／公園／走る　　3．車／交差点／わたる
4．バス／駅前／通る　　5．ひこうき／空／とぶ　　6．ふね／海／わたる

(4) Completion of an activity: ~ already done?

A: もう新聞を読みましたか。
　 Did you already read the newspaper?

B: はい、もう読みました。
　 Yes, I already read it.

A: じゃあ、もう雑誌を読みましたか。
　 Well, have you also already read the magazine?

B: いいえ、まだ**読みません**＊／　まだです。
　 No, I haven't read it yet.

＊ If the answer is negative, the verb must be put in the present tense,
　 because the action has not yet been completed at this point in time. See L.7.

「れんしゅう」

1．日本／行く／中国　　2．日本料理／食べる／お酒／飲む　　3．野菜／買う／くだもの
4．教科書／買う／読む　　5．かな／勉強する／漢字　　6．宿題／する／友だち／会う

(5) Question about the purpose and answer

A: **何をしに**そこへ行きますか。
　 For what purpose are you going there?
B: 友だちに会いに行きます。
　 I'm going there to see my friends.

The **stem of the Masu form** (SdMF) is used before "**に**".

「れんしゅう」

1．町／えいが／見る　　2．会社／仕事／する　　3．学校／日本語／勉強する
4．本屋／ざっし／買う　　5．図書館／本／かりる　　6．郵便局／切手／買う

(6) Invitation to activities or events = V-ませんか

A: 明日(いっしょに)すしを食べませんか。*
Shall we go eat sushi together tomorrow?
B: はい、ぜひ。よろこんで。
Yes, with pleasure!

はい、ありがとう。でも、ちょっと時間がありません。
Thanks, but unfortunately I don't have time.

* Instead of "ませんか", "ましょう" can be used. See L.10.

「れんしゅう」
1．えいが／見る　　2．日本語／勉強する　　3．公園／さんぽする
4．おどる　　　　　5．コンサート／行く　　6．町／出かける

Lesson test

(1) Form the sentences in the past tense.
1．私 / きのう / 町 / 友だち / 会う
2．いっしょ / えいが / 見る / そして / 公園 / さんぽする
3．かれ / ワイン / 飲む / が / わたし / 何 / 飲む (negative)
4．わたし / もう / 日本 / 行く / が / かれ / まだ / 行く (negative)
5．しゅうまつ / 友だち / 海 / およぐ / 行く
6．車 / はし / わたる / そして / 駅 / まで / 走る

(2) Answer the questions.
1．きのう映画を見ましたか。
2．きのうのばんに何をしましたか。
3．もう日本料理を食べましたか。
4．しゅうまつどこへ行きましたか。
5．いつ日本語を勉強しましたか。
6．明日いっしょにコンサートに行きませんか。

(3) Translate the sentences into Japanese.
1．What did you do at the weekend?
2．I went out for sushi with my friends.
3．Have you done the Japanese homework yet?
4．No, not yet.

第６課 だいろっか Dai Ro-kka

いちばんふる　　みやこ

一番古い 都

Ichi-ban furui miyako

Lesson 6　一番古い都

北野　　　：先週　友だちと　奈良へ　旅行しました。
マイヤー　：あ、そうですか。　いかがでしたか。
北野　　　：とても　楽しかったです。
マイヤー　：天気は　いかがでしたか。
北野　　　：少し　さむかったですが、悪くなかったですよ。
マイヤー　：それは　よかったですね。　奈良は　京都より　小さい町ですね。
北野　　　：ええ、奈良は　京都ほど　大きくないです。　でも　京都とおなじぐらい　有名です。
　　　　　　そして　もっと　古い町です。
マイヤー　：奈良は　日本で　一番古い都　でしたね。　奈良で　何を　見ましたか。
北野　　　：東大寺の大仏や　若草山を　見ました。
マイヤー　：鎌倉にも　大仏が　ありますね。　どちらのほうが　大きいですか。
北野　　　：東大寺のほうが　大きいですよ。そして　もっと古いです。
マイヤー　：ああ、そうですか。

Translation of the text

The first capital

Kitano: Last week I travelled to Nara with my friends.
Mayer: Oh really? How was it?
Kitano: It was very nice!
Mayer: How was the weather?
Kitano: It was a bit cold, but it wasn't bad.
Mayer: That's good, right? Nara is smaller than Kyoto, isn't it?
Kitano: Yes, Nara is not as big as Kyoto, but Nara is just as famous as Kyoto
　　　　and even older.
Mayer: Nara was the first capital of Japan, wasn't it? What did you see in Nara?
Kitano: I saw the large Buddha statue in Todaiji Temple and Mount Wakakusa.
Mayer: There is also a large Buddha statue in Kamakura, isn't there? Which one is bigger?
Kitano: The one in Todaiji is bigger than the one in Kamakura and it's even older.
Mayer: Ah, really?

Questions about the text

1．マイヤーさんは先週旅行しましたか。
2．北野さんはどこへ旅行しましたか。
3．天気はいかがでしたか。
4．京都と奈良とでは、どちらのほうが大きいですか。
5．京都が日本で一番古い都ですか。
6．奈良で何を見ましたか。
7．奈良の大仏と鎌倉の大仏とでは、どちらのほうが古いですか。

Vocabulary and idioms

Vocabulary	reading	English
秋　あき	aki	autumn
後で　あとで	ato de	later
暑い　あつい	atsui	hot
大仏　だいぶつ	daibutsu	large Buddha statue
どちら	dochira	which
どうぶつ	doobutsu	animal
エベレスト山　さん	eberesuto-san	Mt. Everest
英語　えいご	eigo	English
フランス・〜語　ご	furansu, ~go	France, French
冬　ふゆ	fuyu	winter
銀　ぎん	gin	silver
ご主人　ごしゅじん	go-shujin	husband of another woman
８月　はちがつ	hachi-gatsu	August
始め　はじめ	hajime	beginning
春　はる	haru	spring
早い　はやい	hayai	early, fast
速い　はやい	hayai	fast (only for speed)
東　ひがし	higashi	east
ほど〜ない	hodo ~nai	not as ~ as
方　ほう	hoo	direction, side, here for the comparative used
細い　ほそい	hosoi	slender, thin
一番　いちばん	ichiban	number 1, here: word for superlative
一年　いちねん	ichi-nen	one year
忙しい　いそがしい	isogashii	busy
鎌倉　かまくら	kamakura	city of Kamakura (west of Tokyo)
簡単な（な）　かんたん（な）	kantan(na)	easy
軽い　かるい	karui	light (weight)
着物　きもの	kimono	kimono (Japanese traditional clothes)
金　きん	kin	gold
昨日　きのう	kinoo / sakujitsu	yesterday
季節　きせつ	kisetsu	seasons
北　きた	kita	north
今週　こんしゅう	konshuu	this week
氷　こおり	koori	ice
国　くに	kuni	country, state
クラス	kurasu	class
今日　きょう	kyoo	today
京都　きょうと	kyooto	Kyoto (city)
南　みなみ	minami	south
都　みやこ	miyako	capital (old term)
もっと	motto	even more
村　むら	mura	village
難しい　むずかしい	muzukashii	difficult
奈良　なら	nara	Nara (city)
なる	naru	become

夏　なつ	natsu	summer
にぎやか（な）	nigiyaka(na)	lively, active
日本　にほん	nihon	Japan
西　にし	nishi	west
乗り物　のりもの	norimono	vehicle
おいしい	oishii	delicious, tasty
奥さん　おくさん	okusan	wife of another man
重い　おもい	omoi	heavy (weight)
おもしろい	omoshiroi	interesting
同じ　おなじ	onaji	same
～と同じぐらい　おなじ	onaji gurai	just as ~ as
多い　おおい	ooi	much, many
パーティー	paatii	party
ロシア	roshia	Russia
旅行（する）　りょこう	ryokoo(suru)	travel, journey
サッカー	sakkaa	soccer
寒い　さむい	samui	cold (only with climate)
世界　せかい	sekai	world
先週　せんしゅう	senshuu	last week
試験　しけん	shiken	exam
親切（な）　しんせつ（な）	shinsetsu(na)	friendly, kind
少し　すこし	sukoshi	a little
少ない　すくない	sukunai	little bit
楽しい　たのしい	tanoshii	funny, cheerful
店員　てんいん	ten'in	sales person
天気　てんき	tenki	weather
テスト	tesuto	test, examination
東大寺　とうだいじ	toodaiji	Todaiji Temple in Nara
遠い　とおい	tooi	far, distant
強い　つよい	tsuyoi	strong
美しい　うつくしい	utsukushii	beautiful (appearance)
ワイン	wain	wine
若い　わかい	wakai	young
若草山　わかくさやま	wakakusayama	Wakakusayama hill in Nara
悪い　わるい	warui	bad
野球　やきゅう	yakyuu	baseball
やさしい	yasashii	sales person
～より	yori	rather than ~

Kanji

Kanji	SCK	English	On-yomi *Kun-yomi*	Usage / Composites
旅	10	Journey	ryo *tabi*	旅行 ryokoo / journey 旅人 tabibito / traveler
天	4	sky heaven	ten *ama*	天気 tenki / weather 天井 tenjoo / blanket
東	8	east	too *higashi*	東京 tookyoo / Tokyo 東洋 tooyoo / Orient, east
西	6	west	sei, sai, zai *nishi*	西洋 seiyoo / West 東西 toozai / east and west
南	9	south	nan *minami*	南北 nanboku / south and north 南極 nankyoku / south pole
北	5	north	hoku *kita*	北極 hokkyoku / north pole 北海道 island of Hokkaidoo
寺	6	temple	ji *tera*	古寺 furudera / an old temple 寺院 jiin / temple
父	4	father	fu *chichi*	父母 fubo / father and mother お父さん o-toosan / father
母	5	mother	bo *haha*	母国 bokoku / motherland お母さん okaasan / mother
若	8	young	jaku, nyaku *waka-i*	若人 wakoodo / young people 若年 jakunen / young (in writing)
安	6	cheap	an *yasu-i*	安心 anshin / to be reassured 安全 anzen / to be sure
番	12	number	ban	番号 bangoo / number 順番 junban / order
便	9	practical	ben, bin *tayo-ri*	便利 benri / practical 不便 fuben / not practical
利	7	profit	ri *toshi*	利用 riyoo / use 利子 rishi / interest
多	6	much	ta *oo-i*	多数 tasuu / large amount, majority 多数決 tasuuketsu / majority decision
少	4	little	shoo *suku-nai, suko-shi*	少年 shoonen / boy 少女 shoojo / girl
悪	11	bad	aku, o *waru-i*	悪人 akunin / evil person, villain 悪口 warukuchi / bad talk

· SC: stroke count of the kanji · stroke sequence of the kanji: see page 213.

Grammar and exercises

(1) Adjectives - past tense of IA and NA

	Basic form	Positive (-katta)	Negative (-ku nakatta)
IA	やすい (cheap) さむい (cold) いい (good)	やす **かった** です さむ **かった** です **よ かった** です	やすく **なかった** です さむく **なかった** です **よく なかった** です
	Basic form	Positive (-deshita)	Negative (-dewa arimasen deshita)
NA	ゆうめい (famous) げんき (healthy) べんり (practical)	ゆうめい **でした** げんき **でした** べんり **でした**	ゆうめい ではありません **でした** げんき ではありません **でした** べんり ではありません **でした**

A: 旅行はいかが（どう）でしたか。
How was the trip?

B: 楽しかったです（よ）。
It was nice.
楽しくなかったです（よ）。
It was not nice.

「れんしゅう」

1．映画／おもしろい　　2．テスト／むずかしい　　3．パーティー／楽しい
4．天気／いい　　　　　5．ごはん／おいしい　　　6．仕事／多い・少ない

A: かれは元気でしたか。
Was he doing well?

B: はい、とても元気でした（よ）。
Yes, he was very well.
いいえ、あまり元気ではありませんでした（よ）。
No, he wasn't doing so well.

「れんしゅう」

1．その町／にぎやか　　2．店員／親切　　　　3．しけん／かんたん
4．その村／静か　　　　5．そのかばん／便利　　6．着物／きれい

(2) Adverbial form of IA and NA

IA and NA can be used as an adverbial form before the verb.
The adverbial form is formed as follows.

	Stem-i	Stem-ku	example	English
IA	早い	早く	かれは早く起きます。	He gets up early.
	いい	よく (AN*)	天気はよくなりました。	The weather got better.
	Stem-na	Stem-ni	example	English
NA	元気な	元気に	かのじょは元気になりました。	She became healthy.
	有名な	有名に	その町は有名になりました。	The city became famous.

「れんしゅう」　In the past tense
IA:　1．この車／速い／走る　　　2．天気／悪い／なる　　　3．仕事／長い／かかる
NA:　1．彼／人／親切／する　　　2．へや／きれい／する　　　3．町／静か／なる

(3) **Comparative:** comparison between two things

奈良は京都より小さいです。
Nara is smaller than Kyoto.

「れんしゅう」

1．かれ／かのじょ／若い　　　2．日本／ドイツ／大きい　　　3．氷／水／かるい
4．きょう／きのう／いそがしい　　5．今週／先週／暑い　　　6．金／銀／高い

Question and answer

A:　京都と奈良と（では）、**どちらのほうが**大きいですか。
　　Which is bigger, Kyoto or Nara?
B:　京都**のほうが**（奈良より）大きいです。
　　Kyoto is bigger than Nara.

どちらのほうが can be used for objects as well as for people and animals.

「れんしゅう」

1．英語／フランス語／やさしい　　　2．イタリア／スペイン／とおい
3．京都／東京／きれい　　　　　　　4．京都／奈良／にぎやか
5．奈良の大仏／鎌倉の大仏／古い　　6．お母さん／お父さん／若い

AはBと おなじぐらい〜です:　A is just as ~ as B

奈良は京都とおなじぐらい有名です。
Nara is as famous as Kyoto.

「れんしゅう」

1．父／母／元気　　　2．ドイツ／ビール／水／安い　　　3．日本／秋／春／いい
4．ご主人／奥さん／やさしい　　　5．カタカナ／ひらがな／やさしい

AはBほど〜くないです (IA)／　〜ではありません (NA):　A is not as ~ as B

奈良は京都ほど大きくないです／大きくありません。
Nara is not as big as Kyoto.
漢字はかなほど簡単ではありません。
Kanji are not as easy as kana.

「れんしゅう」

1．かな／漢字／むずかしい　　2．バス／電車／はやい　　　3．漢字／かな／少ない
4．京都／東京／にぎやか　　　5．バス／電車／便利　　　　6．銀／金／重い

(4) Superlative: comparison between more than two things or in a class

富士山は日本（の中）で一番高いです。
Mt. Fuji is the highest mountain in Japan.

「れんしゅう」
1．エベレスト山／せかい／高い　　2．ロシア／せかい／大きい
3．マイヤーさん／クラス／若い　　4．春／季節／いい
5．兄／家族／大きい　　6．姉／家族／細い

Question and answer

things:　乗り物の中で**何／どれが**一番速いですか。
(animals)　What is the fastest means of transportation?
　　飛行機**が**一番速いです。
　　Airplanes are the fastest.

people:　～さん（あなた）の家族の中で**だれが**一番大きいですか。
　　Who is the tallest in your family?
　　あにが一番大きいです。
　　My older brother is the tallest.

place:　フランスとイギリスとスペイン の中で／とでは **どこが**一番西にありますか。
　　France, England or Spain, which country is the westernmost?
　　スペインが一番西にあります。
　　Spain is the westernmost.

time　6月と7月と8月 の中で／とでは **いつが**一番暑いですか。
　　June, July or August, which month is the hottest?
　　8月が一番暑いです。
　　August is the hottest.

Instead of the individual question words, "どの N が" can be used in general,

such as "どの人が", "どの国が" and "どの山が".

「れんしゅう」
1．飲み物／おいしい／ワイン　　2．友だち／しんせつ／山田さん
3．動物／つよい／ライオン　　4．ハンブルグ／ベルリン／ミュンヘン／南 にある
5．ドイツの町／美しい？？　　6．季節／いい／春、夏、秋、冬？

Lesson test

（１）Make sentences according to the instructions.

1．そのコンピュータ / とても / 高<ruby>高<rt>たか</rt></ruby>い (past tense)

2．きのう / 天気<rt>てんき</rt> / あまり / いい (past tense)

3．かれ / 自転車<rt>じてんしゃ</rt> / 私<rt>わたし</rt> の / 古<rt>ふる</rt>い (comparative)

4．かのじょ / クラス / 中<rt>なか</rt> / 若<rt>わか</rt>い (superlative)

5．奈良<rt>なら</rt> / 京都<rt>きょうと</rt> / 大<rt>おお</rt>きい (not as ~ as ~)

6．きょう / きのう / いそがしい (just as ~ as ~)

7．その 車<rt>くるま</rt> / 道<rt>みち</rt> / とても / 速<rt>はや</rt>い / 走<rt>はし</rt>る (past tense)

（２）Insert the matching words.

1．ビールとワインとでは＿＿＿＿＿＿高<rt>たか</rt>いですか。

　　ワイン＿＿＿＿＿＿高<rt>たか</rt>いです。

2．山田<rt>やまだ</rt>さんと町田<rt>まちだ</rt>さんとでは＿＿＿＿＿＿ながく 働<rt>はたら</rt> きますか。

　　町田<rt>まちだ</rt>さん＿＿＿＿＿＿ 働<rt>はたら</rt> きます。

3．ドイツとフランスとスペインの中<rt>なか</rt>で＿＿＿＿＿＿大<rt>おお</rt>きいですか。

　　＿＿＿＿＿＿大<rt>おお</rt>きいです。

4．くだものの中<rt>なか</rt>で＿＿＿＿＿＿おいしいですか。

　　りんご＿＿＿＿＿＿おいしいです。

5．クラスの中<rt>なか</rt>で＿＿＿＿一番<rt>いちばん</rt>＿＿＿＿＿＿走<rt>はし</rt>りますか。

　　まさとさん＿＿＿＿＿＿走<rt>はし</rt>ります。

（３）Translate the sentences into Japanese.
1．Today was not as cold as yesterday.
2．This bread is tastier than that bread.
3．My older brother is the tallest in my family.

きょうはきのうほど暑<rt>あつ</rt>くないです。

もう元気<rt>げんき</rt>になりましたよ。

富士山<rt>ふじさん</rt>は日本で一番高<rt>いちばんたか</rt>い山です。
そして一番<rt>いちばん</rt>きれいな山ですね。

第７課 だいななか Dai Nana-ka

上野への行き方を聞いています。

Ueno e no ikikata o kiite imasu.

Lesson 7　上野への　行き方を　聞いています。

マイヤー 　：北野さん、すみませんが、上野への　行き方を
　　　　　　　教えてください。

北野 　　　：上野ですね。　まず、そこのバスていで　5番の
　　　　　　　バスに　乗ってください。

マイヤー 　：5番ですね。

北野 　　　：ええ、それで　池袋駅まで　行ってください。

マイヤー 　：はい。

北野 　　　：池袋駅で　バスをおりて、今度は　山手線に　乗りかえてください。

マイヤー 　：はい、山手線ですね。

北野 　　　：そうです。　そこから　8番目の駅が　上野ですよ。

マイヤー 　：わかりました。　ところで　池袋から　上野まで　うんちんはいくらですか。

北野 　　　：それは　知りません　ので、駅員に　聞いてください。

マイヤー 　：はい、そうします。　どうもありがとう。

北野 　　　：どういたしまして。

Translation of the text

Ms. Mayer asks Mr. Kitano for directions to Ueno.
Kitano: Oh, to Ueno. First, please take bus no. 5 at the bus stop.
Mayer: No. 5, right?
Kitano: Yes. Go with it to Ikebukuro station.
Mayer: Okay.
Kitano: At Ikebukuro station please transfer. This time get onto the Yamanote-line!
Mayer: Got it, the Yamanote-line, right?
Kitano: That's right! The eighth station from there (Ikebukuro) is Ueno.
Mayer: All right! By the way, how much is the fare from Ikebukuro to Ueno?
Kitano: I don't know, so please ask the staff at the train station.
Mayer: Yes, I'll do that. Thank you very much!
Kitano: You're welcome!

Questions about the text

1．マイヤーさんは北野さんに何を聞いていますか。
2．何番のバスに乗りますか。
3．そのバスでどこまで行きますか。
4．そこで何に乗りかえますか。
5．上野はそこから何番番目の駅ですか。
6．北野さんは上野までのうんちんを知っていますか。
7．マイヤーさんはどうしますか。

Vocabulary and idioms

vocabulary	reading	English
明るい　あかるい	akarui	bright
秋葉原　あきはばら	akihabara	Akihabara (district of Tokyo)
開く　あく	aku	open
雨、～が降る　あめがふる	ame, - ga furu	rain, raining
売店　ばいてん	baiten	kiosk
晩ご飯　ばんごはん	ban-gohan	dinner
バス停　バスてい	basu-tei	bus stop
美術館　びじゅつかん	bijutsukan	art museum
豚肉　ぶたにく	butaniku	pork
地下鉄　ちかてつ	chikatetsu	subway
中央駅　ちゅうおうえき	chuuoo-eki	Central Station
出口　でぐち	deguchi	exit
電気　でんき	denki	light, power, electricity
動物園　どうぶつえん	doobutsuen	zoo
どういたしまして	doo itashimashite	Here you go! / You're welcome!
どうして	dooshite	why
駅員　えきいん	eki'in	railroad employee
円　えん	en	yen, circle
5番　5ばん	go-ban	number 5
牛肉　ぎゅうにく	gyuuniku	beef
牛乳　ぎゅうにゅう	gyuunyuu	cow's milk
8番目　8ばんめ	hachi-banme	the eighth
はがき	hagaki	postcard
入る　はいる	hairu	go in
晴れる　はれる	hareru	clear up
池袋　いけぶくろ	ikebukuro	Ikebukuro (district of Tokyo)
行き方　いきかた	ikikata	route, directions
いくら	ikuraow	expensive, how much (quantity)
今　いま	ima	now
入（り）口　いりぐち	iriguchi	entrance
鍵　かぎ	kagi	key
鍵がかかっている	kagi ga kakatte iru	be locked
～から	kara	because ～
傘　かさ	kasa	umbrella
ケーキ	keeki	cake
結婚する　けっこん	kekkon-suru	marry
消す　けす	kesu	turn off (light, fire)
消える　きえる	kieru	go out (light, fire)
機械　きかい	kikai	machine
～に～を聞く　きく	～ ni ～o kiku	ask someone about
切符　きっぷ	kippu	ticket
今度　こんど	kondo	this time, next time
コップ	koppu	glass, cup
ください	kudasai	Please give me ～!
暗い　くらい	kurai	dark
曲がる　まがる	magaru	turn

まっすぐ	massugu	straight ahead
～を待つ　まつ	~ o matsu	wait for ~
まず	mazu	first of all
持って行く　もっていく	motteiku	take (objects)
持って来る　もってくる	mottekuru	bring (objects)
持つ　もつ	motsu	have, possess
何回　なんかい	nan-kai	how often ~ ?
習う　ならう	narau	learn (from a teacher)
～ので	node	because ~
乗り変える　のりかえる	norikaeru	change vehicles
乗る　のる	noru	get on, take a means of transportation
お金　おかね	o-kane	money
降りる　おりる	oriru	get out
教える　おしえる	oshieru	teach, instruct
お釣り　おつり	o-tsuri	change (money)
ペン	pen	pen, ballpoint pen
ラジオ	rajio	radio
レストラン	resutoran	restaurant
才（歳）さい	sai	~ years old
咲く　さく	saku	blossom
桜　さくら	sakura	cherry blossom
洗濯（する）せんたく	sentaku(suru)	wash, wash clothes
説明（する）せつめい	setsumei(suru)	explanation, explain
閉まる　しまる	shimaru	close, shut
死ぬ　しぬ	shinu	die
知る　しる	shiru	know
週　しゅう	shuu	week
そうします	soo shimasu	I will do it.
掃除（する）そうじ	sooji-suru	clean, clean up
すみません	sumimasen	Excuse me, please!
住む　すむ	sumu	live
スポーツ	supootsu	sport
手帳　てちょう	techoo	notebook
手紙　てがみ	tegami	letter
テニス	tenisu	tennis
ところで	tokorode	by the way
止まる　とまる	tomaru	stop
止める　とめる	tomeru	~ stop
使う　つかう	tsukau	use
点ける　つける	tsukeru	turn on (light, fire)
点く　つく	tsuku	be lit (electricity comes on)
作る　つくる	tsukuru	make, produce
連れて行く　つれていく	tsureteiku	take (people or animals)
連れて来る　つれてくる	tsuretekuru	bring (people or animals)
上野　うえの	ueno	Ueno (district of Tokyo)
運賃　うんちん	unchin	travel cost, fare
売る　うる	uru	sell
わかりました	wakarimashita	All right!
山手線　やまのてせん	yamanote-sen	Yamanote line in Tokyo (circular line)

Kanji

Kanji	SCK	English	On-yomi *Kun-yomi*	Usage / Composites
左	5	left	sa *hidari*	左右 sayuu / left and right 左側 hidari-gawa / left side
右	5	right	yuu, u *migi*	右側 migi-gawa / right side 右折 u-setsu / turn right
教	11	teach	kyoo *oshi-eru*	教師 kyooshi / teacher 教室 kyooshitsu / classroom
雨	8	rain	u *ame*	風雨 fuu'u / wind and rain 大雨 ooame / heavy rain
目	5	eye	moku *me*	目標 mokuhyoo / destination 目次 mokuji / table of contents
円	4	circle round	en *maru-i*	十円 juu-en / ten yen 百円 hyaku-en / one hundred yen
金	8	gold money	kin *kane*	お金 o-kane / money 料金 ryookin / fee
今	4	now	kon *ima*	今年 kotoshi / this year 今度 kondo / this time
入	2	go in	nyuu *hai-ru, i-reru*	入口 iriguchi / entrance 入学 nyuugaku / to start school
駅	14	train station	eki	中央駅 chuuooeki / main station 駅員 ekiin / railroad employee
口	3	mouth	koo *kuchi*	出口 deguchi / exit 出入口 deiriguchi / entrance and exit
員	10	member	in	会社員 kaisha-in / employee 店員 ten'in / salesperson
週	11	week	shuu	一週間 isshuukan / one week 週末 shuumatsu / weekend
住	7	live	juu *su-mu*	住所 juusho / address 住民 juumin / inhabitant
持	9	have	ji *mo-tsu*	持参 jisan / bring something yourself 支持 shiji / support
知	8	know	chi *shi-ru*	知人 chijin / acquaintance 知識 chishiki / knowledge

· SC: number of strokes of the kanji   · stroke sequence of the kanji: See page 213.

Grammar and exercises

(1) Te-form of verbs: orm of connection with another verb or a sentence

	Ending	Te-Form	Basic form	Masu form	Te-Form	English
1- step verbs	-る	**-て**	起^おきる	起^おきます	起^おきて	get up
			見^みる	見^みます	見^みて	see
			食^たべる	食^たべます	食^たべて	eat
5-step verbs	-う	**-って**	買^かう	買^かいます	買^かって	buy
	-つ		待^まつ	待^まちます	待^まって	wait
	-る		乗^のる	乗^のります	乗^のって	get on
	-む	**-んで**	読^よむ	読^よみます	読^よんで	read
	-ぶ		飛^とぶ	飛^とびます	飛^とんで	fly
	-ぬ		死^しぬ	死^しにます	死^しんで	die
	-く	**-いて**	書^かく	書^かきます	書^かいて	write
	-ぐ	**-いで**	泳^{およ}ぐ	泳^{およ}ぎます	泳^{およ}いで	swim
	-す	**-して**	話^{はな}す	話^{はな}します	話^{はな}して	speak
Irregular verbs	-る	**-て**	する	します	して	do
			くる	きます	きて	come

With 5-step verbs, there are five variations of the te-form depending on the endings of the base form. Exception: 行^いく (go) → **行って**

Various expressions in the Te form

1. Request form

① ～をください: when you want to get an object from the other person

買^かい物^{もの}

buyer: そのラジオをください。
　　　Please give me the radio.

seller: はい、ありがとうございます。2500円^{えん} になります／です。
　　　Yes, with pleasure! Please!　 It costs 2500 yen.

buyer: 10000 円でおねがいします。
　　　To 10000 yen please.

seller: はい、7500 円のおつり になります／です。どうもありがとうございました。
　　　Yes, so you will get 7500 yen back. Thank you very much!

「練^{れんしゅう}習」

1．ペン／240 円／1000 円　　　　2．ケーキ／180 円／500 円

3．時計^{とけい}／3890 円／5000 円　　　4．コップ／370 円／1000 円

5．くつ／4600 円／5000 円　　　6．80 円の切手^{きって}／5枚^{まい}／400 円／1000 円

7．牛肉^{ぎゅうにく}（豚肉^{ぶたにく}）／200 グラム／1280 円／2000 円

② **V(Te form) + ください**: when you ask the other person to do something (action)

A: 中央駅まで行ってください。
　　Please go to the main station.

B: 中央駅ですね。はい、わかりました。
　　To the main station, all right!

「練習」

1．あした／来る　　　　2．ビール／二本／買う　　　3．美術館への行き方／教える

4．この道／まっすぐ行く　5．右／まがる　　　　　　6．左／まがる

7．駅前／止まる（止める）　8．駅の入口（出口）／待つ

2. V(Te form) + います

① **Progressive form:** Someone is in the process of carrying out an action.

A: 今何をしていますか。
　　What are you doing now?

B: 今手紙を書いています。
　　I'm writing a letter right now.

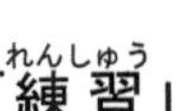

「練習」

1．ごはん／食べる　　　2．日本語／勉強する　　　3．コーヒー／飲む

4．へや／そうじする　　5．せんたくする　　　　　6．はがき／書く

② **State form:** the continuous state of a situation

A: ドアは開いていますか。
　　Is the door open?

B: いいえ、開いていません。／閉まっています。
　　No, it is not open / closed.

「練習」

1．雨／ふる／はれる　　　2．かぎ／かかる　　　3．電気／つく／きえる

4．さくら／もう／さく　　5．てちょう／かばん／入る　　6．南さん／もう／結婚する

③ Routine or regular actions

A: ざっしはどこで売っていますか。
　　Where do they sell magazines?

B: 駅の売店で売っています。
　　They sell them at the station kiosk.

「練習」

1．どんなスポーツ／する／テニス　　　2．どんな* 新聞／読む／日本語の新聞

3．週に何回／日本語／ならう／週に3回　　4．この機械／何／作る／カメラ

However, the masu form is used if the actions are part of the daily routine. See L4.
The question with "don'na" can be asked not only about the property, but also about the variety
when it is used with a verb.

④ **Idiomatic expressions:** common and established expressions

The verbs 住む (to live), 持つ (to have, only for objects) and 知る (to know, to know) are usually used in the Te form.

A: かれはどこに住んでいますか。
　 Where ist he living?
B: かれは京都に住んでいます。
　 He is living in Kyoto.
A: 西さんはいくらお金を持っていますか。
　 How much money do you have, Mr. Nishi?
B: 五千円持っています。
　 I have 5000 yen.
A: かれの名前を知っていますか。
　 Do you know his name?
B: はい、知っています。／ いいえ、知りません。*
　 Yes, I know it / No, I don't know it.

* The masu form must be used for the negative answer.

⑤ **Negative answer to the question about the completion of an action**

Instead of "V (MF)-masen"(L.5), "V (Te-form)-imasen" is used in this case, because the action has not yet been completed and this state is still ongoing. There may also be the nuance that the action is deliberately not carried out, if the masu form is used in the answer.

もうへやをそうじしましたか。⇒ いいえ、**まだしていません**。（いいえ、まだです。）
Have you cleaned the room yet?　No, not yet.

「練習」
1. 昼ごはん／食べる　　　2. 宿題／する　　　3. 今日の新聞／読む
4. 飛行機の切符／買う　　5. 上野／行く　　　6. 友だち／手紙／書く

3. Sentence connection:

① **Enumeration of several actions (verbs) without "そして (and)"**

A: 週末何をしましたか。
　 What did you do at the weekend?
B: 町へ行って、買い物して（から）、レストランでごはんを食べました。
　 I went into town, did some shopping and ate at a restaurant.

· The verb at the end of the sentence does not take the "te form", but the "masu form
· The tense (present or past tense) is determined by the verb at the end of the sentence, whereas the te-form itself is independent of the tense.
· However, the temporal succession of actions exists from the verb at the beginning to the verb at the end of the sentence.
· "kara" is used after the te-form when the after-time is to be emphasized.
　 In English, "te kara" means "after ~" or "afterwards ~".

「練習」

1．友だちに会う／さんぽする／映画を見る　　2．勉強する／泳ぐ／ビール／飲む
3．電車／乗る／上野／行く／買い物する　　4．家／いる／何も／する
5．家／帰る／ばんごはん／食べる／おんがく／聞く／ねる

② Enumerating several properties (adjectives and nouns)

The Te form of adjectives and nouns can be used to list several properties of the subject in
one sentence. The Te-form is used with IA "～くて"　(Attention! いい → よくて)
and the Te form is used for NA and N "で".

東京はどんな町ですか。
What kind of city is Tokyo?
東京は大きくて (IA.)、にぎやかで (NA.)、とてもおもしろい町です。
Tokyo is big, lively and a very interesting city.
彼女はどんな人ですか。
What kind of person is she?
彼女はドイツ人で (N)、23才 (N)で、日本語の生徒です。
She is German, 23 years old and a Japanese student.

「練習」

1．彼女／若い／元気／親切　　2．そのカメラ／新しい／便利／いい
3．その町／古い／静か／きれい　　4．その部屋／小さい／古い／不便
5．彼／日本人／32才／会社員　　6．富士山／日本／一番／高い／美しい／有名

③ Compound verbs with the te-form: V₁-te＋V₂

"TAKE ALONG", "BRING ALONG" and modal phrases with the te-form
In modal phrases, the Te-form is used to show the style or manner in which the action
is performed, with the main verb at the end of the sentence.

A: 東さんは旅行に何を持って行きますか。(持って来る: bring along for items)
　　What are you taking with you on the trip, Mr. Higashi?

B: デジタル・カメラとデジタル・ビデオを持って行きます。
　　I am taking a digital camera and a digital video camera with me.

A: 北さんは動物園にだれを連れて行きますか。(連れて来る: bring along for people/animals)
　　Who are you taking to the zoo, Mr. Kita?

B: 私は子供を連れて行きます。
　　I am taking my child with me.

A: 動物園へ何に乗って行きますか。
　　What do you take to the zoo?

B: バスに乗って行きます。　／ 歩いて行きます。
　　I take the bus. / I walk.

A: 何を使って日本の新聞を読みましたか。
　　What did you use to read the Japanese newspaper?

B: 辞書を使って読みました。
I read the Japanese newspaper with the dictionary.
A: 何を使って漢字を書きましたか。
What did you use to write kanji?
B: コンピュータを使って書きました。
I wrote kanji with the computer.

(2) ～ので／～から (Reason: because ~)

V:　電車に乗る（乗ります）ので／から、きっぷを買ってください。
Please buy a ticket because we are taking a train.

IA:　きょうは天気がいい（です）ので／から、子供とさんぽします。
I'm going for a walk with my children because the weather is nice today.

NA:　かのじょは親切なので／ですから、友だちがたくさんいます。
She has many friends because she is friendly.

N:　次は上野なので／ですから、地下鉄に乗りかえてください。
Please change to the subway because the nearest (station) is Ueno.

「練習」　with the request form
1．映画／見る／きっぷ／買う　　　2．その本／おもしろい／読む
3．このペン／便利／使う　　　　　4．暗い／電気／つける
5．雨／降る／かさ／持って行く　　6．ここ／図書館／静か／する

<u>Question about the reason and the answer to it</u>

どうしてそのカメラを買いますか。　　→　とても便利で、安いですから。
Why do you buy the camera?　　　　　　Because it is very practical and cheap.
どうして日本語を勉強していますか。　→　日本で働きますから。
Why are you learning Japanese?　　　　Because I will work in Japan.

「練習」
1．地下鉄／乗る → 速い／便利　　　2．そのスーパー／買いません → 高い
3．かさ／持って行く → 雨／降る　　4．映画／見ません → おもしろくない
5．きのう／家／いる → 天気／悪い　6．町／行く → 友だち／会う／ビールを飲む

Justification with the te form is also possible if the main clause does not involve any active actions in the main clause.

この町はたくさんスーパーやデパートが**あって**、便利です。
It is convenient to live in this city because there are many supermarkets and department stores.
今日は仕事がたくさん**あって**、とても忙しかったです。
We've been very busy today because we have a lot of work to do.
今日は天気が**よくて** (wrong)、友だちと公園を<u>散歩します</u>(action)。⇒ **いいから／ので**
I'm going for a walk in the park with my friends because it's nice weather out today.

(3) **S₁ が、 S₂** (Introduction)

Sentence 1 with the AP が can be used as an introduction or indication of the topic for sentence 2, and sentence 2 is followed by a request, a question or an explanation. け(れ)ど is sometimes used instead of が.

すみません**が**、駅への行き方を教えてください。
Excuse me! Could you please tell me how to get to the station?
山本です**が**、田中さんはいますか。
My name is Yamamoto. Is Mr. Tanaka here?
その先生です**が**、若くて、とても親切ですよ。
Regarding the teacher, he is young and very nice.

Lesson test

（１）Make the sentences according to the instructions.
1. あした / 9時 / ここ / 来る (request form)
2. ユリアさん / マリアさん / 公園 / さんぽする (progressive form)
3. 私たち / 週に3回 / 日本語 / ならう (habitual action)
4. デパート / もう / 開く / か (state form)
5. 町まで / 電車 / 乗る / 行く / か / 歩く / 行く / か (modal use)
6. きのう / 友だち / 会う / いっしょ / ごはん / 食べる (sentence connection)
7. その車 / 新しい / 速い / 便利 / とてもいい (sentence connection)
8. ドア / 開く / どうぞ / 入る (justification / request form)

（２）Answer the following questions.
1. ～さん（あなた）はどこに住んでいますか。
2. 京都や奈良をよく知っていますか。
3. コンピュータを持っていますか。
4. もう結婚していますか。
5. どんなスポーツをしていますか。
6. きのうの今ごろ何をしていましたか。
7. どうして日本語を勉強していますか。

（３）Translate the sentences into Japanese.
1. Could you please tell me how to go to the station?
2. Take bus no. 7 and please get off in front of the subway station.
3. Where do you sell English newspapers? At the kiosk at the station.
4. Kyoto is old, beautiful, interesting and famous.
5. Should we go to Ueno Park because cherry trees are blooming now?
6. Please turn off the light and leave the room.

第８課 だいはちか Dai Hachi-ka

日本語の試験の前に

Nihongo no shiken no mae ni

Lesson 8　日本語の　試験の　前に

マイヤー　：先生、ちょっと　質問しても　いいですか。
先生　　　：ええ、いいですよ。　どうぞ！
マイヤー　：試験は　ペンで　書かなければ　なりませんか。
先生　　　：いいえ、ペンで　書かなくても　いいですよ。
　　　　　　えんぴつで　書いても　いいです。
マイヤー　：ローマ字で　書いても　いいですか。
先生　　　：いいえ、ローマ字で　書いては　いけません。　かなと　漢字で　書いてください。
マイヤー　：それでは　じしょを　使っても　かまいませんか。
先生　　　：いいえ、いけません。　じしょは　使わないで　ください。
マイヤー　：じゃあ、となりの人と　話しても　かまいませんか。
先生　　　：いいえ、それも　いけません。　となりの人と　話さないで、一人で
　　　　　　やってください。
マイヤー　：あ、はい、わかりました。
先生　　　：じゃあ、始めてください。

Translation of the text

Before the Japanese exam

Mayer:　Sir, I would like to ask a quick question
Sensei:　Yes, of course! Please, go ahead!
Mayer:　Do I have to write this exam with a fountain pen?
Sensei:　No, you don't have to write with a fountain pen. You may write with a pencil.
Mayer:　Can I write it in roomaji?
Sensei:　No, you are not allowed to write in roomaji. Please write in kana and kanji.
Mayer:　And can I use a dictionary?
Sensei:　No, you are not allowed to use a dictionary.
Mayer:　Can I talk to my neighbour?
Sensei:　No, that's not possible either. Please do it alone, without talking to your neighbour.
Mayer:　Ah, yes, okay.
Sensei:　Now please get started!

Questions about the text

1．試験はペンで書かなければなりませんか。
2．ローマ字で書いてもいいですか。
3．辞書を使ってはいけませんか。
4．となりの人と話をしてもかまいませんか。

Vocabulary and idioms

Vocabulary	reading	English
開ける　あける	akeru	open, open up
部長　ぶちょう	buchoo	head of department
外出（する）　がいしゅつ	gaishutsu(suru)	go out
ゲーム	geemu	game
ごみ	gomi	rubbish
午後　ごご	gogo	in the afternoon
午前　ごぜん	gozen	in the morning
始める　はじめる	hajimeru	begin, start
払う、お金を〜　はらう、かね	harau, okane o 〜	pay, pay money
一人で　ひとりで	hitori de	alone
いけません	ikemasen	It is not possible, not allowed
入れる　いれる	ireru	put in
医者　いしゃ	isha	doctor
言う　いう	iu	say
〜に鍵を掛ける　かぎをかける	〜 ni kagi o kakeru	lock up
着る　きる	kiru	dress
答　こたえ	kotae	to answer
答える　こたえる	kotaeru	answer
薬　くすり	kusuri	medicine
窓　まど	mado	window
毎日　まいにち	mainichi	every day
万年筆　まんねんひつ	man'nenhitsu	fountain pen
値段　ねだん	nedan	price
ネクタイ	nekutai	tie
廊下　ろうか	rooka	corridor
ローマ字　じ	roomaji	Latin characters
砂糖　さとう	satoo	sugar
さようなら	sayoonara	Goodbye!
セーター	seetaa	jumper
席　せき	seki	table, place, seat
説明（する）　せつめい	setsumei(suru)	explanation, explain
閉める　しめる	shimeru	close
質問（する）　しつもん	shitsumon(suru)	question, ask
相談（する）　そうだん	soodan(suru)	meeting, discuss
それでは	sore dewa	so, also
捨てる　すてる	suteru	throw away
座わる　すわる	suwaru	sit down
たばこを吸う　すう	tabako o suu	smoke
タクシー	takushii	taxi
立つ　たつ	tatsu	stand up
使う　つかう	tsukau	use
やる	yaru	do (colloquial language)
〜を休む　やすむ	yasumu	take a break, take time off, be absent
予約（する）　よやく	yoyaku(suru)	reservation, reserve
ワイシャツ	waishatsu	shirt
全部　ぜんぶ	zenbu	everything, all

Kanji

Kanji	SCK	English	On-yomi / *Kun-yomi*	Usage / Composites
先	6	front	sen / *saki*	先生 sensei / teacher 先週 senshuu / last week
生	5	Life	sei, shoo / *i-kiru, u-mareru*	学生 gakusei / student 生徒 seito / pupil
勉	10	strive	ben / *tsuto-meru*	勉強 benkyoo / to learn 勉学 bengaku / learning, study
強	11	strong	kyoo / *tsuyo-i*	強力 kyooryoku / strong, powerful 強化 kyooka / reinforcement
水	4	water	sui / *mizu*	水曜日 suiyoobi / Wednesday 水道 suidoo / water pipe
土	3	earth	do, to / *tsuchi*	土曜日 doyoobi / Saturday 土地 tochi / plot of land, earth
毎	6	every	mai / *goto*	毎日 mainichi / every day 毎朝 maiasa / every morning
午	4	noon	go	午前 gozen / morning 午後 gogo / afternoon
後	9	after	go, koo / *ushiro, ato, nochi*	後半 koohan / second half 今後 kongo / from now on
休	6	break	kyuu / *yasu-mu*	休日 kyuujitsu / day of rest 休憩 kyuukei / break
病	10	disease	byoo / *yamai*	病気 byooki / sick, illness 病院 byooin / hospital
院	10	suffix for institutions	in	～医院 iinn / private clinic with the name 入院 nyuuin / admission to hospitals
開	12	open	kai / *hira-ku, a-ku, a-keru*	開始 kaishi / beginning 開店 kaiten / opening of business
閉	11	close	hei, to-jiru / *shi-maru, shi-meru*	閉鎖 heisa / to close 閉店 heiten / close store
乗	9	get on	joo / *no-ru*	乗り物 norimono / means of transportation 乗客 jookyaku / passenger
使	8	use	shi / *tsuka-u*	使用 shiyoo / use 使い方 tsukaikata / method of use
始	8	begin	shi / *haji-meru, haji-maru*	開始 kaishi / beginning 始終 shijuu / always

・ SC: number of strokes of the kanji ・ stroke sequence of the kanji: See page 214.

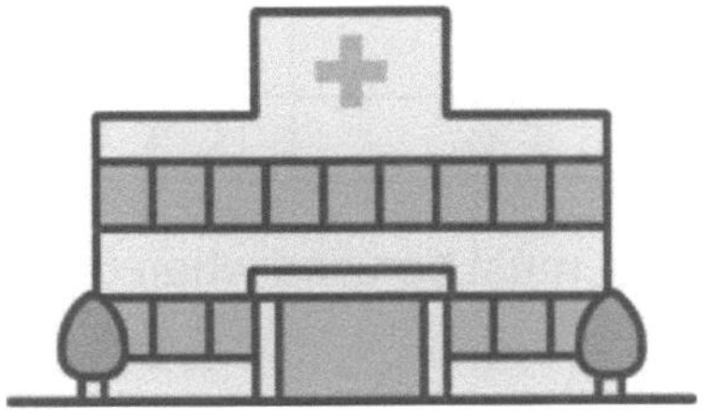

Grammar and exercises

(1) Other uses of the te-form

① Permission: V-てもいいです, V-てもかまいません (may / can)

A: ケーキを食べてもいいですか。
   Can I eat the cake?
B: はい、食べてもいいです。
   Yes, you can eat it.

* You can omit "tabete mo" from the answer.

「練習」
1．水／飲む　　　　2．タクシー／乗る　　　　3．まど／開ける
4．ちょっと／休む　5．家／帰る　　　　　　　6．日本語／説明する

② Prohibition: V-てはいけません (not allowed)

A: ここでたばこをすってもいいですか。
   Can I smoke here?
B: いいえ、すってはいけません。
   No, you are not allowed to smoke here.

* You can omit "sutte wa" from the answer.

「練習」
1．お酒／飲む　　　　2．ふろ／入る　　　　3．ここに／ごみ／すてる
4．ローマ字／書く　　5．ろうか／走る　　　6．辞書／使う

(2) Nai form: nonpolite form of negation　← V-masen (polite negation form)

-step	Basic form	Masu-form	Nai-form		English
1	食べる	食べます	-nai	食べない	do not eat
1	見る	見ます		見ない	do not see
5	会う*	会います		会わない*	do not meet
5	書く	書きます		書かない	do not write
5	話す	話します		話さない	not speak
5	立つ	立ちます	-a-nai	立たない	not stand up
5	読む	読みます		読まない	do not read
5	座る	座ります		座らない	do not sit down
UR	来る	来ます	konai	来ない	do not come
UR	する	します	shinai	しない	do not do

* "-wa nai" must be used when 5-step verbs have the ending "う".

Uses of the nai form

① Negative request: V-ないでください (Please do not ~)

A: この部屋に入ってもいいで
 May I go into this room?
B:いいえ、入らないでください。入ってはいけません。
 No, please don't go in. It is forbidden to enter.

「練習」

1．ここ／たばこ／吸う　　2．午後／外出する　　　3．明日／仕事／休む
4．英語／話す　　　　　5．テスト／万年筆／書く　6．仕事／一人／やる

② Requirement: V-ないといけません (must)

A: 薬を飲まないといけません
 Do I need to take medication?
B: はい、飲まないといけません。
 Yes, you must take it.

You can also use the following forms: "**V-なければなりません**",
"**V-なければいけません**", "**V-なくてはなりません**" and "**V-なくてはいけません**".

Among these, the two forms "V-ないといけません" and "V-なければなりません"
are the most commonly used. However, the first form tends to be used for private,
the second form used for official matters.

「練習」

1．まど／閉める　　　　　　2．ドア／かぎ／かける　3．へや／そうじする
4．毎日／日本語／勉強する　5．医者／行く　　　　　6．ネクタイ／する

③ No requirement: V-なくてもいいです (not mandatory)

A:今、お金をはらわなければなりませんか。
 Do I have to pay now?
B: いいえ、今、はらわなくてもいいです（よ）。
 No, you don't have to pay now.

「練習」

1．せき／予約する　　　　2．病院／行く　　　3．土曜日／働く
4．一人でぜんぶ／する　　5．万年筆／書く　　6．今／質問／答える

④ Negative compound sentence: V-ないで, ~ (not ~, but ~ / without ~ to ~)

A:かれは勉強していますか。
 Is he learning now?
B: いいえ、勉強しないで、遊んでいます。
 He's not learning, but he's playing (a game).

「練習」

1. さんぽする／ねる　　　　　2. 本を読む／コンピュータゲームをする

3. 漢字を書く／ひらがなを書く　　4. ワイシャツを着る／セーターを着る

A: 辞書を使いましたか。
　　Did you use the dictionary?
B: いいえ、辞書を使わないで読みました。
　　No, I read it without using the dictionary.

「練習」

1. 休む／働く　　2. ねだんを聞く／買う　　3. さよならをいう／帰る

4. コーヒー／さとう／入れる／飲む　　5. 部長とそうだんする／する

Negative sentence connection for adjectives and nouns: 〜なくて, 〜 (not 〜, but 〜)

IA: 高くなくて、安いです。　　　　　　　　　It's not expensive, but it's cheap.
NA: 便利では／じゃなくて、不便です。　　　It's not practical, but it's impractical.
N: 　りんごでは／じゃなくて、みかんです。　　It's not an apple, but a tangerine.

The form "V-なくて" can be used like the te-form (see p.82) in the case of justification.
However, there is no action in the second part of the sentence. A state must always be
described.

電気がつかなくて、部屋はとても暗かったです。(correct)
The room was completely dark because the light didn't light up.
その部屋はそうじしていなくて、きれいではありませんでした。(correct)
The room was not clean because it was not cleaned.
バスはもう走っていなくて、駅から家まで歩きました (action)。 (false)
バスはもう走っていなかったので／から、駅から家まで歩きました。(correct)
I walked home from the station because there were no more buses.

Despite the use of the polite blank form (Nai form), all phrases ①, ②, ③ and ④
sound polite because the form of the end of the sentence is in the polite form.

Lesson test

（1） Rewrite the sentences according to the instructions.

1．その部屋に入る。(forbid)

2．あした仕事をする。(no requirement)

3．コンピュータを使う。(requirement)

4．すこし休む。(permission / question)

5．ここでたばこを吸う。(negative request)

6．かのじょは何もいいませんでした。帰りました。(without to)

7．ドイツ語を話しませんでした。日本語を話しました。(not ~, but ~)

（2） Answer the questions about the text.

1．試験はペンで書かなければなりませんか。

2．ローマ字で書いてもいいですか。

3．辞書を使ってもいいですか。

4．となりの人と話してはいけませんか。

（3） Translate into Japanese.

1．May I ask you a question?

2．You must always speak Japanese.

3．He wasn't working today, he was at home.

4．Did you write everything on your own without asking a Japanese person?

何をしなければなりませんか。
手紙を書かなければなりません。

てがみをかく	はたらく	はしる
せんたくする	そうじする	いしゃにいく

第９課 だいきゅうか Dai Kyuu-ka

映画に行かない？
（えいがにいかない）

Eiga ni ikanai?

Lesson 9　映画に　行かない？

まさと：この 間の 日本語の試験 どうだった？

ユリア：ちょっと むずかしかったわ。 日本語を たくさん 読んだり
　　　　書いたり、話したり しなければならなかったの。

まさと：それは たいへんだったね。

ユリア：ええ、でも 私*、けっこう いい成績を もらったのよ。

まさと：あ、そう。 それは よかった。 おめでとう。 よく がんばったね。

ユリア：ありがとう。 やっと ほっとしたわ。

まさと：じゃあ、ユリア、こんどの土曜日時間 ある？

ユリア：あるけど、何？

まさと：友だちと 映画に 行くんだけど、いきぬきに ユリアも いっしょに 行かない？

ユリア：いいわよ。 何か おもしろい映画を やって(い)るの？

まさと：うん、「北見たけし」の 新しい映画、「兄弟」だよ。

ユリア：ああ、今人気の映画ね。 ええ、ぜひ行くわ！ チケットは 予約したほうが いいの？

まさと：いや、しなくても だいじょうぶ だよ。 じゃあ、一時ごろ 家に むかえに
　　　　行くから、待って(い)て！**

ユリア：うん、わかったわ。

> * In everyday language, the AP は for the subject is often omitted.
> ** The Request form is often used in colloquial language without ください.

Translation of the text

Shall we go to the movies?

Masato: How was the last Japanese exam?
Julia:　 It was a bit difficult. We had to read a lot of Japanese, as well as write and speak.
Masato: That must have been exhausting, wasn't it?
Julia:　 Yes, but I got a pretty good grade.
Masato: Oh, that's great! Congratulations! It seems like you put in a lot of effort.
Julia:　 Thank you very much! Now I can finally take a breath of relief.
Masato: So, Julia, are you free on Saturday?
Julia:　 Yes, I'm free. Why?
Masato: I'm going to the movies with friends. Do you want to come too?
Julia:　 Why not! Is there a good movie on now?
Masato: Yes, a new movie by "Takeshi Kitami" called "Kyoodai".
Julia:　 Oh, very popular movie right now, isn't it? Yes, I'd love to go.
　　　　 Is it better to book the tickets?
Masato: No, you don't need to. Well, I'll pick you up around 1 o'clock.
Julia:　 All right!

Questions about the text

1．日本語の試験で何をしなければなりませんでしたか。
2．試験の成績はいかがでしたか。
3．ユリアさんは土曜日に時間がありますか。
4．まさととユリアさんは土曜日に何をしますか。
5．映画の名前は何ですか。
6．チケットを予約しますか。
7．まさとは何時にユリアさんをむかえに行きますか。

Vocabulary and idioms

Vocabulary	**reading**	**English**
美術館　びじゅつかん	bijutsukan	art gallery
文法　ぶんぽう	bunpoo	grammar
だいじょうぶ	daijoobu	no problem, it's alright
ドライブ（する）	doraibu(suru)	go for a drive
服　ふく	fuku	clothes, dresses
がんばる	ganbaru	make an effort, do my best
銀行　ぎんこう	ginkoo	bank
歯医者　はいしゃ	haisha	dentist
花見　はなみ	hanami	look at cherry blossoms
暇(な)　ひま(な)	hima(na)	have time off
ホテル	hoteru	hotel
ほっとする	hotto suru	be reassured
息ぬき　いきぬき	ikinuki	relaxation, refreshment
いや	iya	no (CF)
課長　かちょう	kachoo	head of small department
かなり	kanari	quite
かわいい	kawaii	cute, sweet
～けど、～けれど	kedo, keredo	although ~, It can also be used as an introduction.
けっこう	kekkoo	pretty, good
きたない	kitanai	dirty
この間　あいだ	kono aida	recently, a few days ago
兄弟　きょうだい	kyoodai	brothers, siblings
教授　きょうじゅ	kyooju	professor
まずい	mazui	taste bad, not good
問題　もんだい	mondai	question, task, problem
もらう	morau	get
迎えに行く　むかえにいく	mukae ni iku	come and pick up / go
ミュンヘン	mynhen	Munich
人気　にんき	ninki	popularity, to be popular
覚える　おぼえる	oboeru	memorize, learn by heart
おめでとう	omedetoo	Congratulations!
終わる　おわる	owaru	finish
ピッツァ	pittsa	pizza
練習（する）　れんしゅう	renshuu(suru)	practice, practise
魚　さかな	sakana	fish
成績　せいせき	seiseki	performance, grade
洗濯する　せんたく	sentaku-suru	do laundry
社員　しゃいん	shain	employee
社長　しゃちょう	shachoo	CEO / company boss
塩　しお	shio	salt
そば	soba	buckwheat noodle
スパゲティー	supagettii	spaghetti
正しい　ただしい	tadashii	right, correct
大変(な)　たいへん(な)	taihen(na)	exhausting, serious, terrible
たくさん	takusan	a lot (with verbs)
建物　たてもの	tatemono	building

作る　つくる	tsukuru	make, cook
うん	un	yes (CF)
うるさい	urusai	loud in a negative sense
ううん	uun	no (CF)
上着　うわぎ	uwagi	jacket
やっと	yatto	finally
柔らかい　やわらかい	yawarakai	soft
ずぼん	zubon	trousers

Kanji

Kanji	SCK	English	On-yomi *Kun-yomi*	Usage / Composites
映	9	reflection	ei *utsu-ru, -su*	映画　eiga / motion picture 反映　han'ei / reflection
画	8	image	ga, kaku	画家　gaka / painter 計画　keikaku / plan
月	4	moon, month	gatsu, getsu *tsuki*	月曜日　getsuyoobi / Monday 一か月　ikkagetsu / one month
火	4	fire	ka *hi*	火曜日　kayoobi / Tuesday 火事　kaji / fire, blaze
男	7	man	dan, nan *otoko*	男性　dansei / man 男子　danshi / boy
女	3	woman	jo *on'na*	女性　josei / woman 女子　joshi / girl
子	3	child	shi *ko*	子供　kodomo / child 親子　oyako / parents and children
長	8	long	choo *naga-i*	社長　shachoo / boss 部長　buchoo / head of department
兄	5	older brother	kei, kyoo *ani*	兄弟　kyoodai / sibling 兄さん　niisan / older brother
弟	7	younger brother	tei *otooto*	子弟　shitei / son, children 弟子　deshi / apprentice, pupil
家	10	house	ka, ke *ie*	家庭　katei / family 家族　kazoku / family
手	4	hand	shu *te*	手紙　tegami / letter 手段　shudan / means
紙	10	paper	shi *kami*	用紙　yooshi / form 折り紙　origami / paper folding
答	12	answer	too *kotae*	解答　kaitoo / answer, solution 返答　hentoo / answer, reply
足	7	leg, foot	soku *ashi*	遠足　ensoku / excursion 不足　fusoku / deficiency
待	9	wait	tai *ma-tsu*	招待　shootai / invitation 接待　settai / hospitality
作	7	make	saku, sa *tsuku-ru*	作文　sakubun / essay 作者　sakusha / author

・ SC: Stroke count of the kanji. ・ Stroke sequence of the kanji: See page 214.

Grammar and exercises

Non-polite forms (NPF): familiar form

The polite empty forms consist of the following four forms:
1. basic form (GF) present/positive, 2. nai form (Nai-F) present/negative,
3. ta-form (Ta-F)* preterit/positive, 4. nakatta-form (Nak-F) preterit/negative
The ta form can be derived from the te form by replacing "te" or "de" with "ta" or "da".
This form is used for familiar colloquial language, for written language (newspaper, magazine, books or diary) and for the combined forms. (for example 行かないといけません / must go)

Table of non-polite forms (NPF)

category	tense	verb-F	conjugation	example	English
1-st. verbs	PS-P PS-N PT-P PT-N	BF Nai-F Ta-F Nak-F	-e/i-ru -e/i-nai -e/i-ta -e/i-nakatta	食べる 食べない 食べた 食べなかった	eat do not eat ate did not eat
5-st. verbs	PS-P PS-N PT-P PT-N	BF Nai-F Ta-F Nak-F	-u -a-nai -ta (-da) -a-nakatta	書く 書かない 書いた 書かなかった	write do not write wrote did not write
IV: する	PS-P PS-N PT-P PT-N	BF Nai-F Ta-F Nak-F	-ru -nai -ta -nakatta	する しない した しなかった	do do not do did did not do
IV: 来る	PS-P PS-N PT-P PT-N	BF Nai-F Ta-F Nak-F	-ru -nai -ta -nakatta	来（く）る 来（こ）ない 来（き）た 来（こ）なかった	come do not come came did not come
I-adjective	PS-P PS-N PT-P PT-N	BF Nai-F Ta-F Nak-F	-i -kunai -katta -kunakatta	新しい 新しくない 新しかった 新しくなかった	be new not be new was new was not new
Na-adjective	PS-P PS-N PT-P PT-N	BF Nai-F Ta-F Nak-F	-da -dewa-nai -datta -dewa-nakatta	元気だ 元気ではない 元気だった 元気ではなかった	be healthy not be healthy was healthy was not healthy
noun	PS-P PS-N PT-P PT-N	BF Nai-F Ta-F Nak-F	-da -dewa-nai -datta -dewa-nakatta	魚だ 魚ではない 魚だった 魚ではなかった	be a fish not be a fish was a fish was not a fish

- Exception: ある (BF) ⇒ **ない** (Nai-F) ⇒ あった (Ta-F) ⇒ なかった (Nakatta-F)
- だ is the NPF von です (be).
- じゃ can be used instead of では for the negation of na- adjectives and nouns.

(1) Uses of the non-polite form (NPF)

① Verbs (PS)

A: 月曜日（に）映画を見る（の）？
Are you going to watch a movie on Monday?

B: うん、見るよ。
Yes, I'm going to watch one.

　ううん、見ないよ。
No, I'm not going to watch one.

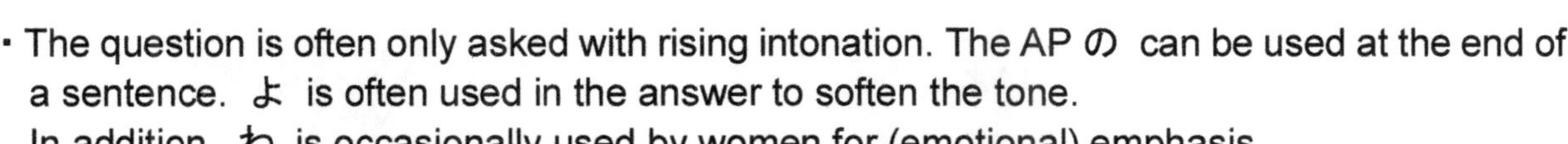

- The question is often only asked with rising intonation. The AP の can be used at the end of a sentence. よ is often used in the answer to soften the tone.
  In addition, わ is occasionally used by women for (emotional) emphasis.

- うん is a familiar form of はい (yes) and ううん is a familiar form of いいえ (no).
  Instead of ううん, you can also say いや.

「練習」
1．火曜日／町／行く　　2．水曜日／そうじ／する　　3．木曜日／日本語／勉強する
4．金曜日／公園／さんぽする　　5．土曜日／学校／行く　　6．日曜日／友だち／会う

② Verbs (PT)

A: きのう何をしたの？
What did you do yesterday?

B: 家で音楽を聞いた（の／んだ）よ。
I was listening to music at home.

　何もしなかった（の／んだ）よ。
I didn't do anything.

- For emphasis, you can use "の" for women and "んだ" for men and women at the end of a sentence.

「練習」
1．お酒／飲む　　2．漢字／練習する　　3．ふく／せんたくする
4．手紙／書く　　5．ごはん／作る　　6．上着／ネクタイ／ずぼん／買う

③ Familiar form of request ← V-masen ka (polite request)

A: 火曜日（に）いっしょに映画に行かない？
Shall we go to the movies together on Tuesday?

B: うん、いいよ／いいわよ。
Yes, gladly! (male / female)

　うん、でも時間が ないんだ／ないの。
Yes, but I don't have time. (male / female)

- The Nai-form is also used with rising intonation when making a request.
- Only men sometimes use "ないか".

「練習」

1．水曜日／テニス／する　　2．木曜日／ごはん／食べに行く　3．金曜日／音楽／聞く
4．土曜日／ドライブ／する　　5．日曜日／花見／行く　　6．月曜日／馬／乗る

④ I adjective (PS)

A:その本はおもしろい？
　Is the book interesting?
B:うん、とてもおもしろいよ。
　Yes, it is very interesting.
　ううん、あまりおもしろくないよ。
　No, it's not so interesting.

「練習」

1．車／はやい　　　　　2．町／古い　　　　3．ごはん／おいしい
4．漢字／むずかしい　　5．川／長い　　　　6．仕事／おもしろい

⑤ I adjective (PT)

A:その本はおもしろかった？
　Was the book interesting?
B:うん、とてもおもしろかったよ。
　Yes, it was very interesting.
　ううん、あまりおもしろくなかったよ。
　No, it was not so interesting.

「練習」

1．試験／やさしい　　2．家／大きい　　　3．旅行／楽しい
4．成績／いい　　　　5．肉／やわらかい　6．答／正しい

⑥ Na adjective (PS)

A:その人は元気？
　Is she/he well?
B:うん、とても元気だよ／よ。
　Yes, she/he is very well.
　ううん、あまり元気では／じゃ ないよ。
　No, she/he is not so well.

1. Na-adjectives are used in the present tense without "だ" in the question.

2. The ending particle "よ" is used in the answer by women and "だよ" by both.
   Instead of ～ではない，～じゃない is also often used.

「練習」

1．女の人／親切　　2．男の人／有名　　3．町／きれい
4．町／しずか　　　5．問題／かんたん　6．ホテル／便利

⑦ Na adjective (PT)

A: <u>その仕事</u>はたいへんだった？
　 Was the work exhausting?
B: うん、かなりたいへんだったよ。
　 Yes, it was quite exhausting.
　 ううん、あまりたいへん では／じゃ なかったよ。
　 No, it wasn't so exhausting.

「練習」
1. 試験／かんたん　　2. きのう／ひま　　3. 町／にぎやか
4. かれ／親切　　　　5. カメラ／便利　　6. 湖／きれい

⑧ Noun (PS)

A: <u>その人</u>は先生？
　 Is she / he a teacher?
B: うん、先生よ／だよ。
　 Yes, she / he is a teacher?
　 ううん、先生では／じゃないよ。会社員よ／だよ。
　 No, she is / he is not a teacher. She/he is an employee.

1. nouns are used in the question in the present tense without "だ".
2. the ending particle "よ" is used in the answer by women and "だよ" by both.
　 Instead of ～ではない, ～じゃない is also often used.

「練習」
1. 女の人／日本人／中国人　　2. 男の人／社長／部長
3. 建物／銀行／郵便局　　　　4. 料理／すし／そば
5. 飲み物／お茶／お酒　　　　6. それ／塩／砂糖

⑨ Noun (PT)

A: <u>その人</u>は教授だった？
　 Was she / he a professor?
B: うん、教授だったよ。
　 Yes, she / he was a professor.
　 ううん、教授では／じゃなかったよ。医者だったよ。
　 No, she / he wasn't a professor. She / He was a doctor.

・This question can not only be asked about a fact in the past, but it can also be asked
　as a general confirmation of the fact.

「練習」
1. 女の人／ドイツ人／イギリス人　　2. 男の人／部長／課長
3. 建物／駅／美術館　　　　　　　　4. 料理／スパゲティー／ピッツァ
5. 漢字の試験／火曜日／水曜日　　　6. 上野までの運賃／いくら／360円

(2) Uses of the ta form / nai form (the combined form)

① **V-た／ない方がいい**: recommendation (it is better to do / not to do ~)

医者に行った方がいい（よ）。（〜た方がいいですよ。）
It is better to go to the doctor.
たばこは吸わない方がいい（よ）。（〜ない方がいいですよ。）
It is better not to smoke.

「練習」
1．その映画／見る　　2．早く／ねる　　3．やさい／たくさん／食べる
4．家／いる　　5．高いから／あのスーパー／買物する　　6．お酒／たくさん／飲む

② **V-たり、V-たりする**: Representative listing of actions (sometimes this, sometimes that)

A: 週末何をする？（〜しますか。）
　　What do you do at the weekend?
B: 本を読んだり、音楽を聞いたりするよ。（〜しますよ。）
　　For example, I read books and listen to music.

「練習」
1．映画／見る／さんぽをする　　2．買物する／レストランに行く
3．友だち／会う／手紙を書く　　4．文法／勉強する／漢字／覚える
5．そうじする／せんたくする　　6．歌／歌う／ダンス／する

Adjectives and nouns can also be used, and at the end of a sentence "da (desu)" can be used instead of "suru (shimasu)".

I-A: 　天気はよかったり、わるかったり**だ**/**です**。（する/します。）
　　　The weather is sometimes good and sometimes bad.
Na-A: ここの店員は親切だったり、親切で（は）なかったり**だ**/**です**。（する/します。）
　　　The sales staff here are sometimes friendly and sometimes unfriendly.
N: 　社員は日本人だったり、ドイツ人だったり、中国人だったり**だ**/**です**。（する/します。）
　　　Some employees are Japanese, some are German and some are Chinese.

「練習」
1．成績／いい／わるい　　2．ごはん／おいしい／まずい
3．部屋／きれい／きたない　　4．町／うるさい／しずか
5．かばん／重い／軽い　　6．仕事／いそがしい／ひま

Lesson test

(1) Rewrite the underlined parts in the NPF.

1．かのじょはいい成績を<u>もらいました</u>。
2．昨日早く家に<u>帰りませんでした</u>。
3．かのじょは有名<u>ではありません</u>が、親切<u>です</u>。
4．お金は<u>あります</u>が、時間が<u>ありません</u>。
5．かのじょは元気<u>でしたか</u>。いいえ、あまり元気<u>ではありませんでした</u>よ。
6．日曜日にいっしょに映画を<u>見ませんか</u>。ええ、でも時間が<u>ありません</u>。

(2) Form the sentences in the NPF according to the instructions.

1．パーティー／話す／歌／歌う　(sometimes this, sometimes that)
2．試験／日本語／読む／書く／話す　(sometimes~, sometimes~ must)
3．試験／成績／いい／わるい　(sometimes~, sometimes~ / past)
4．町／電車／行く　(recommendation)
5．たくさん／やさい／くだもの／食べる　(recommendation)
6．今日／天気／わるい／から／さんぽする　(recommendation / negative)

(3) Translate into Japanese. (in the NPF)

1．Because it was very hot yesterday, we went swimming.
2．We didn't need to book tickets.
3．We often had to work.
4．In the evening, we read books and listened to music, among other things.
5．We had to work a lot today.
6．Would you like to go to the movies and eat Japanese food at the weekend?

お酒をのんだり、歌を歌ったりしましたよ。

第 10 課 だいじゅっか Dai Ju-kka

ケーキを焼くことができる
Keeki o yaku koto ga dekiru

Lesson 10　ケーキを 焼くことが できる

マイヤー　：北野さんは どんなスポーツが できますか。

北野　　　：テニスや スキーや 水泳などが できますよ。

マイヤー　：スポーツマンですね。 みんな じょうずですか。

北野　　　：スキーはまだへたですが、テニスと水泳はとくいですよ。 マイヤーさんは？

マイヤー　：今エアロビクスを していますが、テニスも 始めたいわ。

北野　　　：じゃあ、今度の土曜日、いっしょに やりましょう。 ぼくが 教えますよ。

マイヤー　：ありがとう。 ぜひ おねがいします。

北野　　　：ところで、マイヤーさんは 料理が できますか。

マイヤー　：スパゲティーぐらいは できますが、料理は ちょっと にがて (なん) です。

　　　　　　でも、ケーキを じょうずに 焼くことが できますよ。

北野　　　：あ、それはいいな。 マイヤーさん、ぼくにケーキの焼き方を 教えてください。

マイヤー　：ええ、もちろん いいですよ。 北野さんは ケーキが 好きですか。

　　　　　　日本の男の人は たいてい あまいものが きらいですね。

北野　　　：ええ、でも ぼくは 大好きですよ。

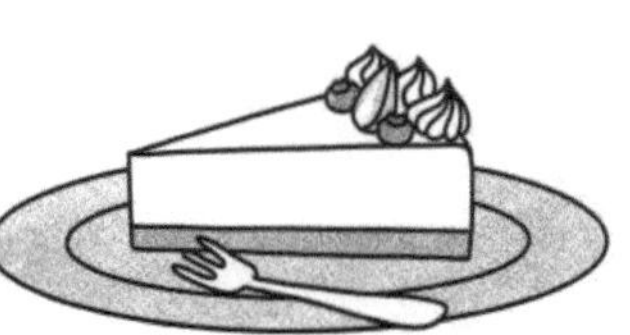

Translation of the text

I can bake cakes.

Mayer: Mr Kitano, what kind of sports do you do?

Kitano: I play tennis, I ski and I swim, for example.

Mayer: Oh, you're very sporty! Are you good at everything?

Kitano: I'm not good at skiing yet, but tennis and swimming are my strengths.
And you, Mrs Mayer?

Mayer: I already do aerobics, but now I want to take up tennis.

Kitano: Well, how about we go and play tennis together this Saturday?
I'll give you some lessons then.

Mayer: Thank you very much! That's very kind of you.

Kitano: By the way, do you like cooking, Mrs Mayer?

Mayer: Oh, I can only cook spaghetti. Cooking is my weakness.
But I like baking cakes.

Kitano: Oh, how nice! Then perhaps you can teach me how to bake cakes one day.

Mayer: Of course! Do you like eating cake?
Most Japanese men don't like sweets, do they?

Kitano: That's true! But I do like sweets very much.

Questions about the text

1．北野さんは水泳ができますか。

2．北野さんはスキーがじょうずですか。

3．マイヤーさんはどんなスポーツをしていますか。

4．マイヤーさんと北野さんは土曜日に何をしますか。

5．マイヤーさんは料理がとくいですか。

6．マイヤーさんは何がじょうずですか。

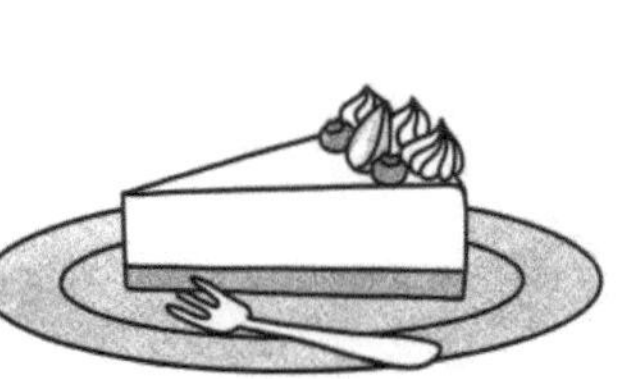

7. マイヤーさんは北野さんに何を教えますか。

8. 北野さんはあまいものが好きですか。

Vocabulary and idioms

Vocabulary	reading	English
甘いもの　あまいもの	amaimono	sweets
案内（する）　あんない	an'nai(suru)	lead, guide, show
バレーボール	bareebooru	volleyball
弁当　べんとう	bentoo	packed lunch
大好き（な）　だいすき	dai-suki(na)	like very much
ダンス、〜をする	dansu, 〜 o suru	dance
できる	dekiru	can
どんな	don'na	which
絵を描く　えをかく	e o kaku	paint / draw a picture
エアロビクス	earobikusu	aerobics
外国語　がいこくご	gaikokugo	foreign language
ギターを弾く　ひく	gitaa o hiku	play guitar
〜ぐらい	gurai	〜 so what
下手（な）　へた	heta(na)	bad at, not skilful
法律　ほうりつ	hooritsu	law
ほしい	hoshii	want to have
インライン・スケート	inrain-sukeeto	inline skate
イタリア語　ご	itariago	Italian
ジョギング	jogingu	jogging
上手（な）　じょうず	joozu(na)	to be good at, to be skilful
柔道　じゅうどう	juudoo	judo
返す　かえす	kaesu	give back
看護士　かんごし	kangoshi	nurse
貸す　かす	kasu	lend something to someone
片付ける　かたづける	katazukeru	tidy up
計算（する）　けいさん	keisan(suru)	calculate
経済　けいざい	keizai	economy
嫌い（な）　きらい	kirai(na)	dislike
コーラ	koora	cola
クラシック	kurasikku	classical music
みんな	min'na	all
もちろん	mochiron	of course
息子　むすこ	musuko	son
娘　むすめ	musume	daughter
な	na	AP for desire and emotion
等　など	nado	etc.
苦手（な）　にがて	nigate(na)	weakness
肉　にく	niku	meat
人形　にんぎょう	ningyoo	doll
お茶を入れる　おちゃいれる	o-cha o ireru	serve tea
おもちゃ	omocha	toy

お願いします　おねがい	o-negai-shimasu	Please do.
ピンポン	pinpon	table tennis
来月　らいげつ	raigetsu	next month
来週　らいしゅう	raishuu	next week
歴史　れきし	rekishi	history
作文　さくぶん	sakubun	essay
政治　せいじ	seiji	politics
写真を撮る　しゃしんをとる	shashin o toru	photograph, take a picture
詩　し	shi	poem
修理（する）　しゅうり	shuuri(suru)	repair
水泳　すいえい	suiei	swimming
好き（な）　すき	suki(na)	like, favourite
スキー	sukii	ski
スポーツマン	supootsu-man	sportsman
数学　すうがく	suugaku	mathematics, arithmetic
たいてい	taitei	mostly
天ぷら　てんぷら	tenpura	tempura: delicately deep-fried vegetables and seafood
手伝う　てつだう	tetsudau	help (at work)
得意（な）　とくい	tokui(na)	strength
腕時計　うでどけい	udedokei	wristwatch
運転（する）　うんてん	unten(suru)	driving, driving a car
歌を歌う　うたをうたう	uta o utau	sing songs
焼き方　やきかた	yakikata	way to bake something
焼く　やく	yaku	bake, roast, burn
洋服　ようふく	yoofuku	European clothes
分かる　わかる	wakaru	understand, know

Kanji

Kanji	SCK	English	On-yomi *Kun-yomi*	Usage / Composites
音	9	sound noise	on *oto*	音楽 ongaku / music 発音 hatsuon / pronunciation
楽	13	cheerful	gaku, raku *tano-shii*	楽器 gakki / musical instrument 楽園 rakuen / paradise
歌	14	song	ka *uta, uta-u*	歌手 kashu / singer 国歌 kokka / national anthem
方	4	direction person	hoo *kata*	方角 hoogaku / direction 地方 chihoo / province
泳	8	swim	ei *oyo-gu*	泳ぐ oyogu / swim 競泳 kyooei / swimming competition
好	6	like	koo *su-ki*	好き suki / like 好物 koobutsu / favourite thing
仕	5	serve	shi *tsuka-eru*	仕事 shigoto / work 仕方 shikata / method
事	8	thing	ji *koto*	事実 jijitsu / truth, fact 工事 kooji / construction

	SC			
料	10	fees	ryoo	料理 ryoori / cooking 料金 ryookin / fees
理	11	theory	ri *kotowari*	理論 riron / theory 論理 ronri / logic
形	7	form	kei, gyoo *katachi*	人形 ninngyoo / doll 三角形 sankakukei / triangle
自	6	itself	ji *mizuka-ra*	自由 jiyuu / free 自分 jibun / self, oneself
転	11	roll	ten *koro-bu*	自転車 jitensha / bicycle 運転 unten / driving
運	12	carry	un *hako-bu*	運動 undoo / movement, sport 運送 unsoo / transport
牛	4	cow	gyuu *ushi*	牛肉 gyuuniku / beef 牛乳 gyuunyuu / cow's milk
肉	6	meat	niku	豚肉 butaniku / pork 肉体 nikutai / body
魚	11	fish	gyo *sakana*	魚屋 sakanaya / fish shop 金魚 kingyo / goldfish

・SC: Number of strokes of the kanji ・Stroke sequence of the kanji: See page 215.

Grammar and exercises

Wa-Ga form 1

The "Wa-Ga form" is a particularly important sentence form that can be used in several variants. In this lesson, you will learn the following expressions with the help of the "Wa-Ga form". Ability, inclination and expression of desire.

(1) Ability:

① N + can: **S wa N ga dekiru.**   (S = subject, N = noun)

A: 北野さんはスキーができますか。
Can you ski, Mr Kitano?
B: はい、（スキーが）できます。
Yes, I can.
いいえ、（スキーが）できません。
No, I cannot.

「練習」

1．テニス　　　　2．水泳　　　　3．野球
4．バレーボール　5．ピンポン　　6．サッカー

The Wa-Wa form can be used when two things are listed in contrast.
This rule also applies to all other Wa-Ga forms

私はテニスはできますが、野球はあまりできません。
I can play tennis, but I'm not so good at baseball.

② V + can: S **wa** V(BF)-koto **ga dekiru**. (koto = nominaliser = to ~)

A: マイヤーさん**は**英語を話すこと**が**できますか。
Can you speak English, Mss. Mayer?
B: はい、（英語を話すことが）できます。
Yes, I can speak English.
いいえ、（英語を話すことが）できません。
No, I can't speak English.

「練習」
1．漢字／書く　　　2．歌／歌う　　　3．コンピュータ／使う
4．車／運転する　　5．お金／私／貸す　6．来月までに*／返す

  * "まで" with the AP に　means "by ~ at the latest".

③ can do well: S **wa** N / V(BF)-koto **ga joozu** desu.

A: 彼女**は**歌**が**じょうずですか。
Can she sing well?
B: はい、（歌が）とてもじょうずです。
Yes, she can sing very well.
いいえ、（歌が）あまりじょうずではありません。
No, she can't sing that well.

「練習」
1．ダンス　　　2．料理　　　3．ギター
4．絵／かく　　5．写真／とる　6．人形／作る

④ can do badly: S **wa** N / V(BF)-koto **ga heta** desu.

A: 彼**は**歌**が**じょうずですか。
Can he sing well?
B: いいえ、（歌が）じょうずではありません。へたです。
No, he can't sing well.

「練習」
1．フランス語　2．運転　　　3．けいさん
4．スポーツ　　5．作文／書く　6．泳ぐ

⑤ Strength: S **wa** N / V(BF)-koto **ga tokui** desu.

A: 彼女**は**何**が**とくいですか。
What is her strength?
B: 彼女**は**料理**が**とくいです。
Cooking is her strength.

「練習」
1．イタリア語　2．漢字　　3．音楽
4．経済　　　　5．法律　　6．英語で手紙／書く

⑥ Weakness: S **wa** N / V(BF)-koto **ga nigate** desu.

A: 町田さん**は**数学**が**とくいですか。
Is mathematics your strong point, Mr. Machida?

B: いいえ、（数学が）とくいではありません。にがてです。
No, math is not my strength, it's my weakness.

「練習」

1．外国語　　　2．漢字　　　3．ダンス
4．政治　　　5．水泳　　　6．そうじする

⑦ N + understand / know: S **wa** N **ga wakaru**.

A: 山田さん**は**英語**が**わかりますか。
Do you understand English, Ms. Yamada?
B: はい、わかります。
Yes, I understand English.
いいえ、わかりません。
No, I don't understand English.

「練習」

1．イタリア語　　　2．先生の説明　　　3．上野への行き方
4．「得意」この漢字の読み方　　　5．ケーキの焼き方

· You don't say "知りません", but "わかりません" if you don't know what you want to do or what will happen.
週末何をしますか。
What will you do at the weekend?
まだわかりません。
I don't know yet.

· "わかりました" also means "agreed" or "all clear".
先生：来週漢字のテストをします。
Teacher: I'll give you a kanji test next week.
生徒：はい、わかりました。
Pupil: All right!

(2) **Taste:**

① like: S **wa** N / V(BF)-koto **ga suki** desu.

A: くだものの中で何**が**好きですか。
Which kinds of fruit do you like?

B: （私**は**）りんご**が**好きです。
I like apples.

「練習」

1．スポーツ／テニス　　　2．勉強／歴史　　　3．音楽／クラシック
4．食べもの／天ぷら　　　5．肉／牛肉　　　6．季節／いつ／春、夏、秋、冬

② do not like: S **wa** N / V(BF)-koto **ga kirai** desu.

A: 大田さん**は**肉が好きですか。
　Do you like meat, Mr. Oota?
B: いいえ、（肉が）好きではありません。きらいです。
　No, I don't like meat.

「練習」
1．魚　　　　　2．やさい　　　　3．コーラ
4．さんぽ　　　5．そうじする　　6．料理を作る

(3) **Expression of desire**:

① wanting to have something: S **wa** N **ga hoshii** desu.

A: ～さん（あなた）**は**自転車が<u>ほしい</u>ですか。　("hoshii" is an I-adjective.)
　Would you like to have a bicycle?
B: はい、（自転車が）<u>ほしい</u>です。
　Yes, I would like one.
　いいえ、（自転車が）<u>ほしくない</u>です。
　No, I don't want one.

・ It can sound too direct if this question is asked of people with whom you need to be
　particularly polite. It is better to ask without "anata":
　「自転車が必要でしょう* か。」or「自転車をさしあげましょう*か。」
　"Do you need a bicycle?" or "Shall I offer you a bicycle?"
　See L16 (presumptive form) and L30 (polite language) in volume 2.

「練習」
1．テレビ　　　2．ステレオ　　　3．コンピュータ
4．飲みもの　　5．大きい家　　　6．腕時計

② V + would like: S **wa** N o / **ga** V(stem of masu-F)-tai desu. ("tai" is an adverb.)

A: （-さん**は**）何が／を<u>食べたい</u>ですか。
　What do you want to eat?
B: 私**は**すし**が**／**を**<u>食べたい</u>です。
　I want to eat sushi.
　何**も**<u>食べたくない</u>です。
　I don't want to eat anything.

Both "が" and "を" can be used after the object. In everyday conversation, however,
を is used more often, while が is used to emphasize the object. "を" must even be used
exclusively when the object is a person.

公園に**子供**を連れて行きたいです。
I would like to take my children to the park.

Instead of "Wa-ga/o form", other forms such as "Wa-e form" or "Wa-ni form" etc. are used
if the verb does not originally use a direct object, i.e. no AP を.

私は東京へ行きたいです。そして友だちに会いたいです。
I want to go to Tokyo. And I want to meet my friends.

「練習」
1．何／する／買いもの　　　2．何／飲む／ビール
3．何／買う／ステレオ　　　4．どんなスポーツ／する／テニス
5．どこへ／旅行する／日本　6．だれ／公園／連れて行く／子供

③ **Wish of a third person** (he / she / it)

1. ~ want to have: S wa ~ o hoshigatte iru.
2. ~ V + want: S wa ~ o V(stem of masu-F)-tagatte iru

After the direct object, が is not used, but only を.
The other AP "ni" or "e" is also used if the verb originally requires it.

A: 彼は何をほしがっていますか。
   What does he want?
B: 彼は新しいカメラをほしがっています。
   He wants a new camera.
A: 彼女は何をしたがっていますか。
   What does she want to do?
B: 彼女は水泳をしたがっています。
   She wants to go swim.

「練習」
1．彼女／辞書／何／買う／ケーキ　　2．彼／旅行かばん／どこ／行く／京都
3．むすこさん／おもちゃ／何／なる／医者　4．むすめさん／洋服／何／なる／かんごし

However, the original forms "hoshii" and "tai" are used in the subordinate clause or
in the quotation.

彼は新しいカメラがほしいから、今アルバイトをしています。
He is now doing a job because he wants a new camera.
彼女は水泳をしたいと言っています。(See L. 13)
She says that she wants to go swimming.

(4) invitation: V-mashoo (Let's ~!)

① The verb form is like the masu form: -masu → -mashoo
It has roughly the same meaning as "V-masen ka" (see L.5)

A: いっしょにテニスをしましょう。
   Let's play tennis together!
B: はい、しましょう。（やりましょう）
   Yes, with pleasure!

   はい、ありがとう。でも、ちょっと時間がありません。
   Yes, thank you, but unfortunately I don't have time.

「練習」
1．ビール／飲む　　　2．料理／作る　　　3．音楽／聞く
4．日本語／勉強する　5．部屋／かたづける　6．花見／行く

***V-mashoo ka:** The interrogative particle "ka" softens the requesting tone.
"-mashoo ka" can therefore be translated as "Shall we ~?".

② Other meaning of "**V-mashoo ka**" (willingness)
"-mashoo ka" can also be used when you want to offer help to your conversation partner.
This means "Should I ~?" in English.

A: お荷物を持ちましょうか。
   Would you like me to carry your luggage?
B: ありがとう。お願いします。持ってください。
   Yes, thank you! That's very kind of you. Please carry it.
   ありがとう。でもけっこうです。
   No, thank you!

「練習」
1．窓／閉める　　　　2．お茶／入れる　　　3．仕事／手伝う
4．日本語／教える　　5．町／案内する　　　6．べんとう／作る

何が食べたいですか。
すしが食べたいですね。

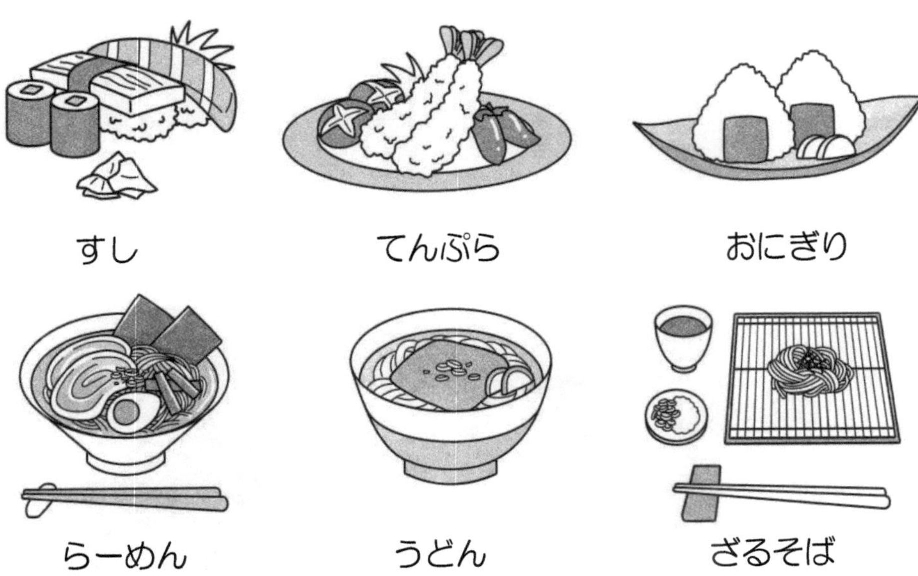

Lesson test

（1）Complete the sentences with the matching words.

1．私たちは天ぷらが ＿＿＿＿＿＿＿＿＿＿＿。(want to eat)

2．彼はスキーが ＿＿＿＿＿＿＿＿＿＿＿。(can)

3．彼女は歌が ＿＿＿＿＿＿＿＿＿＿＿。(strength)

4．彼はまだ日本語を ＿＿＿＿＿＿＿＿＿＿＿。(can't speak well)

5．私は魚が ＿＿＿＿＿＿＿ が、肉が ＿＿＿＿＿＿＿＿ 。(like / dislike)

6．私は日本で ＿＿＿＿＿＿＿＿＿＿＿。(want to work)

7．彼は車の運転が ＿＿＿＿＿＿＿＿＿＿。(can't)

8．彼は数学が ＿＿＿＿＿＿＿＿＿＿。(weakness)

9．弟は新しいかばんを ＿＿＿＿＿＿＿＿＿＿。(want to have)

10．私の友だちは映画を ＿＿＿＿＿＿＿＿＿＿。(want to see)

（2）Answer the questions.

1．ビールとワインとお酒とでは、何が一番好きですか。

2．～さん（あなた）は今何が一番したいですか。

3．～さん（あなた）は何がとくいですか。

（3）Translate into Japanese.

1．I want to meet my friends on Saturday.

2．I like playing tennis, but I'm not that good yet.

3．My mother wants to go to a concert tomorrow.

第11課　Dai Juui-kka

行ったことがありますか。

Itta koto ga arimasu ka.

Lesson 11　行ったことが　ありますか。

マイヤー　：北野さんの　故郷は　どちらですか。

北野　　　：私 の故郷は　信 州 の長野市です

　　　　　　マイヤーさんは　行ったことが　ありますか。

マイヤー　：いいえ、私は　ときどき　旅行することが　ありますが、

　　　　　　長野は　まだ　行ったことが　ないんです。

北野　　　：山に　近くて、冬は　スキー、夏は　キャンプに　便利ですから、

　　　　　　ぜひ　一度　行ってください。

マイヤー　：はい、そうします。　北野さんは　よく　帰るんですか。

北野　　　：いいえ、いそがしくて　時間がない ので、あまり　帰りません。

　　　　　　まあ　1年に2回、正 月とお盆ぐらい　ですね。

マイヤー　：それは　残念ですね。　それで　長野市は　どんな町ですか。

北野　　　：長野市は　信 州の中 心で、歴史が　古くて、きれいな町ですよ。

マイヤー　：見所も　たくさん　ありますか。

北野　　　：ええ、でも、やっぱり　善光寺が　一番有名ですね。

　　　　　　善光寺は　古い 大きなお寺で、全国から　たくさん人が　おとずれます。

マイヤー　：そうですか。　ぜひ　私 も　行きたいです。

　　　　　　それから　長野の食べ物は　いかがですか。

北野　　　：食べ物は「信 州 そば」と「信 州 みそ」が　とても　有名です。

マイヤー　：あ、「信州そば」は　私も　一度　食べたことが　ありますよ。

　　　　　　とても　おいしかったわ。

Translation of the text

Have you ever travelled there?

Mayer: Mr Kitano, what is your hometown?

Kitano: My hometown is the city of Nagano in Shinshuu.
　　　　Have you ever travelled there?

Mayer: No, I travel from time to time, but I've never been to Nagano.

Kitano: Nagano is good for skiing in winter and camping in summer,
　　　　because the mountains are nearby. You should definitely go there one day!

Mayer: I would like to do that. Do you go back there often?

Kitano: No, unfortunately not that often because I don't have much time.
　　　　Just about t twice a year, at New Year's and for the Bon Festival.

Mayer: That's a pity! What is the city of Nagano like?

Kitano: Nagano is the capital of Shinshuu, has a long history and is a beautiful city.

Mayer: Are there many sights there?

Kitano: Yes, quite a few. But the Zenkooji Temple is certainly the most famous.
　　　　It's old and big. Many people from all over the country visit it.

Mayer: Oh, really? I also really want to go there one day. And how is the food in Nagano?

Kitano: In terms of food, "Shinshuu soba" and "Shinshuu miso" are very famous.

Mayer: Yes, I've eaten Shinshuu soba before. It was very tasty

Questions about the text

１．北野さんの故郷はどこですか。
２．マイヤーさんは行ったことがありますか。
３．北野さんはよく故郷に帰りますか。
４．北野さんはいつ故郷に帰りますか。
５．長野はどんな町ですか。
６．見所はどこが有名ですか。
７．食べ物はどんなものが有名ですか。
８．マイヤーさんはまだ信州そばを食べたことがありませんか。

Vocabulary and idioms

Vocabulary	**reading**	**English**
赤ちゃん　あかちゃん	akachan	baby
秋　あき	aki	autumn
青い　あおい	aoi	blue
頭　あたま	atama	head
ビデオ	bideo	video, video camera
病気　びょうき	byooki	sick, illness
知人　ちじん	chijin	acquaintance
力　ちから	chikara	power
中心　ちゅうしん	chuushin	centre
同僚　どうりょう	dooryoo	colleague
鼻　はな	hana	nose
晴　はれ	hare	cheerful, nice weather
広い　ひろい	hiroi	large, wide, broad
居間　いま	ima	living room
いつ	itsu	when
字引き　じびき	jibiki	dictionary
～回　かい	kai	~ times
髪　かみ	kami	hair
考え　かんがえ	kangae	idea, thought
顔　かお	kao	face
希望　きぼう	kiboo	wish, hope
コアラ	koara	koala
子供　こども	kodomo	child
恋人　こいびと	koibito	lover
故郷　こきょう	kokyoo	hometown
曇　くもり	kumori	cloudy
クラスメート	kurasu-meeto	classmates
黒い　くろい	kuroi	black
キャンプ	kyanpu	camping
目　め	me	eye
めったに～ない	mettani ~ nai	rare, seldom
見所　みどころ	midokoro	place of interest

短い　みじかい	mijikai	short
耳　みみ	mimi	ear
味噌　みそ	miso	miso paste
長野市・県　ながのし・けん	nagano-shi, -ken	Nagano city, Nagano prefecture
なる	naru	become
庭　にわ	niwa	garden
登る　のぼる	noboru	climb
お盆　おぼん	o-bon	Bon festival in August
（お）寺　てら	o-tera	temple
訪れる　おとずれる	otozureru	visit
プール	puuru	swimming pool
留学（する）　りゅうがく	ryuugaku(suru)	study abroad
留学生　りゅうがくせい	ryuugakusei	foreign student
背　せ	se	height, body size
信州　しんしゅう	shinshuu	Shinshuu (central area of Japan)
白い　しろい	shiroi	white
正月　しょうがつ	shoogatsu	new year
そば	soba	buckwheat noodles
それで	sorede	and then
食べ物　たべもの	tabemono	food, food stuffs
強い　つよい	tsuyoi	strong
やっぱり	yappari	but, actually
休み　やすみ	yasumi	break, holiday
雪　ゆき	yuki	snow
残念（な）　ざんねん	zan'nen(na)	unfortunately, a pity
全国　ぜんこく	zenkoku	whole country
善光寺　ぜんこうじ	zenkooji	Zenkooji Temple

Kanji

Kanji	SCK	English	On-yomi *Kun-yomi*	Usage / Composites
白	5	white	haku *shiro-i*	白人　hakujin / the white one 白紙　hakushi / white paper, blank
黒	11	black	koku *kuro-i*	黒板　kokuban / blackboard 黒字　kuroji / profit
赤	7	red	seki *aka-i*	赤字　akaji / loss 赤ちゃん　akachan / baby
青	8	blue	sei *ao-i*	青年　seinen / teenager 青春　seishun / youth
回	6	times	kai *mawa-ru*	回数券　kaisuuken / book of tickets 回転　kaiten / turn
度	9	times	do *tabi*	今度　kondo / this time, next time 温度　ondo / temperature
正	5	correct	sei, shoo *tada-shii*	正月　shoogatsu / New Year 正解　seikai / correct answer
年	6	year	nen *toshi*	今年　kotoshi / this year 来年　rainen / next year

	SC				
夏	10	summer	ka *natsu*	夏休み natsuyasumi / summer holidays 初夏 shoka / beginning of summer
冬	5	winter	too *fuyu*	冬休み fuyuyasumi / winter holidays 冬眠 toomin / hibernation
心	4	heart	shin *kokoro*	中心 chuushin / centre 心臓 shinzoo / heart (organ)
野	11	field	ya *no*	平野 heiya / plain 野球 yakyuu / baseball
市	5	city	shi *ichi*	市長 shichoo / mayor 市役所 shiyakusho / city hall
帰	10	return	ki *kae-ru*	帰宅 kitaku / return home 帰国 kikoku / return to the home country
物	8	thing	butsu *mono*	食べ物 tabemono / meal, food 動物 doobutsu / animal
姉	8	thing	shi *ane*	姉妹 shimai / sisters お姉さん oneesan / older sister
妹	8	older sister	mai *imooto*	姉妹 shimai / sisters 妹さん imootosan / younger sister
広	5	wide, spacious,	koo *hiro-i*	広大 koodai / large, spacious 広告 kookoku / advert, advertisement

・ SC: number of strokes of the kanji　・ stroke sequence of the kanji: See page 215.

Grammar and exercises

(1) Wa-Ga form 2

In this case, the "Wa-Ga form" expresses possession, quality, experience and occurrence.

① Possession: S wa N ga aru / iru. (~ have)

"aru" is used for objects and "iru" for people.
"motte iru" (L 7) is also used like "aru" for possession, but "motte iru" is often used for concrete objects such as a camera, computer or a car, while "aru" is often used for abstract objects.

A: マイヤーさん**は**時間**が**ありますか。
　　Do you have time, Mrs Mayer?
B: はい、（時間が）あります。
　　Yes, I have time.
　　いいえ、（時間が）ありません。
　　No, I don't have time.

「練習」
1. お金／たくさん／ぜんぜん　　　2. おもしろい仕事／よく／あまり
3. 長い休み／ときどき／めったに　　4. 質問／一つだけ／ぜんぜん
5. 宿題／毎日／めったに　　　　　　6. いい考え／たくさん／ぜんぜん

買い物で　Shopping

A: このかばん、もっと**大きいの**はありませんか。
   Do you have a slightly larger one of this bag?
B: はい、こちらはいかがですか。
   Yes, how about this one?
A: ああ、いいですね。それをください。
   That's good. Give it to me, please.

- "の" is the noun substitute, e.g. 大きいかばん,
- Here " the AP "は" is used instead of "が" because a larger bag is contrasted with another bag and thematized.

「練習」

1．くつ／小さい　　　　　2．テレビ／安い
3．カメラ／軽い　　　　　4．雑誌／新しい
5．花／きれいな　　　　　6．コンピュータ／便利な

A: マイヤーさん**は／には** 日本人の**友だち**がいますか。
   Do you have any Japanese friends, Ms. Mayer?
B: はい、（日本の友だちが）たくさんいます。
   Yes, I have (many) Japanese friends.
   いいえ、（日本の友だちが）ぜんぜんいません。
   No, I don't have any (at all).

Both　は　and　には　can be used here.

「練習」

1．兄弟（兄、姉、弟、妹）　　2．恋人　　3．子供（息子・娘）
4．赤ちゃん　　5．いいどうりょう　　6．外国人の友だち

② **Characteristic description:** S wa ~ ga ~ da.　(As for S, so ~)

A certain part of the whole (subject) is explained in this sentence form.

A: 長野はどんな町ですか。
   What kind of city is Nagano?

B: 長野は町がきれいです。そして善光寺が有名です。
   Regarding Nagano, the city is beautiful and the Zenkooji Temple is famous.

「練習」

1．ベルリン／町／おもしろい／クーダム／有名
2．友だち／人／髪／長い／目／黒い
3．彼の家／家／居間／広い／庭／きれい
4．日本／天気／夏／暑い／春と秋／とてもいい
5．京都／町／歴史／古い／有名な寺／たくさん／ある
6．あなたの故郷／町　？？

③ **Experience:** S **wa** V-ta (Ta form) **koto ga** aru.　(to have done once)

A: シュミットさん**は**日本へ行ったこと**が**ありますか。
　Have you ever been to Japan, Mr. Schmidt?

B: はい、（日本へ行ったことが）一度あります。
　Yes, I have been to Japan once.

　いいえ、（日本へ行ったことが）一度もありません。
　No, I've never been to Japan.

「練習」
1．日本料理／食べる　　2．イタリア／旅行する　　3．コアラ／見る
4．日本の歌／歌う　　　5．富士山／登る　　　　　6．日本／留学する

④ **Occurrence:** S **wa** V(BF)-**koto ga** aru.　(It happens that ~)

A: マイヤーさん**は**スポーツをすること**が**ありますか。
　Do you sometimes do sports, Ms. Mayer?
B: はい、（スポーツをすること**が**）ときどきあります。
　Yes, sometimes I do (sports).
　いいえ、（スポーツをすること**が**）めったにありません。
　No, I rarely do (sports).

「練習」
1．フランス語／話す　　2．車／運転する　　3．手紙／書く
4．お酒／飲む　　　　　5．病気／なる　　　6．みそ汁／飲む

(2) NPF-n-desu form

The n-desu form is often used in everyday conversation mixed with the masu form when you want to ask the other person questions in any situation and the other person wants to express their opinion or wish in a slightly emphasized answer. Despite the use of the NPF, this form is a polite expression because "desu" is at the end.

	PS-P	PS-N	PT-P	PT-N
V	行く-んです	行かない-んです	行った-んです	行かなかった-んです
IA	高い-んです	高くない-んです	高かった-んです	高くなかった-んです
NA	元気な-んです	元気じゃない-んです	元気だった-んです	元気じゃなかった-んです
N	先生な-んです	先生じゃない-んです	先生だった-んです	先生じゃなかった-んです

"no-desu" can also be used for the formal idiom, e.g. 行くのです.
"n/no-da" is the NPF of "n/no-desu", e.g. 高いん／のだ.

Verb:
A:今日の午後、何を**するんです**か。
　What are you doing this afternoon?
B:映画を**見るんです**よ。
　I'm going to see a movie.

「練習」
1．晩／友だち／会う　　　2．明日／料理／作る
3．朝／公園／ジョギングする　　4．昨日／何も／しない
5．昨日の晩／部屋／そうじする　　6．週末／プール／泳ぐ

I-Adjective:

A:その人はどんな**人なんです**か。
　What kind of person is he/she?
B:背がとても**高いんです**よ。
　He/she is very tall.

「練習」
1．髪／みじかい　　2．顔／白い　　3．目／青い
4．頭／いい　　5．力／強い　　6．鼻／高い

Na-Adjective:

A:その町は**有名なんです**か。
　Is the city famous?
B:いいえ、あまり**有名じゃないんです**よ。
　No, it's not that famous.

「練習」
1．テレビ／便利　　2．人／しんせつ
3．へや／しずか　　4．子ども／元気
5．テスト／簡単　　6．字引／便利

Noun:

A:それはカメラ**なんです**か。
　Is it a camera?
B:いいえ、カメラ**じゃないんです**。ビデオ**なんです**よ。
　No, it's not a camera, it's a video camera.

「練習」
1．それ／新聞／ざっし　　2．その人／ドイツ人／フランス人
3．その町／京都／奈良　　4．それ／豚肉／牛肉
5．明日／雨／雪　　6．きのう／晴れ／くもり

Fill in the blanks with the n-desu form.

① 町田　　：週末何を（　　　　　　　）ですか。
　ユリア　：家で日本語の宿題をしました。
　町田　　：私は友だちと買い物を（　　　　　　　）ですよ。
　ユリア　：何を（　　　　　　　）ですか。
　町田　　：くつとセーターを（　　　　　　　）です。

② ユリア ：先週大学に来ませんでしたね。どこかに（　　　　　　）ですか。
　 町田 ：ええ、奈良へ（　　　　　　）ですよ。
　 ユリア ：ああ、そう（　　　　　　）ですか。いかがでしたか。
　 町田 ：天気もよくて、楽しかったですよ。
　 ユリア ：それはよかったですね。奈良はどんな町（　　　　　　）ですか。
　 町田 ：奈良は日本で一番古い都（　　　　　　）です。
　 ユリア ：奈良で何を（　　　　　　）ですか。
　 町田 ：東大寺の大仏や若草山を（　　　　　　）ですよ。

③ ユリア ：町田さん、テニスですか。
　 町田 ：ええ、週に2～3回は（　　　　　　）です。
　　　　　僕はテニスが大（　　　　　　）ですよ。
　 ユリア ：私もテニスを（　　　　　　）ですが、やったことが（　　　　　　）です。
　 町田 ：じゃあ、ぜひいっしょにやりましょう。僕が教えますよ。
　 ユリア ：はい、ぜひお願いします。

Lesson test

（1）Put the matching words in the Wa-Ga form.

1．週末 ＿＿＿＿＿＿＿＿＿＿＿＿＿ か。 (have free time)
2．私は兄が ＿＿＿＿＿＿＿＿＿ が、姉が ＿＿＿＿＿＿＿＿ 。 (no / two)
3．この町は ＿＿＿＿＿＿＿＿＿＿ 。 (a beautiful park)
4．彼は ＿＿＿＿＿＿＿＿＿ て、 ＿＿＿＿＿＿＿＿＿ 。 (black hair and blue eyes)
5．ドイツは ＿＿＿＿＿＿＿＿＿＿＿ 。 (many breweries)

（2）Form the sentences according to the instructions.

1．彼女／信州そば／食べる (experience)
2．彼／まだ／富士山／登る (experience: negative)
3．私／友だち／テニス／する (from time to time: occurrence)
4．私の子ども／病気／なる (rare: occurrence)

（3）Rewrite the following sentences in the "n-desu form".

1．私はきのう彼に会いました。
2．先生は今日どこにも行きません。
3．たくさん漢字を練習しなければなりませんでした。
4．父はサッカーがじょうずでした。
5．彼女はあまり元気じゃありませんでした。

第12課　Dai Juuni-ka

あぶない 車<ruby>くるま</ruby>？

Abunai kuruma?

Lesson 12　あぶない車？

まさと：　今度 実家に 帰る時、ユリアの 車 を 借りても いいかな。
　　　　　荷物を 運ばなければ ならないんだ。
ユリア：　いいわよ。でも運転する前に、よく車を点検してね。とても古い車だから。
まさと：　うん、そうするよ。
ユリア：　それから車を 使った後は、ちゃんと ガソリンを 入れてね。
まさと：　ああ、もちろん そうするよ。
ユリア：　まさと、運転しながら、携帯電話を かけては いけないわよ。
まさと：　うん、あぶないからね。 かけないよ。
ユリア：　運転しながら、たばこも すってはいけないわよ。
まさと：　うんうん、わかって（い）るよ。
ユリア：　それと、もう一つ。
まさと：　まだ何か あるのかい？
ユリア：　走っている 間 に、変な音を 聞いた時は、すぐ 車からおりて！
まさと：　ええ？
ユリア：　エンジンを かけたままに しないで！ とても きけんだから。
まさと：　ええ？ 何だって？ それ 本当かい？
ユリア：　フフ、、まさか、じょうだんよ！

Translation of the text

A dangerous car?

Masato:　Can you lend me your car when I go to my parents' house?
　　　　　I have to take my luggage there.
Julia:　　No problem! But you have to check the car carefully before you drive it,
　　　　　because it's very old.
Masato:　Okay, I'll do that.
Julia:　　After the drive, please don't forget to fill up the tank.
Masato:　Yes, of course I'll fill up the tank.
Julia:　　You're not allowed to talk on your cell phone while driving.
Masato:　Yes, that's dangerous. I won't talk on the phone.
Julia:　　You're not allowed to smoke while driving either.
Masato:　Yes, yes, I know.
Julia:　　And one more thing.
Masato:　What else?
Julia:　　Get out of the car quickly if you hear a strange noise while you're driving!
Masato:　Excuse me?
Julia:　　Don't leave the engine running! That's extremely dangerous!
Masato:　Huh? What? Is that true?
Julia:　　Ha ha... Of course not! Just a little joke!

Questions about the text

１．まさとはどうしてユリアから 車 を借りますか。
２．いつ車を点検しますか。
３．車を使った後、何をしますか。
４．運転しながら、携帯電話をかけてもいいですか。

5．それから運転しながら、何をしてはいけませんか。
6．いつ車をおりなければなりませんか。
7．それは本当ですか。

Vocabulary and idioms

Vocabulary	reading	English
危ない　あぶない	abunai	dangerous
～間　～あいだ	aida	during ~, as long as ~
洗う　あらう	arau	wash
アルバイト（する）	arubaito(suru)	job, jobbing
遊ぶ　あそぶ	asobu	play
～後で　あとで	ato de	after ~
ちゃんと	chanto	correctly, properly (CF)
地図　ちず	chizu	map, city map
出す	dasu	take out
できる	dekiru	get, create, finish
電話をかける　でんわ	denwa o kakeru	call, make a phone call
出て行く　でていく	deteiku	go out
読書（する）　どくしょ	dokusho(suru)	read books
どうして	dooshite	why
エンジン、～をかける	enjin, ~ o kakeru	engine, ~ start
ガソリン	gasorin	gasoline
ギター	gitaa	guitar
歯　は　～をみがく	ha, ~ o migaku	tooth, brush teeth
運ぶ　はこぶ	hakobu	carry, transport
箸　はし	hashi	chopsticks
変な　へんな	hen-na	strange
弾く　ひく	hiku	play (a musical instrument)
ヒーター	hiitaa	heater
本当　ほんとう	hontoo	true, real
実家　じっか	jikka	parental home
冗談　じょうだん	joodan	joke
～かい	kai	interrogative particle (CF)
～かな	ka na	interrogative particle (CF) question to oneself
かご	kago	basket
会議　かいぎ	kaigi	conference, meeting
会話　かいわ	kaiwa	conversation, talk, dialog
借りる　かりる	kariru	borrow
風　かぜ	kaze	wind
風邪を引く　かぜをひく	kaze o hiku	catch a cold
警察　けいさつ	keisatsu	police, policeman
携帯電話　けいたいでんわ	keitai-denwa	mobile phone
見物（する）　けんぶつ	kenbutsu(suru)	visit
見学（する）　けんがく	kengaku(suru)	visit, visit to ~ learn
景色　けしき	keshiki	landscape
危険な　きけん	kiken-na	dangerous
切符　きっぷ	kippu	ticket

コート	kooto	coat
果物 くだもの	kudamono	fruit
クーラー、〜をつける	kuuraa, 〜 o tsukeru	air conditioning, ~ turn on
窓 まど	mado	window
〜前に まえに	mae ni	before ~
〜まま	mama	leaving like this
まさか	masaka	My goodness!, Of course not -
磨く みがく	migaku	polish
もう一つ もうひとつ	moo hitotsu	one more
〜ながら	nagara	while
何だって？ なん	Nan datte?	What?
眠い ねむい	nemui	tired, sleepy
荷物 にもつ	nimotsu	luggage, package
音 おと	oto	sound, noise
ローマ	rooma	Rome
制服 せいふく	seifuku	uniform
新鮮な しんせん	shinsen(na)	fresh
食事 しょくじ	shokuji	food, meal
小説 しょうせつ	shoosetsu	novel
外 そと	soto	outside
すぐ	sugu	immediately
涼しい すずしい	suzushii	cool (pleasantly)
大使館 たいしかん	taishikan	message
立つ たつ	tatsu	get up (e.g. from a chair)
点検（する） てんけん	tenken(suru)	control, check, examine
手伝う てつだう	tetsudau	help
トイレ	toire	toilet
時 とき	toki	time, here: when ~ (temporal)
点ける つける	tsukeru	turn on, switch on
着く つく	tsuku	arrive
冷たい つめたい	tsumetai	cold (objects)
運動（する） うんどう	undoo(suru)	sport, do sports
うれしい	ureshii	cheerful, happy, rejoice

Kanji

Kanji	SCK	English	On-yomi *Kun-yomi*	Usage / Composites
引	4	pull	in *hi-ku*	引き出し hikidashi / drawer 引力 inryoku / gravitation
練	14	knead	ren *ne-ru*	練習 renshuu / exercise 訓練 kunren / training
習	11	learn	shuu *nara-u*	習字 shuuji / calligraphy 学習 gakushuu / learning
寝	13	sleep	shin *ne-ru*	寝室 shinshitsu / bedroom 寝台 shindai / bed
荷	11	luggage	ka *ni*	荷物 nimotsu / luggage 重荷 omoni / burden

屋	9	loading	oku *ya*	屋内 okunai / inside, in the house 屋外 okugai / the outdoors
暑	12	hot	sho *atsu-i*	暑い atsu-i / hot 暑中見舞い shochuumimai / summer greetings
静	14	quiet	sei *shizu-ka*	静止 seishi / stop 冷静 reisei / prudent, sensible
窓	11	window	soo *mado*	窓 mado / window 同窓 doosoo / to be in the same school year
変	9	change	hen *ka-eru, -waru*	変化 henka / change 変人 henjin / strange person
部	11	part	bu (he)	部屋 heya / room 部分 bubun / part
当	6	hit	too *a-taru, -teru*	本当 hontoo / really, true 不当 futoo / unjust
遊	12	play	yuu *aso-bu*	遊び場 asobiba / playground 遊園地 yuuenchi / amusement park
立	5	stand	ritsu *ta-tsu*	立体 rittai / cube 立場 tachiba / point of view
動	11	move	doo *ugo-ku*	運動 undoo / movement, sport 自動車 jidoosha / car
働	13	work	doo *hatara-ku*	労働 roodoo / labor, work 労働者 roodoosha / worker

· SC: number of strokes of the kanji · stroke sequence of the kanji: See page 216.

Grammar and exercises

Temporal clauses

(1) Simultaneity

① Subordinate clause (SC) **toki,** main clause (MC): when ~ / as ~

Verbs: NPF + toki, ~

The BF is used before "toki" if the action in the SC has not yet been completed at a point in time when the action in the MC is carried out or is carried out simultaneously. It is independent of the tense (time) in the MC.

町へ行く時、バスに乗ります。
I take the bus when I go into town.

きのう寝る時、ちゃんと窓を閉めましたか。
Did you close the windows properly when you went to bed last night?

Ta-form is used before "toki" when the action in the SC is already completed before the action in the MC is carried out. It is independent of the tense in the MC.

朝、人に会った時、「おはようございます」と言います。
People say "Ohayoo-gozaimasu" when they meet someone in the morning.

町へ行った時、上田さんに会いました。
I met Mr. Ueda when I went to the city.

「練習」

1．ごはん／食べる／はしで食べる　　　2．朝／起きる／歯／みがく
3．コーヒー／飲む／ミルクを入れる　　4．電車／乗る／切符／買う
5．奈良／行く／大仏や若草山／見る　　6．かぜ／引く／この薬／飲む (Bitte)

I-adjectives (IA): BF + toki, ~

IA are always used in the basic form, regardless of the tense in the main clause.

PS: 天気が*いい**時**、私はよくさんぽします。
I often go for a walk when the weather is good.
PT: 天気が*いい**時**、私はよくさんぽしました。
I often went for a walk when the weather was good.

The MC "が" must be used after the subject in the SC if there is a different subject in the SC and MC. If the subject in the MC and SC is identical, the subject in the SC is inserted with "は" and can be omitted in the MC. This rule is generally valid for every subordinate clause.

「練習」

1．暑い／よく／クーラー／つける　　　2．ごはん／おいしい／たくさん／食べる
3．仕事／いそがしい／よく／手伝う　　4．風／冷たい／コート／着る
5．寒い／ヒーター／つける　　　　　　6．私／ねむい／コーヒー／飲む

Na-adjectives (NA): BF-na + toki, ~

NA are always used in the basic form with "な", regardless of the tense in the main clause

PS: ひまな**時**、読書します。
I read books when I have time off.
PT: ひまな**時**、読書しました。
I read books when I had time off.

「練習」

1．元気／よく運動をする　　　2．静か／よく勉強できる
3．テスト／かんたん／うれしい　　4．景色／きれい／たくさん／写真をとる

Nouns (N): N-no + toki, ~

N are always used with "の", regardless of the tense in the main clause.

PS: 買い物の**時**、かごを持っていきます。
I take a basket with me when I go shopping.
PT: 買い物の**時**、かごを持っていきました。
I took a basket with me when I went shopping.

「練習」

1．休み／長野へ行く　　　2．学生／よくアルバイトする
3．旅行／地図／持って行く　　4．ごはん／ワインを飲む
5．そうじ／窓／開ける　　　6．試験／静か／する (bit form)

② **SC aida / aida ni, MC:** during / as long as ~

Verbs: "~ te iru aida" is used regardless of the time.

PS: 子どもが寝ている 間／間 に*、本を読みます。
I read the book while my child is sleeping.

PT: 子どもが寝ている間／間 に*、本を読みました。
I read the book while my child was sleeping.

The AP に after "aida" can be omitted and means that the action in the MC continues all the time while the action in SC is carried out. With AP に, on the other hand, the meaning is that the action in MC is not carried out all the time, but within this period.

「練習」

1．電車を待つ／友だちと話す　　2．部長が電話する／外で待つ
3．かぜを引く／会社を休む　　4．日本／住む／たくさん／友達／できる
5．試験／する／話す (ban)　　6．桜／さく／花見／行く (request)

I-adjectives (IA): BF + aida (ni) ~

PS: 天気がいい間に、せんたくしましょう。
Let's do the laundry while the weather is good!

PT: 天気がいい間に、せんたくしました。
I did the laundry while the weather was good.

「練習」

1．それが安い／買う　　2．天気がわるい／家にいる
3．若い／たくさん旅行する　　4．すずしい／公園／さんぽする

Na-adjective (NA): BF-na + aida (ni) ~

PS: 魚を新鮮な間に、食べましょう。
Let's eat the fish while they're fresh!

PT: 魚を新鮮な間に、食べました。
I ate the fish while they were fresh.

「練習」

1．ひま／遊びに行く　　2．静か／作文を書く　　3．外が危険／家にいる

Nouns (N): N + no aida (ni) ~

PS: 休みの間に、漢字をたくさん練習してください。
Please learn a lot of kanji during the vacations.

PT: 休みの間に、漢字をたくさん練習しました。
I learned a lot of kanji during the vacations.

「練習」

1．会議／たばこをすわない　　2．仕事／制服を着る
3．病気／家でよく休む　　4．休み／トイレ／行く

③ SC (stem of Masu-F)-nagara, MC: while ~

This sentence form is only used for verbs when the subject is identical in SC and MC and two active actions are performed simultaneously.

PS: 公園をさんぽし**ながら**、話しませんか。
   Shall we talk while we walk in the park?
PT: 公園をさんぽし**ながら**、話しました。
   We talked while we were walking in the park.

「練習」
1. 歌を歌う／帰る　　　　　　2. コーヒーを飲む／バスを待つ
3. ギター／弾く／歌う　　　　4. 日本語のCDを聞く／会話を練習する
5. 写真をとる／町／見学する　6. 日本／働く／日本語／勉強する

④ V-ta mama, ~ : keeping / unchanged situation ~

This sentence form is used when an action in MC is performed under a condition that was previously caused by another action in SC.

彼はドアを開けた**まま**、出て行きました。
Keeping the door open, he left.

But you can say "**V-ta mama ni suru**" if no temporal clause is used.

彼はドアを開けた<u>まま</u>にしました。　　He left the door open.

「練習」
1. 服を着る／寝る　　　　　2. 電気をつける／部屋を出る
3. いすにすわる／話す　　　4. 私たち／立つ／映画／見る
5. 見る／話す (request form)　　　6. 本／ノート／出す (negative request)

(2) **Before tense:** before ~ (for verbs and nouns)

Verb: BF (always) + mae (ni) ~

The tense of the whole sentence is determined by the verb in the MC. A verb before "前に"
is always used in the **basic form** because it is free from the tense of the sentence and only shows the <u>incompleteness</u> of the action in the SC.

A: ドイツに来る**前**に、どこに住んでいましたか。
   Where did you live before you came to Germany?

B: ドイツに来る**前**に、イギリスに住んでいました。
   I lived in England before I came to Germany.

「練習」
1. ここ／来る／だれ／会う → 友だち　　2. 寝る／何／する → テレビを見る
3. この仕事／始める／何／する → 音楽／聞く
4. 朝ごはん／食べる／何／する → 歯をみがく
5. 車を運転する／何／する → ガソリンを入れる
6. きのう／会社／行く／どこ／行く → 図書館

Noun: N + no mae (ni) ~

A: いつ買い物をしましたか。
　　When did you go shopping?
B: コンサートの前にしました。
　　I went shopping before the concert.

「練習」
1．試験／する／休み　　　　　　2．日本／帰る／正月
3．コーヒー／飲む／仕事　　　　4．大使館／行く／日本旅行
5．おふろ／入る／晩ごはん　　　6．ビール／買う／パーティー

(3) **After tense:** after ~ (for verbs and nouns)

The tense of the whole sentence is also determined by the verb in the MC. A verb before "後で"
is always used in the **Ta form** because it only shows the completeness of the action in the NS.

Verb: Ta form (always) **+ ato (de) ~**

A: 勉強した後で、何をしますか／しましたか。
　　What do you do after learning?
　　What did you do after you had learned?
B: 勉強した後で、スポーツをします／しました。
　　I do sports after learning.
　　I did sport after I had learned.

「練習」
1．働く／映画を見る　　　　　　2．友だち／会う／いっしょに買い物する
3．奈良／着く／大仏／見物する　4．仕事する／ビール／飲みに行く
5．日本語／勉強する／日本／働く　6．町／行く／本屋／雑誌／買う

Noun: N + no ato (de) ~

A: いつその小説を読みましたか。
　　When did you read the novel?
B: 勉強の後で読みました。
　　After learning, I read it.

「練習」
1．音楽／聞く／仕事　　　　　　2．ガソリン／入れる／運転
3．ローマ／行く／イギリス　　　4．くだもの／食べる／食事
5．小説を読む／晩ごはん　　　　6．買い物する／仕事

Lesson test

（1）Connect the sentences with temporal expressions.
1．朝起きました。　雨がふっていました。　（時）
2．さむいです。　ヒーターをつけてください。　（時）
3．私は若くて、元気でした。　よくスポーツをしました。　（時）
4．彼女はごはんを作りました。　私は部屋をそうじしました。　（間）
5．病気です。　働かないで家にいます。　（間）
6．彼は働いています。　彼は日本語を勉強しています。　（ながら）
7．電気をつけます。　部屋を出ていってはいけません。　（まま）
8．彼女は立っています。　長い間話しています。　（まま）
9．私は先生になりました。　ゾミーの会社で働きました。　（前）
10．東京に着きました。　すぐ友だちに電話しました。　（後）

（2）Set the appropriate temporal expressions.
1．車を運転した＿＿＿＿＿＿＿ガソリンを入れてください。
2．彼は服を着た＿＿＿＿＿＿＿寝ていますよ。
3．コーヒーをあつい＿＿＿＿＿＿＿飲んでください。
4．上野に行く＿＿＿＿＿＿＿山の手線に乗りかえてください。
5．電車に乗る＿＿＿＿＿＿＿きっぷを買ってください。
6．母はそうじし＿＿＿＿＿＿＿よく歌を歌います。
7．私は日本にいる＿＿＿＿＿＿＿ドイツ語をぜんぜん話しません。

（3）Translate the following sentences into Japanese.
1．Can you lend me your car when I go to my parents' house?
2．You are not allowed to talk on your cell phone while driving.
3．Don't forget to refuel after the journey.

きょう買い物したあとで、りょうりをつくります。
晩、かれと映画を見たあとで、ワインをのみます。

第13課　Dai Juusan-ka

打ち合わせがしたいと言っていました。

Uchiawase ga shitai to itte imashita.

Lesson 13　打ち合わせがしたいと 言っていました。

北野　　　：今日 シュミットさんと言う 人から 電話がありましたよ。

マイヤー　：あ、ユンケル社の 部長さんです。 私、今度通訳の アルバイトを するんです。

北野　　　：へえ、すごいなあ。 難しくないんですか。

マイヤー　：見本市の案内です から、あまり 難しくないと 思います。
　　　　　　でも、私、来月だと 思っていました。

北野　　　：仕事の都合で、昨日日本に 着いたと 言っていました。

マイヤー　：あ、そうですか。何か ほかに 言っていましたか。

北野　　　：ええ、明日マイヤーさんに 会って、打ち合わせがしたいと
　　　　　　言っていましたよ。

マイヤー　：ああ、でも明日は 予定があって、だめなんです。

北野　　　：それじゃあ、早く シュミットさんに 連絡した方が いいですね。

マイヤー　：ええ、シュミットさん、今日 どこに 泊まると 言っていましたか。

北野　　　：新宿のサンライズホテル(だ)と 言っていました。 電話番号は これです。

マイヤー　：どうもすみません。 北野さん、今から 電話してもいいと 思いますか。

北野　　　：今10時半ですね。 ちょっと遅いけど、だいじょうぶだと 思いますよ。

Translation of the text

He said that he wanted to have a pre-briefing with you.
Kitano: Mr. Schmidt called you today.
Mayer: Oh, that's one of the department heads of Junkel Ltd.
　　　　I'll be working as an interpreter for him soon.
Kitano: Oh, great! Isn't that difficult?
Mayer: I don't think it's that difficult because I'm only accompanying him to a trade fair.
　　　　But I thought that wasn't until next month.
Kitano: He said he arrived in Japan yesterday for work.
Mayer: Oh really! What else did he say?
Kitano: He wants to see you tomorrow and have a pre-briefing with you.
Mayer: Unfortunately, tomorrow doesn't suit me because I already have an appointment.
Kitano: Then it's better to get in touch with him quickly.
Mayer: Yes. Did he tell you where he's staying tonight?
Kitano: Yes, he's staying at the Hotel Sunrise in Shinjuku. Here is the phone number.
Mayer: Thank you very much! Do you think I can still call him?
Kitano: It's half past ten now. Well, it's a bit late, but I think it's all right.

Questions about the text

1．今日だれから電話がありましたか。
2．その人はだれですか。
3．マイヤーさんは何をするんですか。
4．シュミットさんはいつ日本に 着きましたか。
5．シュミットさんは明日マイヤーさんと何がしたいと言っていますか。

6．マイヤーさんは明日時間がありますか。

7．シュミットさんはどこに泊まっていますか。

8．今何時ですか。

Vocabulary and idioms

Vocabulary	reading	English
赤い　あかい	akai	red
案内　あんない	an'nai	guide
帽子　ぼうし	booshi	hat, cap
帽子を被る　ぼうしをかぶる	booshi o kaburu	put on hat
だめ（な）	dame(na)	bad, it does not work
電話がある　でんわ	denwa ga aru	get a call
ごちそうさま	gochisoosama	It tasted good.
へえ	hee	Oh!, Yes?
他に　ほかに	hoka ni	in addition
いらっしゃいませ	irasshaimase	Welcome!
いただきます	itadakimasu	Enjoy your meal!
いってまいります	itte mairimasu	Bye! (Farewell to the person leaving home)
今晩　こんばん	konban	this evening
まぐろ	maguro	tuna
見本市　みほんいち	mihonichi	fair
何か　なにか	nani ka	something
おばさん	oba, obasan	aunt, somewhat older woman
おばあさん	obaasan	grandmother, old woman
おはよう	ohayoo	Good morning!
おじさん	oji, ojisan	uncle, slightly older man
おじいさん	ojiisan	grandfather, old man
お客（さん）　おきゃく	o-kyaku(san)	guest, customer
思う　おもう	omou	mean, think, believe
遅い　おそい	osoi	late, slow
お誕生日おめでとうございます	o-tanjoobi omedetoo gozaimasu	Congratulations on your birthday!
おやすみ（なさい）	oyasumi(nasai)	Have a good night!
連絡（する）　れんらく	renraku(suru)	connection, get in touch with ~
立派（な）　りっぱ（な）	rippa(na)	excellent, very good
先月　せんげつ	sengetsu	last month
信号　しんごう	shingoo	traffic light
新宿　しんじゅく	shinjuku	Shinjuku: district of Tokyo
新幹線　しんかんせん	shinkansen	shinkansen (Japanese bullet train)
祖母　そぼ	sobo	grandmother (own)
祖父　そふ	sofu	grandfather (own)
すごい	sugoi	super
ただいま	tadaima	Hello (greeting to those returning home)
誕生日　たんじょうび	tanjoobi	birthday

泊まる　とまる	tomaru	stay overnight
都合　つごう、〜で	tsugoo, 〜 de	circumstance, because of 〜
（に）ついて	(ni) tsuite	about
通訳　つうやく	tsuuyaku	interpreting
打ち合わせ　うちあわせ	uchiawase	preliminary meeting, pre-briefing
予定　よてい	yotei	plan, intention, appointment
夜　よる	yoru	night

Kanji

Kanji	SCK	English	On-yomi *Kun-yomi*	Usage / Composites
明	8	bright	mei, myoo *aka-rui*	明日　ashita / tomorrow 鮮明　senmei / clear
親	16	friendly parents	shin *oya / shita-shii*	親切　shinsetsu / friendly 両親　ryooshin / parents
切	4	cut	setsu *ki-ru*	切手　kitte / stamp 切符　kippu / ticket, travel ticket
朝	12	morning	choo *asa*	朝ご飯　asagohan / breakfast 毎朝　maiasa / every morning
夜	8	night, evening	ya, *yoru, yo*	夜中　yonaka / midnight 今夜　kon'ya / this night
店	8	store	ten *mise*	店員　ten'in / salesperson 売店　baiten / kiosk
客	9	guest customer	kyaku, kaku	客車　kyakusha / passenger car 乗客　jookyaku / passenger
京	8	capital city Kyoto	kyoo *miyako*	京都　Kyooto / Kyoto 東京　Tookyoo / Tokyo
都	11	capital city	to *miyako*	都会　tokai / big city 都市　toshi / big city
言	7	say	gen, gon *i-u*	言語　gengo / language 方言　hoogen / dialect
思	9	think	shi *omo-u*	思想　shisoo / thought 思考　shikoo / thinking
合	6	fit	goo *a-u*	合計　gookei / sum 合格　gookaku / to pass
打	5	beat	da *u-tsu*	打つ　utsu / beat 打楽器　dagakki / percussion instrument
着	12	arrive, put on	chaku *tsu-ku, ki-ru*	到着　toochaku / arrival 着陸　chakuriku / landing
終	11	end	shuu *o-waru, o-eru*	終日　shuujitsu / the whole day 終了　shuuryoo / end

・SC: number of strokes of the kanji ・stroke sequence of the kanji: see page 216.

Grammar and exercises

(1) Literal speech

Here, a person's statement is repeated by another speaker or communicated to another person. The statement is marked as a quotation by the AP "と".
The subject of the whole sentence can be placed either at the beginning of the sentence or after the AP "と" can be used. Literal speech is divided into direct and indirect speech. At the end of the sentence, the Te-form "言(い)っていました" (said) is usually used when the statement is passed on for information.

Direct speech (DS): ~ to iu / ~ to itte iru

Mr. Schmidt's statement: 私はきのう日本に着きました。
The statement is repeated verbatim in quotation marks 「 」.

シュミットさんは「私はきのう日本に着きました。」と言っていました。

「私はきのう日本に着きました。」とシュミットさんは言っていました。
Mr. Schmidt said: "I arrived in Japan yesterday."

Indirect speech (IS):

The subject of the statement is omitted if it is the same as the subject of the whole sentence. Indirect speech is used more often than direct speech because direct speech sounds rather childish. instead of 言う 聞く, 話す, 書く etc. can also be used at the end of a sentence.

① Indirect speech: ~ to iu / ~ to itte iru

[Verb]

Statement by Mr. Schmidt: 私はきのう日本に着きました。

IS: シュミットさんはきのう日本に着いたと言っていました。

きのう日本に着いたとシュミットさんは言っていました。
Mr. Schmidt said that he arrived in Japan yesterday.

「練習」
1．私は今日友だちに会います。 → 町田さんは＿＿＿＿＿＿＿＿＿＿＿＿＿。
2．子供はもうすぐ帰ります。 → お母さんは＿＿＿＿＿＿＿＿＿＿＿＿＿。
3．今晩はどこへも行きません。 → マリアは＿＿＿＿＿＿＿＿＿＿＿＿＿＿＿。
4．きのう働きませんでした。 → 北野さんは＿＿＿＿＿＿＿＿＿＿＿＿＿＿＿＿。
5．暑い時、いつも帽子をかぶります。 → おばさんは＿＿＿＿＿＿＿＿＿＿＿＿。
6．若い時、ドイツに行ったことがあります。 → おじさんは＿＿＿＿＿＿＿＿。

[I-adjective]

Statement by Mr. Schmidt: おすしはとてもおいしいです。

DS: シュミットさんは「おすしはとてもおいしいです。」と言っていました。
Mr. Schmidt said: " The sushi tastes very delicious to me."
IS: シュミットさんはおすしはとてもおいしいと言っていました。
Mr. Schmidt said that the sushi tastes very delicious to him.

「練習」

1．今日はとても暑かったです。→　町田さんは_______________________。

2．たくさん旅行がしたいです。→　ユリアは_______________________。 *

3．その本はおもしろくないです。→　さとしは_______________________。

4．テストはあまりむずかしくなかったです。→　マリアさんは_______________________。

5．信号はその時まだ赤かったです。→　鈴木さんは_______________________。

6．祖母の料理はとてもおいしかったです。　→　祖父は_______________________。

* Not the wish form "shitagatte iru", but "shitai" must be used, although it is about the wish
 of the third person, because this form is connected to another word. (L. 10)

[Na-adjective / Noun]

Statement by Mr. Schmidt:　この携帯電話はとても便利です。

DS:　シュミットさんは「この携帯電話はとても便利です。」と言っていました。
Mr. Schmidt said: "The mobile phone is very practical."

IS:　シュミットさんはこの携帯電話はとても**便利だと**言っていました。
Mr. Schmidt said that the mobile phone was very practical.

Statement by Mr. Schmidt:　私はユンケル社の部長です。

DS:　シュミットさんは「私はユンケル社の部長です」と言っていました。
Mr. Schmidt said: "I am head of a department at Junkel."

IS:　シュミットさんはユンケル社の**部長だと**言っていました。
Mr. Schmidt said that he was head of a department at Junkel.

「練習」

1．町田さんはとても親切です。→　山川さんは_______________________。

2．東京は静かではありません。→　マイヤーさんは_______________________。

3．私はテニスが好きでした。→　かおりさんは_______________________。

4．彼女は通訳の仕事がきらいではありません。→マイヤーさんは_______________________。

5．彼は有名ではありませんでした。→　マリアさんは_______________________。

6．春は桜がとてもきれいです。→　おばあさんは_______________________。

7．先週病気でした。→　木村さんは_______________________。

8．晩ごはんは日本料理ではありませんでした。→マイヤーさんは_______________________。

② **Attributive use: ~ to iu N** (N that means ~)

今日シュミットさん**という人**から電話がありました。
The person called Schmidt called you today.

「練習」

1．先月／京都／町／行く　　2．きのう／まぐろ／魚／食べる

3．携帯／漢字／むずかしい　　4．まなび／学校／日本語／勉強している

5．田村さん／人／知る／か　　6．彼／サンライズ／ホテル／泊まる

③ **General statement: ~ to iimasu** (One says ~ / That means ~)

The general statement does not use "言っています" but "言います".

店員はお客に「いらっしゃいませ!」と言います。
The sales staff say to the customers: "Irasshaimase!"

ごはんを食べる時、「いただきます」と言って、食べた時、「ごちそうさま」と言います。
Before the meal you say "Itadakimasu" and "Gochisoosama" after the meal.

「携帯電話」を英語で何と言いますか。「mobile phone」と言います。
What does "keitai-denwa" mean in English?　　It means "mobile phone".

「練習」
1．朝起きた時／おはよう／夜寝る時／おやすみ
2．家を出る時／いってまいります／家に帰った時／ただいま
3．たんじょうびに／おたんじょうびおめでとう
4．Just a moment please!／日本語で／ちょっと待ってください
5．おそくなってすみません!／英語で／何／言う／か
6．Tasted good!／日本語で／何／言う／か

(2) **Expression of opinion: NPF+ to omou** (same sentence structure as with literal speech)

A:「携帯電話」についてどう思いますか。
　　What do you think about mobile phones?
B: とても便利だと思います。
　　I think they are very practical.

「練習」
1．新幹線／とても速い
2．京都／とても有名／きれい
3．彼女の絵／とても立派
4．漢字／少しむずかしい／おもしろい
5．彼／若い／親切
6．そのアパート／新しくない／不便

* „と思っています" is used when it is the opinion of the third person.

<u>マイヤーさん</u>はその仕事はあまりむずかしくないと**思って**います。
　Ms. Meyer thinks that the work is not difficult.

A: 日本まで飛行機でどのくらいかかると思いますか。
　　How long do you think it will take to get to Japan by plane?
B: １２時間ぐらいかかると思います。
　　I think it takes about 12 hours.

「練習」
1．新幹線／東京から大阪まで／何時間／かかる → ３時間ぐらい
2．東京から大阪まで／新幹線と飛行機／どちら／便利
3．日本で／ビール一本／いくらだ → ３００円ぐらい
4．日本／今／何時だ → １１時

5．明日／雨がふる → はい
6．北野さんの故郷／どこだ → 長野
7．シュミットさん／明日／マイヤーさん／何／したい → 打ち合わせ

Lesson test

（1）Complete the indirect speech according to the instructions.

1．来週から通訳のアルバイトをします。　（Ms. Mayer says ~）
2．早く部長に連絡しなければなりません。　（Mr. Kitano says ~）
3．きのう町で友だちに会いました。　（Mr. Machida said ~）
4．山田さんはホテルに泊まりませんでした。　（Mr. Yamada said ~）
5．彼女は肉があまり好きではありません。　（Maria often says ~）
6．今日の仕事はとても大変でした。　（Mr. Schmidt said ~）

（2）Answer the questions.

1．日本人は家を出る時、何と言いますか。
2．日本人は家に帰った時、何と言いますか。
3．日本人はごはんを食べる時、何と言いますか。
4．日本人はごはんを食べた時、何と言いますか。
5．「Congratulations!」は日本語で何と言いますか。
6．「だいじょうぶです」はドイツ語で何と言いますか。

（3）Answer the questions with "omoimasu".

1．明日の天気はいかがですか。
2．あなたは今晩映画を見ますか。
3．長野市は何で有名ですか。(L.11)
4．あなたはE・メールについてどう思いますか。
5．京都と奈良とでは、どちらのほうが古いですか。(L.6)
6．北野さんはスポーツの中で何がとくいですか。(L.10)

京都

奈良

第 14 課　Dai Juuyon-ka

陶器（とうき）について書（か）くことにしました。

Tooki ni tsuite kaku koto ni shimashita.

Lesson 14　陶器について　書くことに　しました。

マイヤー　：夏休みの宿題で　日本文化について　レポートを
　　　　　　書くことに　なりました。

北野　　　：へえ、どんなテーマで　書くつもりですか。

マイヤー　：私は日本のお茶が　好きなので、陶器について　書く
　　　　　　ことに　しました。

北野　　　：おもしろいテーマですね。　本を調べて　書くのですか。

マイヤー　：いいえ、本だけで　なくて、じっさいに　陶器の産地を　見学して、書こうと
　　　　　　思っているんです。

北野　　　：あ、それはいいですね。　陶器の産地は　たくさんありますが、どこへ行く
　　　　　　つもりですか。

マイヤー　：有名な「有田焼き」の産地、佐賀県・有田町へ　行くことに　しました。

北野　　　：そうですか。　「有田焼き」は「マイセン焼き」に　大きな影響を　あたえましたね。

マイヤー　：はい、とても興味深いこと　なので、その歴史も　ぜひ調べる　つもりです。

北野　　　：古い時代の　日独文化交流ですね。

マイヤー　：そうですね。それから私、焼き物のコースに　参加して　陶器を　焼こうと
　　　　　　思っているんですよ。

北野　　　：それは　楽しみです。　マイヤーさんの芸術品を　期待していますよ。

Translation of the text

I have decided to write about porcelain.

Mayer: It was decided that the homework for the summer vacation would be to write
　　　　something about Japanese culture.

Kitano: Oh, what kind of topic would you like to write about?

Mayer: I decided to write about porcelain because I like Japanese tea.

Kitano: Interesting! Are you writing the essay with the help of books?

Mayer: No, not just with books, but I intend to actually visit a production site and write about it.

Kitano: That's nice! But there are many places where porcelain is produced.
　　　　Where do you want to go?

Mayer: I have decided to go to Arita in Saga, where the famous Arita porcelain is produced.

Kitano: Ah, that's great! Arita porcelain has had a great influence on Meissen porcelain, didn't it?

Mayer: Yes, that's an interesting thing. I also really want to investigate the history.

Kitano: A cultural exchange between Japan and Germany in ancient times.

Mayer: That's right! By the way, I intend to take part in a pottery course and fire porcelain
　　　　myself.

Kitano: How nice! I am eagerly awaiting your work of art.

Questions about the text

１．マイヤーさんは夏休みのしゅくだいで何をしますか。
２．何について書くつもりですか。
３．何を見学しようと思っていますか。
４．どこへ行くつもりですか。
５．有田焼きは何にえいきょうをあたえましたか。
６．マイヤーさんはどこで陶器を焼こうと思っていますか。

Vocabulary and idioms

Vocabulary	reading	English
有田町　ありたちょう	arita-choo	Arita town (Choo means small town.)
有田焼き　ありたやき	arita-yaki	Arita porcelain
文化　ぶんか	bunka	culture
文化交流　ぶんかこうりゅう	bunka-kooryuu	cultural exchange
中止（する）　ちゅうし	chuushi(suru)	cancel, stop
～だけでなくて、～	dake denakute, ~	not only ~, but ~
影響をあたえる　えいきょう	eikyoo o ataeru	exert influence
延期（する）　えんき	enki(suru)	displacement, shift
芸術品　げいじゅつひん	geijutsu-hin	work of art
池　いけ	ike	pond
時代　じだい	jidai	time, age
実際に　じっさいに	jissai ni	in fact, really
実施（する）　じっし	jisshi(suru)	realization, carry out
変える　かえる	kaeru	change
計画　けいかく	keikaku	plan
期待（する）　きたい	kitai(suru)	expectation, expect
工場　こうじょう	koojoo	factory
コース	koosu	course
興味、～がある　きょうみ	kyoomi, ~ ga aru	interest, be interested in
興味深い　きょうみぶかい	kyoomi-bukai	interesting
マイセン	Maisen	Meissen
店　みせ	mise	store
何でも　なんでも	nan demo	everything, whatever
日独　にちどく	nichi-doku	Japanese-German
のんびりする	nonbiri-suru	live quietly, relax
オリンピック	orinpikku	Olympics
レポート	repooto	report
佐賀県　さがけん	saga-ken	Saga Prefecture in Kyuushuu
産地　さんち	sanchi	production site
～に参加（する）　さんか	sanka(suru)	participation, participate in
成功（する）　せいこう	seikoo	success, ~ have
調べる　しらべる	shiraberu	investigate, research, look up
食堂　しょくどう	shokudoo	dining room, restaurant
すませる	sumaseru	get ready, do
滞在（する）　たいざい	taizai(suru)	stay
楽しみです　たのしみ	tanoshimi desu	look forward to sth.

建てる　たてる	tateru	build
テーマ	teema	theme, subject
陶器　とうき	tooki	porcelain
つもり	tsumori	intend
釣り　つり	tsuri	fishing
焼き物　やきもの	yakimono	porcelain
全部　ぜんぶ	zenbu	everything, all

Kanji

Kanji	SCK	English	On-yomi *Kun-yomi*	Usage / Composites
芸	7	art	gei	芸術 geijutsu / art 芸能 geinoo / artistic skill
術	11	technology	jutsu	技術 gijutsu / technique 手術 shujutsu / surgery
品	9	goods	hin *shina*	品物 shinamono / article, goods 商品 shoohin / goods
文	4	sentence text	bun *aya*	文化 bunka / culture 作文 sakubun / essay
化	4	transformation	ka *ba-keru*	化学 kagaku / chemistry 変化 henka / change
交	6	cross	koo *maji-waru*	交流 kooryuu / exchange 交通 kootsuu / traffic
流	10	flow	ryuu *naga-reru*	上流 jooryuu / upper course of the river 下流 karyuu / lower course of the river
茶	9	tea	cha, sa	茶道 sadoo / tea ceremony 紅茶 koocha / black tea
調	15	examine	choo *shira-beru*	調査 choosa / investigation 調和 choowa / harmony
歴	14	history	reki	歴史 rekishi / history 学歴 gakureki / educational background
史	5	history	shi	史実 shijitsu / historical fact 史跡 shiseki / historical site
代	5	generation representation	dai *yo, shiro*	時代 jidai / time, age 代表 daihyoo / representation
参	8	come by	san *mai-ru*	参加 sanka / participation 参考 sankoo / to consult
加	5	add	ka *kuwa-waru*	増加 zooka / increase 加入 kanyuu / to join the group
焼	12	burn	shoo *ya-ku*	焼き物 yakimono / porcelain 焼失 shooshitsu / to burn down
計	9	plan measure	kei *haka-ru*	計画 keikaku / plan 時計 tokei / clock
止	4	stop	shi *to-maru, -meru*	中止 chuushi / stop, cessation 禁止 kinshi / prohibition

・ SC: number of strokes of the kanji ・ stroke sequence of the kanji: See page 217.

Grammar and exercises

(1) Expression of the will: intention, purpose and decision

① Intention: V(BF) tsumori desu

A: 週末何をするつもりですか。
What are you going to do this weekend?

B: ケーキを焼くつもりです。
I am going to bake a cake.

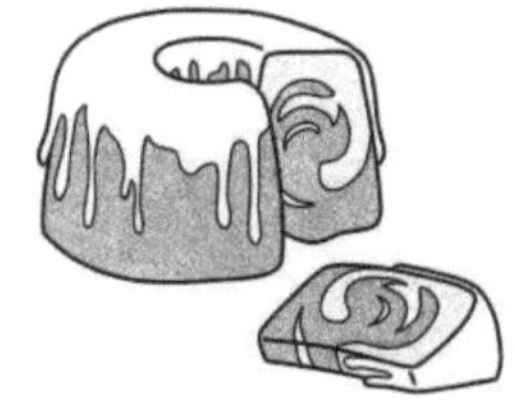

「練習」
1. 映画／見る
2. 宿題／する
3. 友だち／会う
4. 家／のんびりする
5. 京都／お寺／訪れる
6. 池／つり／する

② Not intending to do ~ : 1. V(Nai-F) tsumori desu 2. V(BF) tsumori wa arimasen

1. 今月アルバイトを**しないつもり**です。(normal negation)
   I do not intend to work part-time this month.

2. 今月アルバイトを**するつもりはありません**。(strong negation)
   I do have no intention of working part time this month.

「練習」 Question and answer in two negative forms
1. 明日／映画／見る
2. 今日／そうじ／する
3. 今晩／友だち／会う
4. 休み／料理／作る
5. 週末／何／しない
6. 来年／日本／留学する

③ Unfinished intention: V(BF) tsumori deshita

コンサートに行くつもりでしたが、もう切符がありませんでした。
I actually wanted to go to the concert, but there are no more tickets.

きのう宿題をするつもりでしたが、ねむくてできませんでした。
I wanted to do the homework yesterday, but I couldn't because I was tired.

「練習」
1. 日本／行く／中国／行く
2. 日本料理／食べる／イタリア料理／食べる
3. 友だち／会う／ひま／ない
4. 医者／なる／会社員／なる

④ Subjective imagination (assumption) : Ta-form tsumori desu / Te-iru tsumori desu

In addition to verbs, IA, NA and nouns can also be used.

彼はよく<u>勉強した</u>つもりだが、テストのせいせきはよくなかった。
He imagines that he has learned a lot, but his exam grade was poor.

彼女は何でも<u>知っている</u>つもりだが、本当は何も知らない。
She imagines that she knows everything, but in reality she knows nothing.

彼はまだ<u>若いつもり</u> (IA)で、<u>元気なつもり</u> (NA)だが、本当はもう60才だ。
He imagines that he is still young and healthy, but in reality he is already 60.

それは<u>冗談のつもり</u> (N)でしたが、、、
I only said it as a joke, but...

「練習」

1．がんばる／できない
2．部屋（へや）／よく／そうじする／まだ／きたない
3．電気（でんき）／消す（けす）／つく
4．ドア／かぎ／かける／開く（あく）
5．彼（かれ）／いい医者（いしゃ）／本当（ほんとう）／あまり
6．彼女（かのじょ）／歌（うた）／じょうず／本当（ほんとう）／へた

(2) Familiar form of an invitation: (y)oo*

① The V-(y)oo form is used for requests in a familiar circle: "Let's ~!"
"V-mashoo" is the more polite form of this.　See L.10

	basic form	familiar form	polite form
1-st. V	食べる (eat)	食べよう (-yoo)	食べましょう
5-st. V	飲む (drink)	飲もう (-oo)	飲みましょう
IV1	来（く）る (come)	来（こ）よう (-yoo)	来（き）ましょう
IV2	する (do)	しよう (-yoo)	しましょう

映画を見よう。 → うん、見よう。
Let's see a movie! → Yes, with pleasure!
泳（およ）ぎに行こう。 → うん、行こう。
Let's go for a swim! → Yes, with pleasure!
そうじしよう。 → うん、しよう。
Let's clean up! → Yes, with pleasure!
陶器（とうき）を焼（や）こう。 → うん、でもちょっと時間がないんだ／の（よ）。
Let's fire porcelain! → Yes, but unfortunately I don't have time.

The interrogative particle　か　can be used at the end of a sentence to soften the tone.
映画（えいが）を見ようか。↘　か　is pronounced with descending intonation.

「練習」

1．駅（えき）／電車（でんしゃ）の切符（きっぷ）／買う（か）
2．公園（こうえん）／散歩（さんぽ）する
3．携帯電話（けいたいでんわ）／友（とも）だち／連絡（れんらく）する
4．図書館（としょかん）／本／借りる（か）
5．いっしょ／歌（うた）／歌う（うた）
6．いっしょ／家（いえ）／帰る（かえ）

② Intention: V-(y)oo to omotte iru: intend / want

A:日曜日（にちようび）に何をしようと思（おも）っていますか。
　 What do you want to do on Sunday?
B:映画（えいが）を見ようと思っています。
　 I want to see a movie.

「練習」

1．月曜日（げつようび）／泳（およ）ぎに行く
2．火曜日（かようび）／部屋（へや）をそうじする
3．水曜日（すいようび）／陶器（とうき）について調（しら）べる
4．木曜日（もくようび）／手紙（てがみ）を書く（か）
5．金曜日（きんようび）／宿題（しゅくだい）を全部（ぜんぶ）すませる
6．土曜日（どようび）／コンサートを聞く（き）

(3) Decision

① V-(BF/Nai-F) koto ni suru: to decide (private matter)

A: 何を買うことにしましたか。
   Did you decide to buy something?
B: 自転車を買うことにしました。
   I decided to buy a bicycle.

「練習」

1．どこに行く／イタリア　　　2．いつ行く／来週
3．何で行く／飛行機　　　　　4．だれと行く／友だち
5．そこ／何をする／？　　　　6．どのくらい／滞在する／？

・"N＋にする" is often used when shopping or choosing a menu in a restaurant.

店：　何にしますか。　⇒　この時計にします。
　　　What would you like?　　I would like this watch.
食堂：何にしますか。　⇒　天ぷらそばにします。
　　　What would you like?　　I would like tempura soba.

② V-(BF/Nai-F) koto ni naru: to be decided / determined (official matter)

A: どうなりましたか。What has happened?
B: 計画を変えることになりました。It was decided to change the plan.

「練習」
1．図書館／建てる　　　2．工場／見学する
3．計画／実施する　　　4．計画／中止する
5．計画／延期する　　　6．オリンピック／参加する

③ V-(BF/Nai-F) koto ni natte iru: This form is used if a state is regulated.

日本やイギリスでは車は左側を走ることになっています。
It is regulated that people have to drive on the left-hand side in Japan or England.
この部屋ではタバコを吸ってはいけないことになっています。
It is regulated that you are not allowed to smoke in this room.

「練習」
1．仕事／8時／始まる　　　2．東京／1週間／滞在する
3．毎日／会議／する　　　　4．この会社／制服／着る
5．明日／見本市／案内する　6．試験／間／話す／いけない

Lesson test

（１）Answer the questions according to the instructions.

1．週末何をするつもりですか。　（東京へ行く）
2．東京で何をするつもりですか。　（日本文化について調べる）
3．町でだれに会うつもりですか。　（友だち）
4．友だちと何をするつもりですか。　（買い物する・映画を見る）
5．夏休みに何をしようと思っていますか。　（九州へ旅行する）
6．九州に何で行こうと思っていますか。　（新幹線）
7．九州で何をしようと思っていますか。　（有田焼きの産地を見学する）
8．何を作ろうと思っていますか。　（陶器）

（２）Complete the sentences with either "koto ni suru" or "koto ni naru".

1．４月からその会社で＿＿＿＿＿＿＿＿＿＿＿＿＿＿＿＿＿。
2．雨がふっているので、家に ＿＿＿＿＿＿＿＿＿＿＿＿＿＿＿。
3．彼女が大好きなので、彼女と＿＿＿＿＿＿＿＿＿＿＿＿＿＿＿。
4．大学のとなりに病院を＿＿＿＿＿＿＿＿＿＿＿＿＿＿＿。
5．その計画はお金と時間がたくさんかかるので、＿＿＿＿＿＿＿＿＿。
6．１５００の会社がコンピュータの見本市に＿＿＿＿＿＿＿＿＿＿＿。

（３）Translate the following sentences into Japanese.

1．I decided to write about porcelain because I like Japanese tea.
2．By the way, I intend to take part in a pottery course.
3．I wish you every success in Japan.

マイヤーさんは何をするつもりですか。

夏休みに富士山に登ろうと思っています。

第15課　Dai Juugo-ka

浮世絵展
うきよえてん

Ukiyoe-ten

Lesson 15　浮世絵展

北野　　　：昨日、銀座のデパートで 北斎の展覧会を 見ましたよ。

マイヤー　：ああ、浮世絵ですね。 いかが でしたか。

北野　　　：ええ、とても すばらしかったです。

マイヤー　：一人で 見に行きましたか。

北野　　　：いいえ、北京から 来た ワンさんと いっしょに 行きました。

マイヤー　：そうですか。 北斎は 富士山を たくさん かいた 江戸時代の 浮世絵師ですね。

北野　　　：そうです。 彼の「富嶽三十六景」は とても有名ですが、中でも
　　　　　　「荒波に 小船と 富士山を 力強くかいたの」が 一番印象的でした。

マイヤー　：あ、それは 私も 雑誌に出ていたのを 見たことがあります。
　　　　　　北野さん、浮世絵は もともと どんな意味だか 教えてください。

北野　　　：浮世絵は 「移り変わる世の中の絵」と いう意味です。 浮世絵師たちは 人々の
　　　　　　生活や風俗や風景などを いきいき かいたんです。

マイヤー　：そうですか。 北斎のほかに どんな浮世絵師が いるんですか。

北野　　　：そうですね。 たとえば、美人画をかいた 歌麿、江戸から京都までの 東海道の
　　　　　　風景を かいた 広重、それから 歌舞伎役者を たくさん かいた 写楽などが
　　　　　　有名ですよ。

マイヤー　：たくさん いるんですね。 私も これから いろいろ見て、勉強したいです。
　　　　　　ところで 北野さん、北斎展は いつまで やっているか 知っていますか。

北野　　　：ええ、今月の終り までです。 マイヤーさんも ぜひ 行ってください。

マイヤー　：はい、ぜひ 行きます。

Translation of the text

Exhibition of Ukiyoe

Kitano: Yesterday I saw an exhibition of Hokusai in a department store in Ginza.

Mayer: Oh, that's Ukiyoe, right?　How was it?

Kitano: It was wonderful.

Mayer: Did you go there alone?

Kitano: No, I went together with Wann from Beijing.

Mayer: Oh really? Hokusai is an Ukiyoe master from the Edo period who often drew Mt. Fuji, right?

Kitano: Yes, that's right! His "Fugaku-36-kei" are very well known, but the picture in which a boat on high waves and Mt. Fuji are drawn energetically is the most impressive.

Mayer: I also saw that once in a magazine.
　　　Mr. Kitano, can you explain to me what Ukiyoe originally means?

Kitano: Ukiyoe means pictures of a world that is constantly changing. Ukiyoe masters have drawn the life of the people, the customs and traditions and also the landscapes.

Mayer: I see! And are there other Ukiyoe masters besides Hokusai?

Kitano: Yes, for example Utamaro, who drew beautiful women, Hiroshige, who drew the landscapes from Edo to Kyoto, or Sharaku, who drew many Kabuki actors, are very famous.

Mayer: There are many! I would like to see them too. By the way, do you know until
when this exhibition will take place?
Kitano: Until the end of the month. Please make sure you go.
Mayer: Yes, definitely!

Questions about the text

１．北野さんはどこで北斎の展覧会を見ましたか。

２．一人で見ましたか。

３．北斎は何をたくさんかきましたか。

４．マイヤーさんは「富嶽三十六景」を見たことがありますか。

５．浮世絵の意味は何ですか。

６．北斎のほかにどんな浮世絵師が有名ですか。

７．北斎展はいつまでやっていますか。

葛飾北斎

Vocabulary and idioms

Vocabulary	reading	English
荒波　あらなみ	aranami	high, wild wave
暖かい　あたたかい	atatakai	warm
美人画　びじんが	bijinga	pictures of beautiful women
ビル	biru	buildings
無事　ぶじ	buji	without problem
力強い　ちからづよい	chikara-zuyoi	strong
～に出る　でる	~ ni deru	appear (in the newspaper or magazine)
どうして	dooshite	why
江戸時代　えどじだい	edojidai	Edo period
富嶽三十六景	Fugaku-36-kei	36 Ukiyoe images of Mount Fuji by Hokusai
風景　ふうけい	fuukei	landscape
風俗　ふうぞく	fuuzoku	custom
銀座　ぎんざ	ginza	Ginza (district of Tokyo)
日　ひ	hi	day, sun
広重　ひろしげ	Hiroshige	Andoo Hiroshige: Ukiyoe master
人々　ひとびと	hitobito	people
北斎　ほくさい	Hokusai	Katsushika Hokusai: Ukiyoe master
～行き　いき	iki	journey to ~
いきいき	ikiiki	alive, lively
意味　いみ	imi	meaning
印象的（な）　いんしょうてき	inshooteki(na)	impressive
いろいろ（な）	iroiro(na)	various
事務所　じむしょ	jimusho	office
かける	kakeru	hang up, carry
歌舞伎　かぶき	kabuki	Kabuki theater
描く　かく／えがく	kaku / egaku	paint, designate
考える　かんがえる	kangaeru	think, consider
子　こ	ko	child
小船　こぶね	kobune	small boat
今月　こんげつ	kongetsu	this month

これから	korekara	from now on
めがね	megane	glasses
もの・〜の	mono / no	thing / noun substitute
もともと	motomoto	originally
長い間　ながいあいだ	nagai aida	long time
中でも　なかでも	naka demo	underneath
終り　おわり	owari	end
北京　ペキン	pekin	Peking
背広　せびろ	sebiro	suit
生活(する)　せいかつ	seikatsu(suru)	life, living (everyday life)
写楽　しゃらく	Sharaku	Tooshuusai Sharaku: Ukiyoe master
すばらしい	subarashii	wonderful
すきやき	sukiyaki	stew (beef, tofu and vegetables etc.)
座る　すわる	suwaru	sit down
たとえば	tatoeba	for example
天気予報　てんきよほう	tenki-yohoo	weather report
展覧会　てんらんかい	tenrankai	exhibition
東海道　とうかいどう	tookaidoo	route from Edo to Kyoto or Osaka
次　つぎ	tsugi	nearest(s)
浮世絵師　うきよえし	ukiyoe-shi	Ukiyoe master
浮世絵展　うきよえてん	ukiyoe-ten	Ukiyoe exhibition
生まれる　うまれる	umareru	be born
歌麿　うたまろ	Utamaro	Kitagawa Utamaro: Ukiyoe master
移り変わる　うつりかわる	utsurikawaru	change, to transform
分かる　わかる	wakaru	understand
忘れる　わすれる	wasureru	forget
役者　やくしゃ	yakusha	actor
やる	yaru	make, take place, perform
世の中　よのなか	yononaka	world

Kanji

Kanji	SCK	English	On-yomi *Kun-yomi*	Usage / Composites
力	2	power	ryoku *chikara*	力強い chikarazuyo-i / strong 馬力 bariki / horsepower
絵	12	picture painting	kai e	絵画 kaiga / painting 絵本 ehon / picture book
美	9	beautiful	bi *utsuku-shii*	美術 bijutsu / art 美人 bijin / beautiful woman
意	13	meaning	i	意味 imi / meaning 意見 iken / opinion
味	8	taste	mi *ajii*	興味 kyoomi / interest 美味 bimi / tasted good
他	5	other(s)	ta *hoka*	他人 tanin / the stranger 他方 tahoo / on the other side

	SC			
風	9	wind	fuu *kaze*	風景 fuukei / landscape 台風 taifuu / typhoon
景	12	landscape	kei, ke *kage*	景色 keshiki / landscape 景気 keiki / economic condition
道	12	road street	doo *michi*	道路 dooro / road 水道 suidoo / water pipe
活	9	active live	katsu *i-kiru*	生活 seikatsu / life 活動 katsudoo / action, activity
銀	14	silver	gin	銀座 ginza / Ginza (district of Tokyo) 銀色 gin'iro / silver color
座	10	sit sit down	za *suwa-ru*	座席 zaseki / sit, place 星座 seiza / constellation
船	11	ship	sen *fune*	船長 senchoo / captain of a ship 船室 senshitsu / cabin
雑	14	mixed	zatsu, zoo	雑誌 zasshi / magazine 雑草 zassoo / weed
誌	14	magazine	sh	週刊誌 shuukanshi / weekly magazine 日誌 nisshi / official diary
建	9	build	ken *ta-teru*	建物 tatemono / building 建築 kenchiku / construction

・ SC: number of strokes of the kanji ・ stroke sequence of the kanji: see page 217.

Grammar and exercises

(1) Attributive clause

In Japanese, an attributive clause must always be formed where <u>a relative clause</u> is used in English. The noun of the main clause is connected directly to the attributive clause (without AP) and is described precisely and concretely by the attributive clause.

The verb of the attributive clause is used at the end of the attributive clause in the NPF.
After the subject in the attributive clause, "が" must be used if the subject in the attributive and main clause (at the end) is not the same. If it is the same, "は" is used.

Normal sentence: 私 はきのう町で映画を見ました。
I saw a movie in town yesterday.
Attributive clause: （私 が）きのう町で見た + 映画
The movie I saw in town yesterday

The attributive clause is used as subject (S), predicate (P) and object (O) as follows.

S: <u>（私が）きのう町で見た映画</u>* はとてもおもしろかったです。
　The movie I saw yesterday in town was very interesting.
P: それは<u>（私が）きのう町で見た映画</u>です。
　It's the movie I saw yesterday in town.
O: マリアさんは<u>（私が）きのう町で見た映画</u>をまだ見ていません。
　Maria hasn't seen the movie I saw in town yesterday.

* 映画 can be replaced by "の" if it is clear from the context that you are talking about
　the movie. きのう町で見た**の**はとてもおもしろかったです。

「練習」 as subject
1．彼女（かのじょ）／レストラン／食べた／もの／スパゲティー
2．今日（きょう）／じむしょ／来た（き）／人／シュミットさん
3．先週（せんしゅう）／行った（い）／町／とてもきれい
4．そこ／止（と）まっている／地下鉄（ちかてつ）／上野行き（うえのいき）
5．この子（こ）／生（う）まれた／日（ひ）／4月（がつ）／暖（あたた）かい／日（ひ）
6．彼女（かのじょ）／住（す）む／アパート／小（ちい）さい／きれい

「練習」 as predicate
1．先生（せんせい）／そのいす／座（すわ）っている／人
2．これ／彼女（かのじょ）／きのう／焼（や）いた／ケーキ
3．その建物（たてもの）／マイヤーさん／勉強（べんきょう）している／大学（だいがく）
4．それ／彼（かれ）／先月（せんげつ）／買（か）った／車
5．山川さん／せびろ／着（き）る／めがね／かけた／人
6．その陶器（とうき）／マイヤーさん／有田町（ありたちょう）／焼（や）いた／もの

「練習」 as object
1．山田さん／いう／人／知（し）っている／か
2．きのう／そこ／見（み）た／こと／私／話（はな）してください
3．彼女（かのじょ）／長（なが）い間（あいだ）／考（かんが）えていた／こと／話（はな）した
4．私／図書館（としょかん）／かりた／本／今晩（こんばん）／読（よ）む
5．浮世絵（うきよえ）／いう／漢字（かんじ）／忘（わす）れた
6．私／焼（や）いた／ケーキ／食（た）べませんか

(2) **Indirect question** (relative clause)

① **Interrogative clause** (Subordinate clause) か、main clause

This is not a real question, but a relative clause that contains an interrogative clause.
The interrogative clause (subordinate clause) is used in the NPF before the main clause. Both
"が" and "は" can be used after the subject in the indirect interrogative clause, but "が" must be
used if the interrogative word なに or だれ is the subject in the subordinate clause.

それが**何**（なん）だか／**何**（なに）か、私は知（し）っています。
I know what it is.
それを**だれ**が*したか、知っていますか。
Do you know who made it?

その人は**どこ**に住（す）んでいるか、知りません。
I don't know where she/he lives.
その漢字（かんじ）は**どう**書（か）くか、教（おし）えてください。
Please show me how to write the kanji.
つぎの電車（でんしゃ）が**いつ**来（く）るか、言（い）ってください。
Please tell me when the next train is coming.

彼は今日**どうして**来なかったか、わかりません。
I don't know why he didn't come today.

「練習」

1．この電車／京都／いつ／着く／駅員／聞いてください
2．彼女／電話番号／何番／知る／か
3．あなた／今日／どこ／行った／言ってください
4．そのへや／中／だれ／いる／知らない
5．彼女／今日／大学／どうして／休んだ／知る／か
6．そのごはん／どう／作る／教えましょう
7．どの／辞書／一番／いい／店員／聞きましょう
8．彼／どんな／仕事／している／私たち／説明した

② Interrogative clause (NPF) **かどうか、〜**: Subordinate clause with "whether" + main clause

V：　彼女は今日来るかどうか、まだわかりません。
　　I don't know yet if she will come today.
IA：　その料理がおいしいかどうか、言ってください。
　　Please tell me if the food is delicious
NA：　彼らが元気かどうか、知りたいです。
　　I want to know if they're well.
N：　つぎの駅は新宿かどうか、知っていますか。
　　Do you know if the nearest station is Shinjuku?

「練習」

1．あの人／英語／話す／知る／か
2．あなた／その展覧会／見たい／言う (request form)
3．かれ／そのこと／知る／知りません
4．かれら／日本／ぶじ／着いた／知る／たい
5．あした／天気／いい／天気予報／見る (invitation)
6．試験／むずかしかった／言う (request form)
7．車／ガソリン／入っている／ちゃんと／調べる (request form)
8．私／夏休み／故郷／帰る／まだ／わからない

Lesson test

（１）Connect the sentences with the attributive form.

1．電車はそこに止まっています。　電車に乗ってください。

2．きのう映画を見ました。　とてもおもしろかったです。

3．その人はあそこで電話をかけています。その人は川中先生です。

4．私はそのくつがほしかったです。　今日そのくつをデパートで買いました。

5．その料理はすきやきと言います。　今晩それを食べました。

6．彼女はそこに住んでいます。　その町はとてもきれいです。

7．山田さんはそこで働いています。　会社はそのビルです。

（２）Complete the following indirect questions.

1．北野さんのこきょうは＿＿＿＿＿＿＿＿＿＿＿＿＿言ってください。　→　長野市です。

2．マイヤーさんは＿＿＿＿＿＿＿＿＿＿＿＿＿知っていますか。　→　東京に住んでいます。

3．映画が＿＿＿＿＿＿＿＿＿＿＿＿＿教えてください。　→　７時１５分です。

4．日本まで飛行機で＿＿＿＿＿＿＿＿＿＿＿＿＿言ってください。　→１１時間ぐらいです。

5．ふじさんの漢字は＿＿＿＿＿＿＿＿＿＿＿＿＿知っていますか。　→　「富士山」です。

6．あなたはきのう町で＿＿＿＿＿＿＿＿＿＿＿＿＿言ってください。　→　木村さんです。

（３）Form whether sentences.

1．そのカメラ／便利／店員／聞く／ましょう

2．彼／その会社／働く／まだ／わかりません

3．友だち／パーティー／来る／知る／か

4．田中さん／事務所／いる／電話する／聞く／ください

あなたは何年だか知っていますか。

Appendix

Answers to the questions on the text

L. 1
1．Mayer-san desu.
2．Kitano-san desu.
3．Hai, soo desu. Gakusei desu.
4．Iie, soo de wa arimasen. Kaishain desu.
5．Zomy desu.

L. 2
1．Hai, genki desu.
2．Hai, Kitano-san mo genki desu.
3．Ookiku nai desu ga, kireina apaato desu.
4．Iie, amari shizuka de wa arimasen.
5．Iie, taihen benri desu.
6．Hai, chikai desu.

L. 3
1．Mittsu arimasu.
2．Yooshitsu to washitsu to daidokoro ga arimasu.
3．Iie, arimasen. Demo shawaa ga arimasu.
4．345 no 7890 desu
5．5-nin kazoku desu.
6．Chichi to haha to ani to ane ga imasu.
7．6-nin kazoku desu.
8．Chichi to haha to imooto ga hitori to otooto ga futari imasu.

L. 4
1．朝6時に起きます。
2．ごはんを食べます。そしてみそしるを飲みます。
3．パンを食べます。そしてコーヒーを飲みます。
4．7時ごろ出ます。
5．バスと電車で行きます。
6．1時間半ぐらいかかります。
7．新聞やざっしを読みます。
8．おんがくを聞きます。

L. 5
1．家で日本語のしゅくだいをしました。
2．ともだちと買い物をしました。
3．デパートで買いました。
4．公園をさんぽしました。
5．すしを食べました。
6．いいえ、まだです。まだ食べません。
7．日本料理を食べに行きます。

L. 6
1．いいえ、しませんでした。
2．奈良へ旅行しました。
3．少しさむかったですが、わるくなかったです。

4．京都のほうが大きいです。

5．いいえ、奈良が日本で一番古いみやこです。

6．東大寺の大仏や若草山を見ました。

7．奈良の大仏のほうが古いです。

L. 7

1．上野への行き方を聞いています。

2．5番のバスに乗ります。

3．池袋まで行きます。

4．山手線に乗り変えます。

5．8番目の駅です。

6．いいえ、知りません。

7．駅員にうんちんを聞きます。

L. 8

1．いいえ、ペンで書かなくてもいいです。えんぴつで書いてもいいです。

2．いいえ、いけません。かなと漢字で書かなければなりません。

3．はい、辞書を使ってはいけません。

4．いいえ、いけません。一人でしなければなりません。

L. 9

1．日本語を読んだり、書いたり、話したりしなければなりませんでした。

2．けっこういい成績でした。

3．はい、あります。

4．映画を見に行きます。

5．「兄弟」です。

6．いいえ、しません。

7．1時に迎えに行きます。

L. 10

1．はい、できます。

2．いいえ、まだじょうずではありません。

3．エアロビクスをしています。

4．テニスをします。

5．いいえ、とくいではありません。

6．ケーキを焼くことがじょうずです。

7．ケーキの焼き方を教えます。

8．はい、大好きです。

L. 11

1．長野市です。

2．いいえ、まだありません。

3．いいえ、忙しいので、あまり帰りません。

4．正月とお盆に帰ります。

5．歴史が古くて、きれいな町です。

6．善光寺が一番有名です。

7．信州そばと信州みそが有名です。

8．いいえ、食べたことがあります。

L. 12

1．荷物を運ばなければならないからです。

2．運転する前に点検します。

3．ガソリンを入なければなりません。

4．いいえ、いけません。

5．たばこを吸ってはいけません。

6．へんな音を聞いた時、すぐおりなければなりません。

7．いいえ、じょうだんです。

L. 13

1．シュミットさんから電話がありました。

2．ユンケル社の部長さんです。

3．通訳のアルバイトをします。

4．きのう着きました。

5．打ち合わせがしたいと言っています。

6．いいえ、もう予定があります。

7．新宿のサンライズホテルに泊まっています。

8．今１０時半です。

L. 14

1．日本文化についてレポートを書きます。

2．陶器について書くつもりです。

3．陶器の産地を見学しようと思っています。

4．佐賀県・有田町へ行くつもりです。

5．マイセン焼きに影響をあたえました。

6．焼き物のコースで焼こうと思っています。

L. 15

1．銀座のデパートで見ました。

2．北京から来たワンさんといっしょに見ました。

3．富士山をたくさん描きました。

4．はい、雑誌で見たことがあります。

5．「移り変わる世の中の絵」という意味です。

6．歌麿や広重や写楽などが有名です。

7．今月の終わりまでやっています。

Resolution of the exercises

L. 1

(1)
1. Sore wa kuruma desu ka. Hai, soo desu. Kuruma desu.
   Sore mo kuruma desu ka. Iie, soo dewa arimasen. Densha desu,
2. Sore wa kamera desu ka. Hai, soo desu. Kamera desu.
   Sore mo kamera desu ka. Iie, soo dewa arimasen. Video desu,
3. Sore wa sutereo desu ka. Hai, soo desu. Sutereo desu.
   Sore mo sutereo desu ka. Iie, soo dewa arimasen. Terebi desu,
4. Sore wa konpyuuta desu ka. Hai, soo desu. Konpyuuta desu.
   Sore mo konpyuuta desu ka. Iie, soo dewa arimasen. Fakkusu desu,

(2)
1. Sore wa nan desu ka. Kore wa terebi desu.
2. Sore wa nan desu ka. Kore wa fakkusu desu.
3. Sore wa nan desu ka. Kore wa tokei desu.
4. Sore wa nan desu ka. Kore wa nihongo no hon desu.

(3)
1. Anata wa nihonjin desu ka.
   Hai, soo desu.
2. Anata wa chuugokujin desu ka.
   Iie, soo de wa arimasen. Amerikajin desu.
3. Anata wa sensei desu ka.
   Hai, soo desu.
4. Anata wa seito desu ka.
   Iie, soo de wa arimasen. Gakusei desu.
5. Anata wa kaishain desu ka.
   Hai, soo desu.
6. Anata wa Kitano-san desu ka.
   Iie, soo de wa arimasen. Kawada desu.

(5)
1. Are wa nan'no hana desu ka. Are wa bara no hana desu.
2. Are wa nan'no hon desu ka. Are wa nihongo no hon desu.
3. Are wa nan'no shinbun desu ka. Are wa eigo no shinbun desu.
4. Are wa nan'no kaisha desu ka. Are wa konpyuuta no kaisha desu.

(6)
1. Kore wa dare no kamera desu ka. Sore wa kare no kamera desu.
2. Kore wa dare no kuruma desu ka. Sore wa kanojo no kuruma desu.
3. Kore wa dare no terebi desu ka. Sore wa Kawada-san no terebi desu.
4. Kore wa dare no tokei desu ka. Sore wa Yamada-san no tokei desu.

(7)
1. Kono hana wa dare no hana desu ka. Sono hana wa Mori-san no (hana) desu.
   Kono hana wa nan no hana desu ka. Sono hana wa bara no hana desu.
2. Kono shinbun wa dare no shinbun desu ka. Sono shinbun wa Kitano-san no (shinbun) desu.
   Kono shinbun wa nan no shinbun desu ka. Sono shinbun wa eigo no shinbun desu.
3. Kono hon wa dare no hon desu ka. Sono hon wa Hayashi-san no (hon) desu.
   Kono hon wa nan no hon desu ka. Sono hon wa konpyuuta no hon desu.
4. Kono kuruma wa dare no kuruma desu ka. Sono kuruma wa kaisha no (kuruma) desu.
   Kono kaisha wa nan no kaisha desu ka. Sono kaisha wa sutereo no kaisha desu.
1. Kono kuruma wa Kitano-san no (kuruma) desu.
2. Sono kaisha wa kamera no kaisha desu.
3. Kono hito wa Mayer-san desu.
4. Ano yama wa Fuji-san desu.

L. 2

(1)

① 1. Anata no shoogakkoo wa atarashii desu ka.
   Hai, atarashii desu. / Iie, atarashikunai desu. Furui desu.
2. Toshokan wa chikai desu ka.
   Hai, chikai desu. / Iie, chikakunai desu. Tooi desu.
3. Anata no jidoosha wa takai desu ka.
   Hai, takai desu. / Iie, takakunai desu. Yasui desu.
4. Anata no machi wa ookii desu ka.
   Hai, ookii desu./ Iie, ookikunai desu. Chiisai desu.

② 1. Sore wa atarashii gakkoo desu ka.
   Hai, atarashii gakkoo desu. / Iie, atarashii gakkoo de wa arimasen. / Iie, atarashikunai gakkoo desu.
2. Sore wa furui hon desu ka.
   Hai, furui hon desu. / Iie, furui hon de wa arimasen. / Iie, furukunai hon desu.
3. Sore wa takai konpyuuta desu ka.
   Hai, takai konpyuuta desu. / Iie, takai konpyuuta de wa arimasen. / Iie, takakunai konpyuuta desu.
4. Sore wa yasui apaato desu ka.
   Hai, yasui apaato desu. / Iie, yasui apaato de wa arimasen. / Iie, yasukunai apaato desu.

(2)
① 1. Sono hana wa kirei desu ka.
   Hai, kirei desu. / Iie, kirei de wa arimasen.
2. Sono machi wa shizuka desu ka.
   Hai, shizuka desu. / Iie, shizuka de wa arimasen.
3. Sono hito wa genki desu ka.
   Hai, genki desu. / Iie, genki de wa arimasen.
4. Sono hito wa yuumei desu ka.
   Hai, yuumei desu. / Iie, yuumei de wa arimasen.

② 1. Sore wa kireina machi desu ka.
   Hai, kireina machi desu. / Iie, kireina machi de wa arimasen.
2. Sore wa shizukana machi desu ka.
   Hai, shizukana machi desu. / Iie, shizukana machi de wa arimasen.
3. Sono hito wa genkina hito desu ka.
   Hai, genkina hito desu. / Iie, genkina hito de wa arimasen.
4. Sono hito wa yuumeina hito desu ka.
   Hai, yuumeina hito desu. / Iie, yuumeina hito de wa arimasen.

(3)
① 1. Kono machi wa ikaga desu ka.
   Totemo furui desu. / Amari furukunai desu.
2. Kono kamera wa ikaga desu ka.
   Totemo benri desu. / Amari benri de wa arimasen.
3. Kono kuruma wa ikaga desu ka.
   Totemo hayai desu. / Amari hayakunai desu.
4. Kono hana wa ikaga desu ka.
   Totemo kirei desu. / Amari kirei de wa arimasen.

② 1. Sore wa don'na hana desu ka.
   Totemo kireina hana desu. / Amari kireina hana de wa arimasen.
2. Sore wa don'na apaato desu ka.
   Totemo shizukana apaato desu. / Amari shizukana apaato de wa arimasen.
3. Sore wa don'na gakkoo desu ka.
   Totemo furui gakkoo desu. / Amari furui gakkoo de wa arimasen.
4. Sore wa don'na kamera desu ka.
   Totemo yasui kamera desu. / Amari yasui kamera de wa arimasen.
(4)
1. Kono jidoosha wa hayai desu ne. → Ee, soo desu ne.
2. Sono machi wa amari kirei dewa arimasen yo. → Aa, soo desu ka.
3. Ano Toshokan wa atarashii desu ne. → Ee, soo desu ne.
4. Kono apaato wa totemo benri desu yo. → Aa, soo desu ka.

L. 3
(1)
1. Apaato ni dare ga imasu ka. Schmidt-san to Maria-san ga imasu.
2. Ie ni dare ga imasu ka. Tanaka-san to Kimura-san ga imasu.
3. Kyooshitsu ni dare ga imasu ka. Sensei to gakusei ga imasu.
4. Niwa ni nani ga imasu ka. Inu to neko to uma ga imasu.

1. Kono heya ni nani ga arimasu ka. Sutereo ya konpyuuta ga arimasu.
2. Sono heya ni nani ga arimasu ka. Hondana ya sofaa ga arimasu.
3. Ano heya ni nani ga arimasu ka. Tsukue ya isu ga arimasu.
4. Anata no machi ni nani ga arimasu ka. Byooin ya yuubinkyoku ya kooen ga arimasu.

(2)
1. Koko ni nihonjin ga nan-nin imasu ka.   Hitori imasu.
2. Soko ni doitsujin ga nan-nin imasu ka.   Futari imasu.
3. Asoko ni gakusei ga nan-nin imasu ka.   3(san)-nin imasu.
4. Soko ni sofaa ikutsu arimasu ka.   Hitotsu arimasu.

5. Asoko ni kami ga nan-mai arimasu ka.   5(go)-mai arimasu.
6. Soko ni kuruma ga nan-dai arimasu ka.   6(roku)-dai arimasu.
7. Soko ni hon ga nan-satsu arimasu ka.   7(nana)- satsu arimasu
8. Asoko ni pen ga nanbon arimasu ka.   4(yon)-hon arimasu.

(3)
1. Minami-san wa doko ni imasu ka.   Kaisha ni imasu.
2. Machida-san wa doko ni imasu ka.   Daigaku ni imasu.
3. Inu to neko wa doko ni imasu ka.   Niwa ni imasu.
4. Sensei wa doko ni imasu ka.   Kyooshitsu ni imasu.
5. Okaasan wa doko ni imasu ka.   Daidokoro ni imasu.
6. Kodomo wa doko ni imasu ka.   Chuugakkoo ni imasu.

1. Kaban wa doko ni arimasu ka.   Tsukue no shita ni arimasu.
2. Konpyuuta wa doko ni arimasu ka.   Tsukue no tonari ni arimasu.
3. Depaato wa doko ni arimasu ka.   Eki no mae ni arimasu.
4. Toshokan wa doko ni arimasu ka.   Yuubinkyoku no ushiro ni arimasu.
5. Terebi wa doko ni arimasu ka.   Sutereo to denwa no aida ni arimasu.
6. Furo wa doko ni arimasu ka.   Heya no oku ni arimasu.
7. Gakkoo wa doko ni arimasu ka.   Kooen no mukae ni arimasu.
8. Byooin wa doko ni arimasu ka.   Eki no chikaku ni arimasu.

L. 4

(1) あさ何時におきますか。ばん何時にねますか。

1. 7時におきます。10時半にねます。

2. 7時半におきます。11時半ごろねます。

3. 8時10分前におきます。11時45分にねます。

4. 6時15分におきます。12時すぎにねます。

(2) 1. 何を食べますか。パンを食べます。何をのみますか。ジュースをのみます。
コーヒーも／はのみますか。いいえ、コーヒーはのみません。

2. 何を食べますか。たまごを食べます。何をのみますか。おさけをのみます。
ビールも／はのみますか。いいえ、ビールははのみません。

3. 何を食べますか。やさいを食べます。何をのみますか。おちゃをのみます。
こうちゃも／はのみますか。いいえ、こうちゃはのみません。

4. 何を食べますか。くだものを食べます。何をのみますか。みずをのみます。
ミルクも／はのみますか。いいえ、ミルクはのみません。

(3) 何時に家を出ますか。　何で会社に行きますか。　何時に家に帰りますか。

1. 朝7時半に出ます。バスで行きます。晩5時ごろ帰ります。

2. 朝7時に出ます。車で行きます。晩6時半ごろ帰ります。

3. 朝8時15分に出ます。自転車で行きます。晩7時ごろ帰ります。

4. 朝8時20分に出ます。あるいて行きます。晩9時10分ごろ帰ります。

(4)

1. 家からえきまでどのくらいかかりますか。バスで10分ぐらいかかります。

2. 家からがっこうまでどのくらいかかりますか。じてんしゃで15分ぐらいかかります。

3. 家からこうえんまでどのくらいかかりますか。あるいて5分ぐらいかかります。

4. 家から郵便局までどのくらいかかりますか。車で20分ぐらいかかります。

5. 家からベルリンまでどのくらいかかりますか。電車で4時間ぐらいかかります。

6. 家から町までどのくらいかかりますか。自動車で1時間半ぐらいかかります。

(5)

1. 台所で何をしますか。ごはんを食べます。

2. 会社で何をしますか。はたらきます。

3. 学校で何をしますか。日本語をべんきょうします。

4. へやで何をしますか。テレビを見ます。

5. としょかんで何をしますか。本を読みます。

6. スーパーで何をしますか。おかしとのみものを買います。

L. 5

(1) きょうどこへ行きましたか。だれと行きましたか。～で何をしましたか。

1. 町へ行きました。友だちと行きました。えいがを見ました。

2. 大学へ行きました。一人で行きました。日本語をべんきょうしました。

3. 外国へ行きました。一人で行きました。仕事をしました。

4. うみへ行きました。父と行きました。およぎました。

5. デパートへ行きました。母と行きました。くつしたを買いました。

6. きっさてんへ行きました。友だちと行きました。コーヒーをのみました。

(2)

1. 何を食べましたか。何も食べませんでした。

2. 何を飲みましたか。何も飲みませんでした。

3. 何を見ましたか。何も見ませんでした。

4. 何を聞きましたか。何も聞きませんでした。

5. 何を読みましたか。何も読みませんでした。

6. 何を書きましたか。何も書きませんでした。

7. 何を話しましたか。何も話しませんでした。

8. 何をしましたか。何もしませんでした。

(3)

1. かのじょは道をあるきました。　　　2. かれは公園をはしりました。

3. 車 はこうさてんをわたりました。　　4. バスは駅前をとおりました。

5. ひこうきは空をとびました。　　　　6. ふねは海をわたりました。

(4)

1. もう日本へ行きましたか。はい、もう行きました。じゃあ、もう中国へ行きましたか。
いいえ、まだ行きません。／まだです。

2. もう日本料理を食べましたか。はい、もう食べました。じゃあ、もうお酒を飲みましたか。
いいえ、まだ飲みません。／まだです。

3. もう野菜を買いましたか。はい、もう買いました。じゃあ、もうくだものを買いましたか。
いいえ、まだ買いません。／まだです。

4. もう教科書を買いましたか。はい、もう買いました。じゃあ、もう読みましたか。いいえ、まだ
読みません。／まだです。

5. もうかなを勉強しましたか。はい、もう勉強しました。じゃあ、もう漢字を勉強しましたか。
いいえ、まだ勉強しません。／まだです。

6. もう宿題をしましたか。はい、もう宿題をしました。じゃあ、もう友だちに会いましたか。
いいえ、会いません。／まだです。

(5)

1. 何をしに町へ行きますか。えいがを見に行きます。

2. 何をしに会社へ行きますか。仕事をしに行きます。

3. 何をしに学校へ行きますか。日本語をべんきょうしに行きます。

4. 何をしに本屋へ行きますか。ざっしを買いに行きます。

5. 何をしにとしょかんへ行きますか。本をかりに行きます。

6. 何をしにゆうびんきょくへ行きますか。切手を買いに行きます。

(6) いっしょに～ませんか。

1. いっしょにえいがを見ませんか。
2. いっしょに日本語をべんきょうしませんか。
3. いっしょに公園をさんぽしませんか。
4. いっしょにおどりませんか。
5. いっしょにコンサートに行きませんか。
6. いっしょに町へ出かけませんか。

L. 6
(1)
1. えいがはいかが（どう）でしたか。おもしろかったです。おもしろくなかったです。
2. テストはいかが（どう）でしたか。むずかしかったです。むずかしくなかったです。
3. パーティーはいかが（どう）でしたか。たのしかったです。たのしくなかったです。
4. 天気はいかが（どう）でしたか。よかったです。よくなかったです。
5. ごはんはいかが（どう）でしたか。おいしかったです。おいしくなかったです。
6. 仕事はいかが（どう）でしたか。おおかったです。おおくなかったです。すくなかったです。

1. その町はにぎやかでしたか。はい、とてもにぎやかでしたよ。いいえ、あまりにぎやかでは
ありませんでした。
2. 店員は親切でしたか。はい、とても親切でしたよ。いいえ、あまり親切ではありませんでした。
3. しけんはかんたんでしたか。はい、とてもかんたんでしたよ。いいえ、あまりかんたんでは
ありませんでした。
4. その村はしずかでしたか。はい、とてもしずかでしたよ。いいえ、あまりしずかではありません
でした。
5. そのかばんは便利でしたか。はい、とても便利でしたよ。いいえ、あまり便利ではありません
でした。
6. そのきものはきれいでしたか。はい、とてもきれいでしたよ。いいえ、あまりきれいでは
ありませんでした。

(2)
1. この車は速く走りました。　2. 天気は悪くなりました。　3. 仕事は長くかかりました。
1. かれは人に親切にしました。　2. へやをきれいにしました。　3. 町は静かになりました。

(3)
1. かれはかのじょより若いです。　2. 日本はドイツより大きいです。
3. こおりはみずよりかるいです。　4. きょうはきのうよりいそがしいです。
5. 今週は先週より暑いです。　6. 金は銀より高いです。

1. 英語とフランス語とでは、どちらのほうがやさしいですか。～のほうがやさしいです。
2. イタリアとスペインとでは、どちらのほうがとおいですか。～のほうがとおいです。
3. 京都と東京とでは、どちらのほうがきれいですか。～のほうがきれいです。
4. 京都と奈良とでは、どちらのほうがにぎやかですか。京都のほうがにぎやかです。
5. 奈良の大仏と鎌倉の大仏とでは、どちらのほうが古いですか。奈良の大仏のほうが古いです。
6. お母さんとお父さんとでは、どちらのほうが若いですか。～のほうが若いです。

1. 父は母とおなじぐらい元気です。
2. ドイツで（は）ビールは水とおなじぐらい安いです。
3. 日本で（は）秋は春とおなじくらいいいです。

4. ご主人は奥さんとおなじくらいやさしいです。
5. カタカナはひらがなとおなじくらいやさしいです。

1. かなは漢字ほどむずかしくないです。
2. バスは電車ほどはやくないです。
3. 漢字はかなほどすくなくないです。
4. 京都は東京ほどにぎやかではありません。
5. バスは電車ほどべんりではありません。
6. 銀は金ほど重くないです。

(4)
1. エベレスト山はせかい(の中)で一番高いです。
2. ロシアはせかい(の中)で一番大きいです。
3. マイヤーさんはクラス(の中)で一番若いです。
4. 春は季節(の中)で一番いいです。
5. 兄は家族(の中)で一番大きいです。
6. 姉は家族(の中)で一番細いです。

1. 飲み物の中で何が一番おいしいですか。ワインが一番おいしいです。
2. 友だちの中でだれが一番しんせつですか。山田さんが一番しんせつです。
3. 動物の中で何が一番つよいですか。ライオンが一番つよいです。
4. ハンブルグとベルリンとミュンヘンの中でどこが一番南にありますか。ミュンヘンが一番南にあります。
5. ドイツの町の中でどの町が一番うつくしいですか。～が一番うつくしいです。
6. 季節の中でいつが一番いいですか。～が一番いいです。

L. 7
(1) 1. Request form
① 1. そのペンをください。はい、ありがとうございます。240円になります／です。
    1000円でおねがいします。はい、760円のおつりになります／です。
  2. そのケーキをください。はい、ありがとうございます。180円になります／です。
    500円でおねがいします。はい、320円のおつりになります／です。
  3. その時計をください。はい、ありがとうございます。3890円になります／です。
    5000円でおねがいします。はい、1110円のおつりになります／です。
  4. そのコップをください。はい、ありがとうございます。370円になります／です。
    1000円でおねがいします。はい、630円のおつりになります／です。
  5. そのくつをください。はい、ありがとうございます。4500円になります／です。
    5000円でおねがいします。はい、500円のおつりになります／です。
  6. 80円の切手を5まいください。はい、ありがとうございます。400円になります／です。
    1000円でおねがいします。はい、600円のおつりになります／です。
  7. 牛肉(豚肉)を200グラムください。はい、ありがとうございます。1280円になります／です。
    2000円でおねがいします。はい、720円のおつりになります／です。
② 1. あした 来てください。あしたですね。はい、わかりました。
  2. ビールを二本買ってください。ビール二本ですね。はい、～
  3. 美術館への行き方を教えてください。美術館ですね。はい、～
  4. この道をまっすぐ行ってください。まっすぐですね。はい、～
  5/6. 左／右にまがってください。左／右ですね。はい、～

7. 駅前でとまって（とめて）ください。駅前ですね。はい、〜
8. 駅の入口（出口）で待ってください。入口（出口）ですね。はい、〜

2. V(Te form)＋imasu

① 1. ごはんを食べています。
2. 日本語を勉強しています。
3. コーヒーを飲んでいます。
4. へやをそうじしています。
5. せんたくしています。
6. はがきを書いています。

② 1. 雨はふっていますか。いいえ、ふっていません。晴れています。
2. かぎはかかっていますか。いいえ、かかっていません。
3. 電気はついていますか。いいえ、ついていません。きえています。
4. さくらはもうさいていますか。いいえ、まださいていません。
5. てちょうはかばんに入っていますか。いいえ、入っていません。
6. 南さんはもう結婚していますか。いいえ、まだ（結婚）していません。

③ 1. どんなスポーツをしていますか。テニスをしています。
2. どんな新聞を読んでいますか。日本語の新聞を読んでいます。
3. 週に何回日本語を習っていますか。週に３回習っています。
4. この機械で何を作っていますか。カメラを作っています。

⑤ 1. もうひるごはんを食べましたか。いいえ、まだ食べていません。
2. もう宿題をしましたか。いいえ、まだしていません。
3. もうきょうの新聞を読みましたか。いいえ、まだ読んでいません。
4. もう飛行機の切符を買いましたか。いいえ、まだ買っていません。
5. もう上野に行きましたか。いいえ、まだ行っていません。
6. もう友だちに手紙を書きましたか。いいえ、まだ書いていません。

3. Sentence connection
1. 友だちに会って、さんぽして、映画を見ました。
2. 勉強して、泳いで、ビールを飲みました。
3. 電車に乗って、上野へ行って、買い物しました。
4. 家にいて、何もしませんでした。
5. 家に帰って、晩ごはんを食べて、おんがくを聞いて、ねました。

1. かのじょはどんな人ですか。（かのじょは）わかくて、元気で、親切な人です。
2. そのカメラはどんなカメラですか。新しくて、便利で、いいカメラです。
3. その町はどんな町ですか。古くて、しずかで、きれいな町です。
4. その部屋はどんな部屋ですか。小さくて古くて不便な部屋です。
5. かれは人ですか。かれは日本人で、32さいで、会社員です。
6. 富士山はどんな山ですか。日本で一番高くて、美しくて、有名な山です。

(2)
1. 映画を見ます／見るので／から、きっぷを買ってください。
2. その本はおもしろいので／から、読んでください。
3. このペンは便利なので／ですから、使ってください。

4. くらいので／から、電気をつけてください。

5. 雨がふっています／いるので／から、かさを持っていってください。

6. ここは図書館なので／ですから、しずかにしてください。

1. どうして地下鉄に乗りますか。→ 速くて、便利ですから。

2. どうしてそのスーパーで買いませんか。→ 高いですから。

3. どうしてかさを持って行きますか。 → 雨は降っていますから。

4. どうして映画を見ませんか。 → おもしろくないですから。

5. どうしてきのう家にいましたか。→ 天気が悪かったですから。

6. どうして町へ行きますか。→ 友だちに会って、ビールを飲みますから。

L. 8

(1)

① 1. 水を飲んでもいいですか。はい、飲んでもいいです。

2. タクシーに乗ってもいいですか。はい、乗ってもいいです。

3. まどを開けてもいいですか。はい、開けてもいいです。

4. ちょっと休んでもいいですか。はい、休んでもいいです。

5. 家に帰ってもいいですか。はい、帰ってもいいです。

6. 日本語で説明してもいいですか。はい、（日本語で説明しても）いいです。

② 1. お酒を飲んでもいいですか。いいえ、飲んではいけません。

2. おふろに入ってもいいですか。いいえ、入ってはいけません。

3. ここにごみをすててもいいですか。いいえ、すててはいけません。

4. ローマ字で書いてもいいですか。いいえ、書いてはいけません。

5. ろうかを走ってもいいですか。いいえ、走ってはいけません。

6. 辞書を使ってもいいですか。いいえ、使ってはいけません。

(2)

① 1. ここでたばこを吸ってもいいですか。いいえ、吸わないでください。

2. 午後外出してもいいですか。いいえ、外出しないでください。

3. 明日仕事を休んでもいいですか。いいえ、休まないでください。

4. 英語で/を話してもいいですか。いいえ、英語で/を話さないでください。

5. テストをまんねんひつで書いてもいいですか。いいえ、まんねんひつで書かないでください。

6. 仕事を一人でやってもいいですか。いいえ、一人でやらないでください。

② 1. まどを閉めないといけませんか。はい、閉めないといけません。

2. かぎをかけないといけませんか。はい、かけないといけません。

3. へやをそうじしないといけませんか。はい、（そうじ）しないといけません。

4. 毎日勉強しないといけませんか。はい、（勉強）しないといけません。

5. 医者に行かないといけませんか。はい、行かないといけません。

6. ネクタイをしないといけませんか。はい、しないといけません

③ 1. 席を予約しなければなりませんか。いいえ、予約しなくてもいいですよ。

2. 病院へ行かなければなりませんか。いいえ、行かなくてもいいですよ。

3. 土曜日働かなければなりませんか。いいえ、働かなくてもいいですよ。

4. 一人でぜんぶしなければなりませんか。いいえ、一人でしなくてもいいですよ。

5. まんねんひつで書かなければなりませんか。いいえ、まんねんひつで書かなくてもいいですよ。

6. 今、質問に答えなければなりませんか。いいえ、今答えなくてもいいですよ。

④ 1. かれはさんぽしていますか。いいえ、さんぽしないで、ねています。

2. かれは本を読んでいますか。いいえ、本を読まないで、コンピュータゲームをしています。

3. かれは漢字を書いていますか。いいえ、漢字を書かないで、ひらがなを書いています。

4. かれはワイシャツを着ていますか。いいえ、ワイシャツを着ないで、セーターを着ています。

1. 休みましたか。いいえ、休まないで働きました。

2. ねだんを聞きましたか。いいえ、ねだんを聞かないで買いました。

3. さよならをいいましたか。いいえ、さよならをいわないで帰りました。

4. コーヒーにさとうを入れましたか。いいえ、さとうを入れないで飲みました。

5. 部長とそうだんしましたか。いいえ、部長とそうだんしないでしました。

L. 9
(1) ① Verbs (PS)
1. 火曜日に町へ行くの？　うん、行くよ。ううん、行かないよ。

2. 水曜日にそうじをするの？　うん、するよ。ううん、しないよ。

3. 木曜日に日本語を勉強するの？　うん、するよ。ううん、しないよ。

4. 金曜日に公園をさんぽするの？　うん、するよ。ううん、しないよ。

5. 土曜日に学校に行くの？　うん、行くよ。ううん、行かないよ。

6. 日曜日に友だちに会うの？　うん、会うよ。ううん、会わないよ。

② Verbs (PT)

1. お酒を飲んだ（の/んだ）よ。

2. 漢字を練習した（の/んだ）よ。

3. ふくをせんたくした（の/んだ）よ。

4. 手紙を書いた（の/んだ）よ。

5. ごはんを作った（の/んだ）よ。

6. 上着とネクタイとずぼんを買った（の/んだ）よ。

③ Familiar form of request

1. 水曜日いっしょにテニスをしない？

2. 木曜日いっしょにごはんを食べに行かない？

3. 金曜日いっしょに音楽を聞かない？

4. 土曜日いっしょにドライブをしない？

5. 日曜日いっしょに花見に行かない？

6. 月曜日いっしょに馬に乗らない？

④ I adjectives (PS)

1. その車ははやい？　うん、とてもはやいよ。ううん、あまりはやくないよ。

2. その町は古い？　うん、とても古いよ。ううん、あまり古くないよ。

3. そのごはんはおいしい？　うん、とてもおいしいよ。ううん、あまりおいしくないよ。

4. その漢字はむずかしい？　うん、とてもむずかしいよ。ううん、あまりむずかしくないよ。

5. その川は長い？　うん、とても長いよ。ううん、あまり長くないよ。

6. その仕事はおもしろい？うん、とてもおもしろいよ。ううん、あまりおもしろくないよ。

⑤ I adjectives (PT)

1. 試験はやさしかった？　うん、とてもやさしかったよ。ううん、あまりやさしくなかったよ。

2. その家は大きかった？うん、とても大きかったよ。ううん、あまり大きくなかったよ。

3. 旅行は楽しかった？うん、とても楽しかったよ。ううん、あまり楽しくなかったよ。

4. 成績はよかった？うん、とてもよかったよ。ううん、あまりよくなかったよ。

5. その肉はやわらかかった？うん、とてもやわらかかったよ。ううん、あまりやわらかくなかったよ。

6. その答はただしかった？うん、（とても）ただしかったよ。ううん、（あまり）ただしくなかったよ。

⑥ Na adjectives (PS)

1. その女の人は親切？うん、とても親切よ／だよ。ううん、あまり親切じゃないよ。

2. その男の人は有名？うん、とても有名よ／だよ。ううん、あまり有名じゃないよ。

3. その町はきれい？うん、とてもきれいよ／だよ。ううん、あまりきれいじゃないよ。

4. その町はしずか？うん、とてもしずかよ／だよ。ううん、あまりしずかじゃないよ。

5. その問題はかんたん？うん、とてもかんたんよ／だよ。ううん、あまりかんたんじゃないよ。

6. そのホテルは便利？うん、とても便利よ／だよ。ううん、あまり便利じゃないよ。

⑦ Na adjectives (PT)

1. その試験は簡単だった？うん、かなり簡単だったよ。ううん、あまり簡単じゃなかったよ。

2. きのうはひまだった？うん、かなりひまだったよ。ううん、あまりひまじゃなかったよ。

3. その町はにぎやかだった？うん、かなりにぎやかだったよ。ううん、あまりにぎやかじゃ
   なかったよ。

4. かれは親切だった？うん、かなり親切だったよ。ううん、あまり親切じゃなかったよ。

5. そのカメラは便利だった？うん、かなり便利だったよ。ううん、あまり便利じゃなかったよ。

6. そのみずうみはきれいだった？うん、かなりきれいだったよ。ううん、あまりきれいじゃ
   なかったよ。

⑧ nouns (PS)

1. その女の人は日本人？うん、日本人よ／だよ。ううん、日本人じゃないよ。中国人よ／だよ。

2. その男の人は社長？うん、社長よ／だよ。ううん、社長じゃないよ。部長よ／だよ。

3. その建物は銀行？うん、銀行よ／だよ。ううん、銀行じゃないよ。郵便局よ／だよ。

4. その料理はすし？うん、すしよ／だよ。ううん、すしじゃないよ。そばよ／だよ。

5. その飲み物はお茶？うん、お茶よ／だよ。ううん、お茶じゃないよ。お酒よ／だよ。

6. それは塩？うん、塩よ／だよ。ううん、塩じゃないよ。砂糖よ／だよ。

⑨ nouns (PT)

1. その女の人はドイツ人だった？うん、ドイツ人だったよ。ううん、ドイツ人じゃなかったよ。
   イギリス人だったよ。

2. その男の人は部長だった？うん、部長だったよ。ううん、部長じゃなかったよ。課長だったよ。

3. その建物は駅だった？うん、駅だったよ。ううん、駅じゃなかったよ。美術館だったよ。

4. その料理はスパゲティーだった？ うん、スパゲティーだったよ。ううん、スパゲティーじゃ
   なかったよ。ピッツァだったよ。

5. その漢字の試験は火曜日だった。うん、火曜日だったよ。ううん、火曜日じゃなかったよ。
   水曜日だったよ。

6. 上野までの運賃はいくらだった。360円だったよ。

(2)

①1. その映画を見たほうがいいよ。

2. 早く寝たほうがいいよ。

3. やさいをたくさん食べたほうがいいよ。

4. 家にいたほうがいいよ。

5. 高いから、あのスーパーで買物しないほうがいいよ。

6. お酒をたくさん飲まないほうがいいよ。

②1. 映画を見たり、さんぽをしたりするよ。／しますよ。
2. 買物したり、レストランに行ったりするよ。／しますよ。
3. 友だちに会ったり、手紙を書いたりするよ。／しますよ。
4. 文法を勉強したり、漢字を覚えたりするよ。／しますよ。
5. そうじしたり、せんたくしたりするよ。／しますよ。
6. 歌を歌ったり、ダンスをしたりするよ。／しますよ。

1. 成績はよかったり、わるかったりする（だ）。／します（です）。
2. ごはんはおいしかったり、まずかったりする（だ）。／します（です）。
3. へやはきれいだったり、きたなかったりする（だ）。／します（です）。
4. 町はうるさかったり、しずかだったりする（だ）。／します（です）。
5. かばんは重かったり、かるかったりする（だ）。／します（です）。
6. 仕事はいそがしかったり、ひまだったりする（だ）。／します（です）。

L. 10
(1)
① 1. あなたはテニスができますか。
2. あなたは水泳ができますか。
3. なたは野球ができますか。
4. あなたはバレーボールができますか。
5. あなたはピンポンができますか。
6. あなたはサッカーができますか。
② 1. あなたは漢字を書くことができますか。
2. あなたは歌を歌うことができますか。
3. あなたはコンピュータを使うことができますか。
4. あなたは車を運転することができますか。
5. あなたはお金を私に貸すことができますか。
6. あなたは来月までに返すことができますか。
③ 1. 彼女はダンスがじょうずですか。
2. 彼女は料理がじょうずですか。
3. 彼女はギターがじょうずですか。
4. 彼女は絵をかくことがじょうずですか。
5. 彼女は写真をとることがじょうずですか。
6. 彼女は人形を作ることがじょうずですか。
④ 1. 彼はフランス語がじょうずですか。
2. 彼は運転がじょうずですか。
3. 彼はけいさんがじょうずですか。
4. 彼はスポーツがじょうずですか。
5. 彼は作文を書くことがじょうずですか。
6. 彼は泳ぐことがじょうずですか。
⑤ 1. 彼女はイタリア語がとくいです。
2. 彼女は漢字がとくいです。
3. 彼女は音楽がとくいです。
4. 彼女は経済がとくいです。
5. 彼女は法律がとくいです。

6. 彼女は英語で手紙を書くことがとくいです。

⑥ 1. あなたは外国語がとくいですか。

2. あなたは漢字がとくいですか。

3. あなたはダンスがとくいですか。

4. あなたは政治がとくいですか。

5. あなたは水泳がとくいですか。

6. あなたはそうじすることがとくいですか。

⑦ 1. あなたはイタリア語がわかりますか。

2. あなたは先生の説明がわかりますか。

3. あなたは上野へ行き方がわかりますか。

4. あなたはこの漢字の読み方がわかりますか。

5. あなたはケーキの焼き方がわかりますか。

(2)

① 1. スポーツの中で何が好きですか。私はテニスが好きです。

2. 勉強の中で何が好きですか。私は歴史が好きです。

3. 音楽の中で何が好きですか。私はクラシックが好きです。

4. 食べ物の中で何が好きですか。私は天ぷらが好きです。

5. 肉の中で何が好きですか。私はとり肉が好きです。

6. 季節の中でいつが好きですか。春／夏／秋／冬が好きです。

② 1. あなたは魚が好きですか。

2. あなたはやさいが好きですか。

3. あなたはコーラが好きですか。

4. あなたはさんぽが好きですか。

5. あなたはそうじすることが好きですか。

6. あなたは料理をつくることが好きですか。

(3)

① 1. あなたはテレビがほしいですか。

2. あなたはステレオがほしいですか。

3. あなたはコンピュータがほしいですか。

4. あなたは飲み物がほしいですか。

5. あなたは大きい家がほしいですか。

6. あなたはうで時計がほしいですか。

② 1. あなたは何が/をしたいですか。私は買い物が/をしたいです。何もしたくないです。

2. あなたは何が/を飲みたいですか。私はビールが/を飲みたいです。何も飲みたくないです。

3. あなたは何が/を買いたいですか。私はステレオが/を買いたいです。何も買いたくないです。

4. あなたはどんなスポーツが/をしたいですか。私はテニスが/をしたいです。何もしたくないです。

5. あなたはどこへ旅行したいですか。私は日本へ旅行したいです。どこにも旅行したくないです。

6. あなたはだれを公園に連れて行きたいですか。子供を連れて行きたいです。だれも連れて行き
   たくないです。

③ 1. 彼女は何をほしがっていますか。彼女は辞書をほしがっています。
   彼女は何を買いたがっていますか。彼女はケーキを買いたがっています。

2. 彼は何をほしがっていますか。彼は旅行かばんをほしがっています。

   彼はどこへ行きたがっていますか。彼は京都へ行きたがっています。

3. むすこさんは何をほしがっていますか。むすこはおもちゃをほしがっています。

むすこさんは何になりたがっていますか。むすこは医者になりたがっています。

4. むすめさんは何をほしがっていますか。むすめは洋服をほしがっています。
むすめさんは何になりたがっていますか。むすめはかんごしになりたがっています。

(4)

①1. いっしょにビールを飲みましょう。はい、飲みましょう。

2. いっしょに料理を作りましょう。はい、作りましょう。

3. いっしょに音楽を聞きましょう。はい、聞きましょう。

4. いっしょに日本語を勉強しましょう。はい、(勉強)しましょう。

5. いっしょに部屋をかたづけましょう。はい、かたづけましょう。

6. いっしょに花見に行きましょう。はい、行きましょう。

②1. 窓を閉めましょうか。

2. お茶を入れましょうか。

3. 仕事をてつだいましょうか。

4. 日本語をおしえましょうか。

5. 町をあんないしましょうか。

6. べんとうを作りましょうか。

L. 11
(1)

① 1. (－さんは)お金たくさんがありますか。
はい、たくさんあります。いいえ、ぜんぜんありません。

2. (－さんは)仕事がおもしろいありますか。はい、よくあります。いいえ、あまりありません。

3. (－さんは)長い休みがありますか。はい、ときどきあります。いいえ、めったにありません。

4. (－さんは)質問がありますか。 はい、一つだけあります。いいえ、ぜんぜんありません。

5. (－さんは)宿題がありますか。はい、毎日あります。いいえ、めったにありません。

6. (－さんは)はいい考えがありますか。はい、たくさんあります。いいえ、ぜんぜんありません。

1. このくつ、もっとちいさいのはありませんか。

2. このテレビ、もっとやすいのはありませんか。

3. このカメラ、もっとかるいのはありませんか。

4. この雑誌、もっとあたらしいのはありませんか。

5. この花、もっときれいなのはありませんか。

6. このコンピュータ、もっとべんりなのはありませんか。

1. (－さんは)兄弟がいますか。はい、たくさんいます。いいえ、ぜんぜんいません。

2. (－さんは)恋人がいますか。はい、います。いいえ、ぜんぜんいません。

3. (－さんは)子供(むすこさん・むすめさん)がいますか。はい、たくさんいます。 いいえ、
ぜんぜんいません。

4. (－さんは)赤ちゃんがいますか。はい、います。 いいえ、いません。

5. (－さんは)いいどうりょうがいますか。はい、たくさんいます。 いいえ、ぜんぜんいません。

6. (－さんは) 外国人の友だちがいますか。はい、たくさんいます。 いいえ、ぜんぜんいません。

② 1. ベルリンはどんな町ですか。ベルリンは町がおもしろいです。そしてクーダムが有名です。

2. 友だちはどんな人ですか。友だちは髪が長いです。そして目が黒いです。

3. 彼の家はどんな家ですか。彼の家は居間が広いです。そして庭がきれいです。

4. 日本はどんな天気ですか。日本は夏が暑いです。そして春と秋がとてもいいです。

5. 京都はどんな町ですか。 京都は歴史が古くて、有名な寺がたくさんあります。
6. あなたの故郷はどんな町ですか。？？

③ 1. あなたは日本料理を食べたことがありますか。
2. あなたはイタリアへ旅行したことがありますか。
3. あなたはコアラを見たことがありますか。
4. あなたは日本の歌を歌ったことがありますか。
5. あなたは富士山に登ったことがありますか。
6. あなたは日本に留学したことがありますか。

④ 1. あなたはフランス語を話すことがありますか。
2. あなたは車を運転することがありますか。
3. あなたは手紙を書くことがありますか。
4. あなたはお酒を飲むことがありますか。
5. あなたは病気になることがありますか。
6. あなたはみそしるを飲むことがありますか。

(2)
1. 晩友だちに会うんですよ。
2. あした料理を作るんですよ。
3. 朝公園をジョギングするんですよ。
4. きのう何もしなかったんですよ。
5. きのうの晩へやをそうじしたんですよ。
6. 週末プールで泳ぐんですよ。

1. 髪がとてもみじかいんですよ。
2. 顔がとても白いんですよ。
3. 目が(とても)青いんですよ。
4. 頭がとてもいいんですよ。
5. 力がとても強いんですよ。
6. 鼻がとても高いんですよ。

1. そのテレビは便利なんですか。
2. その人は親切なんですか。
3. そのへやは静かなんですか。
4. その子どもは元気なんですか。
5. そのテストはかんたんなんですか。
6. その字引は便利なんですか。
   いいえ、あまり～じゃないんですよ。

1. それは新聞なんですか。いいえ、新聞じゃないんです。雑誌なんですよ。
2. その人はドイツ人なんですか。いいえ、ドイツ人じゃないんです。フランス人なんですよ。
3. その町は京都なんですか。いいえ、京都じゃないんです。奈良なんですよ。
4. それは豚肉なんですか。いいえ、豚肉じゃないんです。牛肉なんですよ。
5. 明日は雨なんですか。いいえ、雨じゃないんです。雪なんですよ。
6. きのうははれだったんですか。いいえ、はれじゃなかったんです。くもりだったんですよ。

①したん、したん、買ったん、買ったん　②行ったん、行ったん、だったん、なん、なん、したん、見たんです　③しているん、好きなん、始めたいん、ないん

L. 12
(1)
①1.　ごはんを食べる時、はしで食べます。／食べました。
2.　朝起きた時、歯をみがきます。／みがきました。
3.　コーヒーを飲む時、ミルクを入れます。／入れました。
4.　電車に乗る時、きっぷを買います。／買いました。
5.　奈良へ行った時、大仏や若草山を見ます。／見ました。
6.　かぜを引いた時、このくすりを飲んでください。

1.　暑い時、よくクーラーをつけます／ました。
2.　ごはんがおいしい時、たくさん食べます／ました。
3.　仕事がいそがしい時、よく手伝います／ました。
4.　風がつめたい時、コートを着ます。／着ました。
5.　寒い時、ヒーターをつけます。／つけました。
6.　私はねむい時、コーヒーを飲みます。／飲みました。

1.　元気な時、よく運動をします／ました。
2.　静かな時、よく勉強できます／ました。
3.　テストがかんたんな時、うれしいです／かったです。
4.　けしきがきれいな時、たくさん写真をとります。／とりました。

1.　休みの時、長野へ行きます／行きました。
2.　学生の時、よくアルバイトします／しました。
3.　ごはんの時、ワインを飲みます／飲みました。
4.　旅行の時、地図を持っていきます。／持っていきました。
5.　そうじの時、まどを開けます。／開けました
6.　試験の時、静かにしてください。

②1.　電車を待っている間、友だちと話します／ました。
2.　部長が電話している間、外で待ちます／ました。
3.　かぜを引いている間、会社を休みます／ました。
4.　日本にすんでいる間に、たくさん友だちができます／ました。
5.　試験をしている間、話してはいけません。
6.　桜がさいている間に、花見に行きましょう。

1.　それが安い間に、買います／ました。
2.　天気がわるい間、家にいます／ました。
3.　若い間に、たくさん旅行します／ました。
4.　すずしい間に、公園をさんぽします／ました。

1.　ひまな間に、遊びに行きます／ました。
2.　静かな間に、作文を書きます／ました。
3.　外が危険な間、家にいます／ました。

1. 会議の間、たばこをすわないでください。／すいませんでした。
2. 仕事の間、制服を着てください。／着ました。
3. 病気の間、家でよく休んでください。／休みました。
4. 休みの間に、トイレに行ってください。／行きました。

③ 1. 歌を歌いながら、帰りませんか／ました。
2. コーヒーを飲みながら、バスを待ちませんか／待ちました。
3. ギターをひきながら、歌いませんか。／歌いました。
4. 日本語のCDを聞きながら、会話を練習しませんか／しました。
5. 写真をとりながら、町を見学するしませんか／しました。
6. 日本で働きながら、日本語を勉強しませんか／しました。

④ 1. 彼は服を着たまま、寝ました。
2. 彼は電気をつけたまま、部屋を出ました。
3. いすにすわったまま、話しました
4. 私たちは立ったまま、映画を見ました。
5. 見たまま（を）／話してください。
6. 本とノートを出したままにしないでください。

(2)
1. ここに来る前に、だれに会いましたか。ここに来る前に、友だちに会いました。
2. 寝る前に、何をしましたか。寝る前に、テレビを見ました。
3. この仕事をする前に、何をしましたか。この仕事をする前に、音楽を聞きました。
4. 朝ごはんを食べる前に、何／しましたか。朝ごはんを食べる前に、歯をみがきました。
5. 車を運転する前に、何をしましたか。車を運転する前に、ガソリンを入れました。
6. きのう会社に行く前に、どこへ行きましたか。　→　きのう会社に行く前に、図書館へ行きました。

1. いつ試験をしましたか。休みの前にしました。
2. いつ日本に帰りましたか。正月の前に帰りました。
3. いつコーヒーを飲みましたか。仕事の前に飲みました。
4. いつ大使館に行きましたか。日本旅行の前に行きました。
5. いつおふろに入りましたか。晩ごはんの前に入りました。
6. いつビールを買いましたか。パーティーの前に買いました。

(3)
1. 働いた後で、何をしますか。働いた後で、映画を見ます。
2. 友だちに会った後で、何をしますか。友だちに会った後で、いっしょに買い物します。
3. 奈良に着いた後で、何をしますか。奈良に着いた後で、大仏を見物します。
4. 仕事をした後で、何をしますか。仕事をした後で、ビールを飲みに行きます。
5. 日本語を勉強した後で、何をしますか。日本語を勉強した後で、日本で働きます。
6. 町へ行った後で、何をしますか。町へ行った後で、本屋で雑誌を買います。

1. いつ音楽を聞きましたか。仕事の後で聞きました。
2. いつガソリンを入れましたか。運転の後で入れました。
3. いつローマに行きましたか。イギリスの後で行きました。

4. いつくだものを食べましたか。食事の後で食べました。

5. いつ小説を読みましたか。晩ごはんの後で読みました。

6. いつ買い物しましたか。仕事の後でしました。

L. 13

(1)

①1. 町田さんは今日友だちに会うと言っていました。

2. お母さんは子供はもうすぐ帰ると言っていました。

3. マリアは今晩はどこへも行かないと言っていました。

4. 北野さんはきのう働かなかったと言っていました。

5. おばさんは暑い時、いつもぼうしをかぶると言っていました。

6. おじさんは若い時、ドイツに行ったことがあると言っていました。

1. 町田さんは今日はとても暑かったと言っていました。

2. ユリアはたくさん旅行がしたいと言っていました。

3. さとしはその本はおもしろくないと言っていました。

4. マリアさんはテストはあまりむずかしくなかったと言っていました。

5. 鈴木さんは信号はそのときまだ赤かったと言っていました。

6. 祖父は祖母の料理はとてもおいしかったと言っていました。

1. 山川さんは町田さんはとても親切だと言っていました。

2. マイヤーさんは東京は静かではないと言っていました。

3. かおりさんはテニスが好きだったと言っていました。

4. マイヤーさんは通訳の仕事がきらいではないと言っていました。

5. マリアさんは彼は有名ではなかったと言っていました。

6. おばあさんは春はさくらがとてもきれいだと言っていました。

7. 木村さんは先週病気だったと言っていました。

8. マイヤーさんは晩ごはんは日本料理ではなかったと言っていました。

②

1. 先月京都という町へ行きました。

2. きのうまぐろという魚を食べました。

3. 携帯という漢字は難しいです。

4. まなびという学校で日本語を勉強しています。

5. 田村さんという人を知っていますか。

6. 彼はサンライズというホテルに泊まっています。

③

1. 朝起きた時、「おはよう」と言って、夜寝る時、「おやすみ」と言います。

2. 家を出る時、「いってまいります」と言って、家に帰った時、「ただいま」と言います。

3. 誕生日に「おたんじょうびおめでとう！」と言います。

4. 「Just a moment please!!」は日本語で「ちょっと待ってください」と言います。

5. 「おそくなってすみません」は英語で何と言いますか。「I apologize for being late. 」
   と言います。

6. 「Tasted good!」は日本語で何と言いますか。「ごちそうさま」といいます。

(2)
1. 新幹線についてどう思いますか。とても速いと思います。
2. 京都についてどう思いますか。とても有名できれいだと思います。
3. 彼女の絵についてどう思いますか。とても立派だと思います。
4. 漢字についてどう思いますか。少しむずかしいけど、おもしろいと思います。
5. 彼についてどう思いますか。若くて親切だと思います。
6. そのアパートについてどう思いますか。新しくなくて、不便だと思います。

1. 新幹線で東京から大阪まで何時間かかると思いますか。3時間ぐらい かかると思います。
2. 東京から大阪まで新幹線と飛行機と、どちらの方が便利だと思いますか。？
3. 日本でビール一本いくらだと思いますか。３００円ぐらいだと思います。
4. 日本は今何時だと思いますか。11時だと思います。
5. あした雨がふると思いますか。はい、ふると思います。
6. 北野さんの故郷はどこだと思いますか。長野だと思います。
7. シュミットさんは明日マイヤーさんと何がしたいと思っていますか。打ち合わせをしたいと思っています。

L. 14
(1) ① 週末何をするつもりですか。
1. 映画を見るつもりです。
2. 宿題をするつもりです。
3. 友だちに会うつもりです。
4. 家でのんびりするつもりです。
5. 京都のお寺をおとずれるつもりです。
6. 池でつりをするつもりです。
② 1. 明日映画を見ないつもりです。～見るつもりはありません。
2. 今日そうじをしないつもりです。～するつもりはありません。
3. 今晩友だちに会わないつもりです。～会うつもりはありません。
4. 休みに料理を作らないつもりです。～作るつもりはありません。
5. 何もしないつもりです。～するつもりはありません。
6. 来年日本に留学しないつもりです。～するつもりはありません。
③ 1. 日本に行くつもりでしたが、中国に行きました。
2. 日本料理を食べるつもりでしたが、イタリア料理を食べました。
3. 友だちに会うつもりでしたが、ひまがありませんでした。
4. 医者なるつもりでしたが、会社員になりました。
④ 1. がんばったつもりですが、できませんでした。
2. 部屋をよくそうじしたつもりですが、まだきたないです。
3. 電気を消したつもりですが、ついていました。
4. ドアにかぎをかけしたつもりですが、開いていました。
5. 彼はいい医者のつもりですが、本当はあまりよくないです。
6. 彼女は歌がじょうずなつもりですが、本当はへたです。

(2)
① 1. 駅で電車の切符を買おう。　うん、買おう。
2. 公園を散歩しよう。　うん、しよう。
3. 携帯電話で友だちに連絡しよう。　うん、しよう。
4. 図書館で本を借りよう。　うん、借りよう。
5. いっしょに歌を歌おう。うん、歌おう。
6. いっしょに家に帰ろう。　うん、帰ろう。

② 日曜日（火曜日,,,）に何をしようと思っていますか。
1. 泳ぎに行こうと思っています。
2. 部屋をそうじしようと思っています。
3. 陶器について調べようと思っています。
4. 手紙を書こうと思っています。
5. 宿題を全部すませようと思っています。
6. コンサートを聞こうと思っています。

(3)①
1. どこに行くことにしましたか。イタリアに行くことにしました。
2. いつ行くことにしましたか。来週行くことにしました。
3. 何で行くことにしましたか。飛行機で行くことにしました。
4. だれと行くことにしましたか。友だちと行くことにしました。
5. そこで何をすることにしましたか。？
6. どのくらい滞在することにしましたか。？

② どうなりましたか。
1. 図書館を建てることになりました。
2. 工場を見学することになりました。
3. 計画を実施することになりました。
4. 計画を中止することになりました。
5. 計画を延期することになりました
6. オリンピックに参加することになりました。

③
1. 仕事は８時に始まることになっています。
2. 東京に１週間滞在するることになっています。
3. 毎日会議をすることになっています。
4. この会社では制服を着ることになっています。
5. 明日見本市を案内することになっています。
6. 試験の間（は）話してはいけないことになっています。

L. 15
(1)
1. 彼女がレストランで食べたものはスパゲティーです。
2. 今日事務所に来た人はシュミットさんです。
3. 先週行った町はとてもきれいです。

4. そこに止まっている地下鉄は上野行きです。

5. この子が生まれた日は4月のあたたかい日でした。

6. 彼女が住んでいるアパートは小さいですが、きれいです。

1. 先生はそのいすに座っている人です。

2. これは彼女がきのう焼いたケーキです。

3. その建物はマイヤーさんが勉強している大学です。

4. それは彼が先月買った車です。

5. 山川さんはせびろを着て、めがねをかけた人です。

6. その陶器はマイヤーさんが有田町で焼いたものです。

1. 山田さんと言う人を知っていますか。

2. きのうそこで見たことを私に話してください。

3. 彼女は長い間考えていたことを話しました。

4. 私は図書館で借りた本を今晩読みます。

5. 浮世絵という漢字を忘れました。

6. 私が焼いたケーキを食べませんか。

(2)
①
1. この電車が京都にいつ着くか駅員に聞いてください。

2. 彼女の電話番号が何番(だ)か知っていますか。

3. あなたは今日どこへ行ったか言ってください。

4. そのへやの中にだれがいるか知りません。

5. 彼女がきょう大学をどうして休んだか知っていますか。

6. そのごはんをどう作るか教えましょう。

7. どの辞書が一番いいか、店員に聞きましょう。

8. 彼はどんな仕事をしているか、私たちに説明しました。

②
1. あの人は英語を話すかどうか知っていますか。

2. あなたはその展覧会を見たいかどうか言ってください。

3. かれがそのことを知っているかどうか知りません。

4. かれらが日本に無事着いたかどうか知りたいです。

5. あした天気がいいかどうか天気予報を見ましょう。

6. 試験がむずかしかったかどうか言ってください。

7. 車にガソリンが入っているかどうか、ちゃんと調べてください。

8. 私は夏休みに故郷に帰るかどうか、まだわかりません。

Resolution of the lesson tests

L. 1
(1)
1. wa, soo   2. wa, soo dewa   3. Kore   4. Sono, wa, no, no   5. nan no, no
(2)
1. Hai, soo desu. Sore wa pen desu.
2. Iie, soo dewa arimasen.
3. Kore wa nihongo no hon desu.
4. Are wa kamera desu.
5. Kore wa Mayer-san no kamera desu.
6. (Kare wa) Kitano-san desu.
7. Iie, kaishain desu.
8. Watashi wa ~ desu.
9. Watashi wa gakusei / kaishain desu.
10. Watashi wa doitsu-jin / nihon-jin desu.
(3)
1. Hajimemashite, Yamada desu. Doozo yoroshiku!
2. Kochirakoso doozo yoroshiku!
3. Watashi no meishi desu.
4. (Anata wa) doitsu no gakusei-san desu ka. Hai, soo desu.
5. Watashi wa Nihon-Shinbun no kaishain desu.

L. 2
(1)
1. atarashii desu.
2. atarashiku nai desu, kirei desu.
3. shizukana
4. amari takaku nai desu.
5. chiisai desu, benri desu.
(2)
1. Iie, amari chikaku nai desu.
2. Iie, amari yuumei de wa arimasen.
3. Iie, amari yoku nai desu.
4. Iie, amari genki de wa arimasen.
5. Iie, amari atarashiku nai desu.
(3)
1. Sore wa ookii machi desu.
2. Kore wa kireina hana desu.
3. Mori-san wa wakai hito desu.
4. Kyoto wa totemo furui machi desu.
5. Kore wa amari benrina konpyuuta dewa arimasen.
(4)
1. Sono shinbun wa atarashii desu ka.
2. Anata no konpyuuta wa benri desu ka.
3. Kono terebi wa ikaga desu ka.
4. Sore wa don'na kuruma desu ka.

L. 3
(1)
1. Koko ni nihonjin ga 3-nin to doitsu-jin ga 5-nin imasu.
2. Heya (no naka) ni nani ga arimasu ka. Tsukue ga futatsu to terebi ga 1-dai arimasu.
3. Tsukue no ue ni hon ga 3-satsu to nooto ga 2-satsu to tokei ga hitotsu arimasu.
4. Jisho wa doko ni arimasu ka. Jisho wa kaban no naka ni arimasu.

5．Tanaka-san wa doko ni imasu ka. Tanaka-san wa kaisha ni imasu.
6．Niwa ni ki ga 5-hon arimasu. Soshite inu ga 2-hiki to neko ga 3-biki imasu.
(2)
1．Hai, arimasu. / Iie, arimasen.
2．~tsu arimasu. / Zenzen arimasen.
3．Hai, imasu. / Iie, imasen.
4．Hai, arimasu. Zugspitze(-san) desu.
5．Hai, arimasu. Rhein(-gawa) ya Donau(-gawa) desu.
6．~satsu arimasu. / Takusan arimasu. / amari (zenzen) arimasen.
(3)
1．Heya (no naka) ni nani ga arimasu ka.

2．Heya (no naka) ni tsukue to hondana to terebi ga arimasu.

3．Tanaka-san wa doko ni imasu ka.
4．Kare wa eki no mae ni imasu.
5．Tsukue no ue ni hon ga nan-satsu arimasu ka. 5-satsu arimasu.
6．Machi (no naka) ni suupaa ya kireina kooen ya eki (nado) ga arimasu.

L．4
(1)
1．に　2．を　　3．に、を　　4．は、で、に　　5．の、で、や、を
6．から、まで　7．から、まで　　8．に、に
(2)
1．パン／ごはんをたべます。
2．～をのみます。
3．でんしゃ／バス／くるまでいきます。or あるいていきます。
4．8時間ぐらいはたらきます。
5．スーパー／デパートでかいものします
6．テレビをみます。／ほんをよみます。／おんがくをききます。
(3)
1．いえからえきまであるいてどのぐらいかかりますか。
2．わたしはばん（に）パンとりんごをたべます。
3．コーヒーをのみません。
4．いえでテレビをみます。そしておんがくをききます。
5．１１時ごろねます。

L．5
(1)
1．わたしはきのうまちでともだちにあいました。
2．いっしょにえいがをみました。そしてこうえんをさんぽしました。
3．かれはワインを飲みましたが、わたしは何ものみませんでした。
4．わたしはもう日本へいきましたが、かれはまだいきません。
5．しゅうまつともだちとうみにおよぎにいきました。
6．くるまははしをわたりました。そしてえきまではしりました。
(2)
1．はい、見ました。／いいえ、見ませんでした。
2．e.g. 日本語をべんきょうしました。／なにもしませんでした。
3．はい、もう食べました。／いいえ、まだ食べません。（いいえ、まだです。）
4．e.g. ともだちの家に行きました。／どこにも行きませんでした。
5．e.g. わたしはきのうのばん日本語をべんきょうしました。
6．はい、よろこんで。／ありがとう。でも時間がありません。

(3)
1．週末何をしましたか。
2．友だちとすしを食べに行きました。
3．もう日本語のしゅくだいをしましたか。
4．いいえ、まだです。

L. 6
(1)
1．そのコンピュータはとても高かったです。
2．きのうの天気はあまりよくなかったです。
3．かれの自転車は私のより古いです。
4．かのじょはクラスの中で一番若いです。
5．奈良は京都ほど大きくないです。
6．きょうはきのうとおなじぐらいいそがしいです。
7．その車は道をとてもはやく走りました。
(2)
1．どちらの方が ／ の方が
2．どちらの方が ／ の方がながく
3．どこが一番 ／ スペインが一番
4．何が一番 ／ が一番
5．だれが一番 ／ はやく ／ が一番はやく
(3)
1．きょうはきのうほど寒くなかったです。
2．このパンはあのパンよりおいしいです。
3．私の兄は家族の中で一番大きいです。

L. 7
(1)
1．あした9時にここに（へ）来てください。
2．ユリアさんはマリアさんと公園をさんぽしています。
3．私たちは週に3回日本語を習っています。
4．デパートはもう開いていますか。
5．町まで電車に乗って行きますか、歩いて行きますか。
6．きのう友だちに会って、いっしょこごはんを食べました。
7．その車は新しくて、速くて、便利で、とてもいいです、
8．ドアは開いていますから（ので）、どうぞ入ってください。
(2)
1．わたしは～に住んでいます。
2．はい、よく知っています。／いいえ、あまり／ぜんぜん知りません。
3．はい、持っています。／いいえ、持っていません。
4．はい、（もう）けっこんしています。／いいえ、（まだ）けっこんしていません。
5．e.g. テニスをしています。／ 何もしていません。
6．e.g. 日本語をべんきょうしていました。／何もしていませんでした。
7．e.g. 日本ではたらきたいからです。
(3)
1．駅への行き方を教えてください。

２．７番のバスに乗って、地下鉄の駅でおりてください。

３．英語の新聞はどこで売っていますか。駅の売店で売っています。

４．京都は古くて、きれいで、おもしろくて、有名です。

５．いまさくらがきれいにさいていますから、上野公園に行きませんか。

６．電気を消して、部屋を出てください。

L. 8

(1)

１．その部屋に入ってはいけません。

２．あした仕事をしなくてもいいです。

３．コンピュータを使わないといけません。／コンピュータを使わなければなりません。

４．すこし休んでもいいですか。

５．ここでたばこをすわないでください。

６．彼女は何も言わないで、帰りました。

７．ドイツ語を話さないで、日本語を話しました。

(2)

１．いいえ、試験はペンで書かなくてもいいです。鉛筆で書いてもいいです。

２．いいえ、ローマ字で書いてはいけません。

３．いいえ、辞書を使ってはいけません。

４．はい、となりの人と話してはいけません。

(3)

１．しつもんしてもいいですか。

２．いつも日本語を話さなければなりません。

３．かれはきょうはたらかないで、家にいました。

４．日本人に聞かないで一人でぜんぶ書きましたか。

L. 9

(1)

１．もらった　　２．かえらなかった　　３．では／じゃない、だ　　４．ある、ない

５．だった、じゃなかった　６．見ない、ないんだ／ないの

(2)

１．パーティーで話したり、歌を歌ったりする。

２．試験で日本語を読んだり、書いたり、話したりしなければならない。

３．試験のせいせきはよかったり、わるかったりだった／でした。

４．町へ電車で行ったほうがいい。

５．たくさんやさいやくだものを食べたほうがいい。

６．きょうの天気はわるいから、さんぽしないほうがいい。

(3)

１．きのうはとても暑かったので、泳ぎに行った。

２．切符（チケット）を予約しなくてもよかった。

３．たくさんアルバイトしなければならなかった。

４．晩に私たちは本を読んだり、音楽を聞いたりした。

５．きょうたくさんはたらかなければならなかった。

６．週末映画を見たり、日本料理を食べたりしない。

L. 10

(1)

1．食べたいです　2．できます　3．とくいです　4．じょうずに話すことができません

5．好きです、きらいです　6．働きたいです　7．できません

8．にがてです　9．ほしがっています　10. 見たがっています

(2)

1．e. g. ワインとが一番好きです。

2．e. g. 旅行が一番したいです。

3．e. g. 英語がとくいです。

(3)

1．私は土曜日に友だちに会いたいです。

2．私はテニスがすきですが、まだあまりじょうずではありません。

3．私の母はあしたコンサートに行きたがっています。

L. 11

(1)

1．時間(ひま)があります

2．いません、二人います

3．公園がきれいです

4．髪が黒く、目が青いです

5．ビールの会社がたくさんあります

(2)

1．彼女は信州そばを食べたことがあります。

2．彼はまだ富士山に登ったことがありません。

3．私はときどき友だちとテニスをすることがあります。

4．私の子供はめったに病気になることがありません。

(3)

1．私はきのう彼にあったんです。

2．先生は今日どこにも行かないんです。

3．たくさん漢字を勉強しなければならなかったんです。

4．父はサッカーがじょうずだったんです。

5．かのじょはあまりげんきじゃなかったんです。

L. 12

(1)

1．朝起きた時、雨がふっていました。

2．さむい時、ヒーターをつけてください。

3．私は若くて元気な/だった時、よくスポーツをしました。

4．彼女がごはんを作っている間 (に)、私は部屋をそうじしました。

5．病気の間 (は)、働かないで家にいます。

6．彼は働きながら、日本語を勉強しています。

7．電気をつけたまま、部屋を出ていってはいけません。

8．彼女は立ったまま、長い間話しています。

9．私は先生になる前に、ゾミーの会社で働きました。

10. 東京に着いた後で、すぐ友だちに電話しました。

(2)
1．後で　　2．まま　　3．間に　　4．時　　5．前に　　6．ながら　　7．間

(3)
1．実家に行く時、（君の）車を借りてもいいかな。
2．運転しながら、携帯電話をかけてはいけないよ。
3．車を使った後は、ちゃんとガソリンを入れてね。

L. 13

(1)
1．マイヤーさんは来週から通訳のアルバイトをすると言っています。
2．早く部長に連絡しなければならないと北野さんは言っています。
3．町田さんはきのう町で友だちに会ったと言っていました。
4．山田さんはホテルに泊まらなかったと言っていました。
5．マリアさんはあまり肉が好きではないとよく言っています。
6．今日の仕事はとてもたいへんだったとシュミットさんは言っていました。

(2)
1．「行ってまいります」と言います。
2．「ただいま」と言います。
3．「いただきます」と言います。
4．「ごちそうさま」と言います。
5．「おめでとうございます」と言います。
6．「It's all right.」と言います。

(2)
1．いい／わるい／雨が降る　と思います。
2．はい、見ると思います。／いいえ、見ないと思います。
3．善光寺で有名だと思います。
4．とてもはやくて、便利だと思います。
5．奈良のほうが古いと思います。
6．テニスと水泳がとくいだと思います。

L. 14

(1)
1．東京へ行くつもりです。
2．日本文化について調べるつもりです。
3．友だちに会うつもりです。
4．買い物して、映画を見るつもりです。
5．九州へ旅行しようと思っています。
6．新幹線で行こうと思っています。
7．有田焼きの産地を見学しようと思っています。
8．とうきを作ろうと思っています。

(2)
1．働くことになりました
2．いることにしました
3．結婚することにしました
4．建てることになりました
5．中止する／変えることになりました

６．参加することになりました

(3)

１．私は日本のお茶が好きなので、陶器について書くことにしました。

２．それから焼き物のコースに参加しようと思っています。

３．日本での成功を期待しています。

L. 15

(1)

１．そこに止まっている電車に乗ってください。

２．きのう見た映画はとてもおもしろかったです。

３．あそこで電話をかけている人は川中先生です。

４．私がほしかったくつを今日デパートで買いました。

５．すきやきという料理を今晩食べました。

６．彼女が住んでいる町はとてもきれいです。

７．山田さんが働いている会社はそのビルです。

(2)

１．どこ(だ)か　　　２．どこに住んでいるか　　　３．何時に始まるか

４．どのくらいかかるか　　　５．どう書くか　　　６．だれに会ったか

(3)

１．そのカメラが便利かどうか店員に聞きましょう。

２．彼はその会社で働くかどうかまだわかりません。

３．友だちがパーティーにくるかどうか知っていますか。

４．田中さんが事務所にいるかどうか電話をして聞いてください。

Table of sentence forms

L	Categories	Sentence forms	English
01	Being verb (present tense)	～です	be
	Positive, PV	S は P です	S is P.
	Negative, NV	S は P ではありません	S is not P.
	Question, Q	S は P ですか	Is S P?
02	adjective (present tense)	A です	Be A
	I-adjective, predicative, PV	S は IA いです	S is IA.
	IA, predicative, NV	S は IA くないです	S is not IA.
	IA, predicative, Q	S は IA いですか	Is S IA.
	IA, attributive, PV	S は IA い N です	S is IA+N.
	IA, attributive, NV	S は IA い N ではありません	S is not IA+N.
	Na adjective, predicative, PV	S は NA です	S is NA.
	NA, predicative, NV	S は NA ではありません	S is not NA.
	NA, predicative, Q	S は NA ですか	Is S NA?
	NA, attributive, PV	S は NA な N です	S is NA+N.
	NA, attributive, NV	S は NA な N ではありません	S is not NA+N.
03	being there (existence)		
	human / animal, PV	S がいます	S is there.
	human / animal, NV	S がいません	S is not there.
	other things, PV	S があります	There is ~.
	other things, NV	S がありません	There is no (-e, -en). ~.
	location: human, animal	S は～にいます	S is ~.
	location: other	S は～にあります	S is located ~.
04	verbs (present tense)		
	masu form (MF), PV	S は V ます	S makes ~.
	masu form (MF), NV	S は V ません	S does not do.
	masu form (MF), Q	S は V ますか	Does S do ~?
05	verbs (preterite)		
	MF, PV	S は V ました	S did do.
	MF, NV	S は V ませんでした	S did not do.
	MF, F	S は V ましたか	Did S do?
	total negation	S は IW も V ませんでした	S did not go at all~.
	spatial movement	～を V(あるく, はしる etc.)	walk, run in / on ~
	completion, PV	S はもう V ました	S has ~ already ~.
	completion, NV	S はまだ V ません／まだです	S has ~ not yet ~.
	intention of walking	S は V(MF)に行きます	S is going to do ~.
	Iinvitation to activities	V ませんか	Shall we ~?
06	adjectives (past tense)		
	IA, predicative, PV	S は IA かったです	S was IA.
	IA, predicative, NV	S は IA くなかったです	S was not IA.
	NA, predicative, PV	S は NA でした	S was NA.
	NA, predicative, NV	S は NA ではありませんでした	S was not NA.
	adverbial form: IA	IA く V ます	IA＋V
	adverbial form: NA	NA に V ます	NA＋V
	comparative	S は T より～です	S is ~er than T.
	comparative (question and answer)	S と T と(では)、どちらのほうが～ですか。S のほうが～です。	What is ~er, S or T?

	not as ~ as	S は T ほど～ないです。	S is ~er.
	just as ~ as	S は T とおなじぐらい～です。	S is not as ~ as T.
	superlative	S は～の中で一ばん～です	S is just as ~ as T.
	superlative (question and answer)	～の中で、FW が一ばん～ですか	S is ~most in ~.
07	Te form 1	V て	
	request form	ください	Please ~!
	progressive form	S は V ています	S is doing ~ right now.
	state form	S は V ています	S is open. (e.g.)
	regular action (NPF)	S は V ています	make ~ regularly
	sentence connection	S は～て，～て，～ます	S makes ~, ~ and ~.
	justification	S は～ので、～／S はから、～	~ because S ~.
	introduction	～が、～	As far as ~ is concerned, ~
08	Te form 2	V て	
	permission	V ても-いいです／かまいません	may
	prohibition	V てはいけません	not allowed
	nai form (Nai-F)	V ない	negation (NPF)
	negative request	V ないでください	Please do not ~
	require	V ないといけません V なければなりません V なければいけません V なくてはなりません	must
	no requirement	V なくてもいいです	do not have to
	negative compound sentence	V ないで，～	not ~, but ~ / without ~
09	non-polite forms, NPF		
	V: PS, PV (BF)	S は V(r)u	S does ~.
	V: PS, NV (Nai-F)	S は V ない	S does not do.
	V: PT, PV (Ta-F)	S は V た	S has ~ done.
	V: PT, NV (Nakatta-F)	S は V なかった	S has ~ not done.
	IA: PS, PV (BF)	S は IA い	S is IA.
	IA: PS, NV (Nai-F)	S は IA くない	S is not IA.
	IA: PT, PV (Ta-F)	S は IA かった。	S was IA.
	IA: PT, NV (Nakatta-F)	S は IA くなかった	S was not IA.
	NA: PS, PV (BF)	S は NA だ	S is NA.
	NA: PS, NV (Nai-F)	S は NA ではない	S is not NA.
	NA: PT, PV (Ta-F)	S は NA だった	S was NA.
	NA: PT, NV (Nakatta-F)	S は NA ではなかった	S was not NA.
	N: PS, PV (BF)	S は N だ	S is N.
	N: PS, NV (Nai-F)	S は N ではない	S is not N.
	N: PT, PV (Ta-F)	S に N だった	S was N.
	N: PT, NV (Nakatta-F)	S に N ではなかった	S was not S was A. N.
	Recommendation	V たほうがいい V ないほうがいい	it is better to do it is not better to do
	Enumeration of actions	V たり、V たりする	sometimes ~, sometimes ~
10	Wa Ga Form 1		
	ability (to be able)	S は O ができる	S can do.
	ability (to be skillful)	S は O がじょうずだ	S can do well ~.
	ability (not being skillful)	S は O がへただ	S can do badly ~.
	strength	S は O がとくいだ	my strength is ~.

	weakness	S は O がにがてだ	my weakness is ~.
	understanding, knowledge	S は O がわかる	S understands ~. S knows ~.
	taste (like)	S は O がすきだ	S likes ~.
	taste (dislike)	S は O がきらいだ	S does not like ~.
	expression of desire 1	S は O がほしい	S wants t to have ~.
	expression of desire 2	S は O が V たい	S wants to do.
	third person wish 1	S は O をほしがっている	She/he wants to have ~.
	third person's wish 2	S は O を V たがっている	She/he wants to do.
	request	V(SoMF)ましょう	Let's ~!
	willingness (assistance)	V(SoMF)ましょうか	Shall I ~?
11	Wa Ga Form 2		
	property	S は O がある／いる	S has ~.
	property description	S は O が A だ	As regards S, O is ~.
	experience	S は O を V(Ta-F)ことがある	S has done ~ once.
	occurrence	S は O を V(BF)ことがある	It happens that ~
	NPF-n-desu Form	S は～ん(の)だ	S does ~, S is ~.
12	Temporal: simultaneity 1	～とき、～	~, when ~ / ~, when ~
	simultaneity 2	～あいだ(に)、～	~, during ~ / ~, while ~
	simultaneity 3	V(MF)ながら、～	~, while ~
	simultaneity 4	V た(Ta-F)まま、～	under a state ~ make
	before tense	V(BF)まえ(に)、～	before ~
	after tense	V(Ta-F)あと(で)、～	after ~
13	literal speech		
	direct speech	「～」と S はいった	S said, " ~. ".
	indirect speech	～(NPF)と S はいった	S said that ~.
	attributive use	～という N	N, which is called ~
	general statement	S は～という	People say that ~
	expression of opinion	S は～とおもう	S think that ~
14	expression of will		
	intention	V(BF)つもりだ	S intends / wants
	imagination	V(Ta-F)つもりだ	S imagines that ~
	invitation (familiar form)	V(y)oo.	Let's ~!
	intention	V(y)oo とおもっている	S has an intention, ~
	decision	V(BF)ことにする	S decides
	determination	V(BF)ことになる	to be decided / determined
	rule	V(BF)ことになっている	A state is regulated,
15	attributive clause	Sentence (NPF)-N は～ S は sentence (NPF)-N を～ S は sentence (NPF)-N だ	N, which ~, is ~ S do ~ N, which ~ S is N, which ~
	indirect question with a QW	S が QW～(NPF)か、～	MC, what/who/where/when ~
	indirect question with whether ~	S が～(NPF)かどうか、～	MC, whether ~

Vocabulary index (Japanese – English)

Vocabulary (Roomaji) / Japanese / English / Lesson

* IImportant vocabulary for beginners is also listed as a supplement without having been used in a lesson.

A

aa ああ ach 2
abunai 危ない dangerous 12
achira あちら the person over there 1
ageru あげる lift up, give as a gift
aida 間 between 3, while 12
aisatsu あいさつ greeting 1
aji 味 flavour
akachan 赤ちゃん baby 11
akai 赤い red 13
akarui 明るい light 7
akeru 開ける open, open up 8
aki 秋 autumn 6
akihabara 秋葉原 Akihabara (city district of Tokyo) 7
aku 開く open, open 7
amaimono 甘いもの sweets 10
amari ~ masen あまり～ません not so 2
ame, - ga furu 雨、〜が降る rain, raining 7
amerika-jin アメリカ人 American 1
an'nai(suru) 案内(する) lead, show 10
anata あなた you, you 1
anatagata あなたがた, anatatachi あなたたち you 1
ane 姉 older sister (own) 3
ani 兄 older brother (own) 3
ano あの sono その the＋noun over there 1
aoi 青い blue 11
apaato アパート flat 2
aranami 荒波 high, wild wave 15
arau 洗う wash 12
are あれ that over there 1
arigatoo gozaimasu ありがとうございます Thank you! 1
arita-yaki 有田焼き Arita-porcelain 14
aru ある there is (for objects) 3
arubaito(suru) アルバイト(する) jobbing 12
aruite 歩いて on foot 4
aruku 歩く to walk 4
asa 朝 morning, in the morning 4
asagohan 朝ご飯 breakfast 4
asatte 明後日 the day after tomorrow
ashi 足 leg, foot
ashita, asu 明日 tomorrow 5
asobu 遊ぶ play 12
asoko あそこ there, over there 1
atama 頭 head 11
atarashii 新しい new 2
atatakai 暖かい warm 15
ato de 後で later 6
ato de ～後で after ~ 12
atsui 暑い hot 6
au ～に会う~ meet 5

B

baiten 売店 kiosk 7
ban 晩 evening, evening 4
bangohan 晩ご飯 dinner 4
bara ばら rose 1
bareebooru バレーボール volleyball 10
basu バス bus 4
basu-tei バス停 bus stop 7
bataa バター butter
benkyoo(suru) 勉強(する)learn 4
benri-na 便利な practical 2
bentoo 弁当 packed lunch , bento10
bideo ビデオ video, video camera 1
biru ビル building 15
biiru ビール beer 4
bijinga 美人画 pictures of beautiful women 15
bijutsukan 美術館 art museum 7
boku ぼく me (male) 2
boorupen ボールペン ballpoint pen 1
booshi 帽子 hat, cap, ~ o kaburu 〜を被る put on hat 13
botan ボタン button
buchoo 部長 head of department 8
buji 無事 without problem 15
bunka 文化 culture 14
bunka-kooryuu 文化交流 cultural exchange 14
bunpoo 文法 grammar 9
butaniku 豚肉 pork 7
byooin 病院 hospital, doctor's office 3
byooki 病気 sick, illness 11

C

chanto ちゃんと correct, neat 12
chairo 茶色 brown
chawan 茶碗 rice bowl
chichi 父 one's own father 3
chigau 違う different, wrong
chiisai 小さい small 2
chijin 知人 acquaintance 11
chikai 近い close, nearby 2
chikaku ni 近くに nearby (with a verb) 3
chikara 力 power, strengh11
chikara-zuyoi 力強い powerful 15
chikatetsu 地下鉄 subway 7
chizu 地図 map, city map 12
choodo ちょうど exact, straight
chotto ちょっと a little bit 4
~chuu ～中 just about to, kaigichuu 会議中 just be in the meeting
chuugakkoo 中学校 middle school 3
chuugoku-jin 中国人 Chinese (person) 1
chuui(suru) 注意(する) watch out, take care
chuuoo-eki 中央駅 main station 7
chuushin 中心 center 11
chuushi(suru) 中止(する) stop, cancel 14

D

dai 台 counting word for machine, device, car 3
daibutsu 大仏 large Buddha statue 6
daidokoro 台所 kitchen 3
daigaku 大学 university 1
daijoobu だいじょうぶ it works, no problem 9

dai-kazoku 大家族 large family 3
daitai だいたい almost, approximately
dai-suki(na) 大好き(な) like very much 10
dakara だから therefore
dake だけ only 3
dame(na) だめ(な) bad, it doesn't work 13
dandan だんだん gradually
dansu (o suru) ダンス(をする) dance, to dance 10
dare だれ who 1
dareka だれか anyone 5
dare mo ~ nai, だれも〜ません(ない) nobody ~ 3
dare no だれの whose 1
thatu 出す take out 12, hand in, send off
de で AP for the remedy, AP for the place of action 4
deguchi 出口 exit 7
dekakeru 出かける go out, go away 5
dekiru 1 できる can 10
dekiru 2 できる to make ready, to create 12
demo でも but (for two sets) 2
denki 電気 light, current, electricity 7
denki ga tsuku 電気が点く The light goes on. 7
denki o tsukeru 電気を点ける turn on the light 7
densha 電車 train, train 1
denwa 電話 telephone 3
denwa o suru / kakeru 電話をする・かける to call, make a phone call 12
denwa-bangoo 電話番号 phone number 3
depaato デパート department store 3
deru 〜を出る to go out, to leave 4
deru 〜に出る to appear 15
desukara ですから therefore 4
dete iru 出ている stand (in the newspaper) 15
dete-iku 出て行く go out 12
dewa では therefore
dochira どちら which 1
doitsu ドイツ Germany 1
doitsujin ドイツ人 German 1
doko どこ where 1
dokoka どこか somewhere 5
doko nimo ~ nai どこにも〜ない nowhere 5
dokusho(suru) 読書(する) read books 12
donata どなた who = dare 1
don'na どんな what for, which (question about the property) 2
dono どの which 1
donogurai どのぐらい how much 4
doo どう how 2
doo itashimashite どういたしまして You're welcome! 7
doobutsu 動物 animal 6
doobutsuen 動物園 zoo 7
doomo どうも very much, thank you! 1
dore どれ which 1
dooryoo 同僚 colleague 11
dooshite どうして why 7
doozo yoroshiku どうぞよろしく very pleasant! 1
doraibu(suru) ドライブ(する) take a ride 9
doyoobi 土曜日 Saturday 3

E

e o kaku 絵を描く draw 10
earobikusu エアロビクス aerobics 10
eberesuto-san エベレスト山 Mountain Everest 6
edojidai 江戸時代 Edo time 15
ee ええ yes 2
eiga 映画 movie 5
eigo 英語 English 1
eikyoo o ataeru 影響をあたえる exerting influence 14
eki 駅 station 2
eki'in 駅員 railway employee 7
ekimae 駅前 in front of the station 5
en 円 yen, district 7
enjin, ~ o kakeru エンジン、〜をかける engine, ~ start 12
enki 延期(する) displacement, displace 14
enpitsu 鉛筆 pencil 1

F

fakkusu ファックス fax 1
fooku フォーク fork
fuben-na 不便な impractical 2
fueru 増える increase
Fugaku-36-kei 富嶽三十六景 36 Ukiyoe pictures of the Mount Fuji by Hokusai 15
fuirumu フイルム film
fuji-san 富士山 Mt. Fuji 1
fukai 深い deep
fuku 服 clothes, dresses 9
fuku 吹く blow
fun 分 minute 4
fune 船 ship 5
furansu/~go フランス・〜語 France, French 6
furo ふろ bath, bathroom 3
furui 古い old 2
futoi 太い thick (for long things)
futsuu 普通 normal
fuukei 風景 landscape 15
fuutoo 封筒 envelope
fuuzoku 風俗 custom 15
fuyu 冬 winter 6

G

ga 1 が 1 but 2
ga が AP for the subject 3
gaikoku 外国 foreign country 5
gaikokugo 外国語 foreign language 10
gaishutsu(suru) 外出(する) go out 8
gakkoo 学校 school 2
gakusei 学生 student 1
ganbaru がんばる to make an effort 9
gasorin ガソリン gasoline 12
gatsu 〜月 name of the month
gawa: migigawa, hidarigara 側:右側、左側 side : right side, left side
geemu ゲーム game 8
geijutsu-hin 芸術品 work of art 14
genkan 玄関 entrance hallway
genki-na 元気な healthy 2
getsuyoobi 月曜日 Monday 3
gijutsu 技術 technique

gin 銀 silver 6
ginkoo 銀行 bank 9
ginza 銀座 Ginza (district of Tokyo) 15
gitaa ギター guitar 12
gitaa o hiku ギターを弾く Guitar playing 10
go-ban 5番 number 5 7
gochisoosama ごちそうさま It tasted good. 13
gogo 午後 in the afternoon 4
gohan ご飯 food, rice 4
gomenkudasai ごめんください greeting during a visit
gomi ごみ garbage 8
goro ころ approximately (only for time) 4
go-shujin ご主人 husband of the other person
gozen 午前 in the morning 4
gurai ～ぐらい ~ something like that 10
gurai, kurai ぐらい、くらい about 4
gyuuniku 牛肉 beef 7
gyuunyuu 牛乳 cow's milk 4

H

ha, ~ o migaku 歯、～をみがく tooth, brushing teeth 12
hachi-banme 8番目 the eighth 7
hachi-gatsu 8月 August 6
hagaki はがき postcard 7
haha 母 Your own mother 3
hai, はい, yes 1
hai 杯 counting word for cup with contents 3
hairu 入る inside 7
haisha 歯医者 dentist 9
hajimaru 始まる start
hajime 始め beginning 6
hajimemashite はじめまして Hello! (only when getting to know each other) 1
hajimeru 始める start ~ 8
hajimete 初めて for the first time
hakkiri はっきり clearly
hako 箱 box, crate
hakobu 運ぶ carry, transport 12
haku はく put on (pants, shoes, socks)
hakubutsukan 博物館 museum
han 半 half (time) hanbun 半分 half 4
hana 花 flower 1
hana 鼻 nose 11
hanami 花見 view of the cherry blossoms 9
hanasu 話す speak 5
hanbun 半分 half
hantai(suru) 反対(する) be against it
harau, okane o ~ 払う、お金を pay, pay money 8
hare 晴 nice weather 11
hareru 晴れる become more cheerful, clean up 7
haru 春 spring 6
hashi 橋 bridge 5
hashi 箸 chopsticks 12
hashiru 走る running, riding 5
hatachi 二十歳 twenty years old
hatake 畑 field
hataraku 働く work 4
hayai 速い fast 2
hayai 早い early, fast 6
hayashi 林 grove, here: Family name 1

hazukashii はずかしい be ashamed of oneself
hee へえ Oh!, Oh!, Yes? 13
hen-na 変な funny, strange 12
heta(na) 下手(な) bad at something, not skilful 10
heya 部屋 room 3
hi 日 day, sun 15
hi 火 fire
hidari 左 left 3
higashi 東 east 6
hiitaa ヒーター heating 12
hijooni 非常に very, extremely
hiki 匹 counting word for animals
hikidashi 引き出し drawer
hikkosu 引っ越す to move
hikoojoo 飛行場 airport
hikooki 飛行機 plane 5
hiku 引く pull
hiku 弾く play an instrument (piano, violin, etc.) 12
hikui 低い low
hima 暇 have free time 9
hiraku 開く open, go up
hiroi 広い large, wide, broad, spacious 11
hiru 昼 noon, midday 4
hiruma 昼間 during the day
hirugohan 昼ご飯 lunch 4
hisashiburi ひさしぶり after a long time, not seen for a long time.
hito 人 human 1
hitobito 人々 people 15
hitori de 一人で alone 5
hitsuyoo(na) 必要(な) necessary
hodo ~ nai ほど～ない not as ~ as 6
hoka ni 他に also 13
hon 本 book 1
hon'ya 本屋 bookshop 5
hondana 本棚 bookshelf 3
hontoo 本当 true, really 12
hoo 方 direction, page 6
hooritsu 法律 law 10
hoshii ほしい ~ want to have 10
hosoi 細い thin 6
hoteru ホテル hotel 9
hotondo ほとんど fast
hotto suru ほっとする be reassured 9

I

ichiban 一番 number 1, here: Word for superlative 6
ichi-nen 一年 one year 6
ie ni kaeru 家に～ go home 4
ie, uchi 家 house, flat 4
igirisu-jin イギリス人 English people 1
ii いい good 2
iie, いいえ, no 1
iie, mada desu いいえ、まだです No, not yet. 5
ikaga いかが like 2
ike 池 pond 14
ikemasen いけません It is not possible, not allowed 8
iki ～行き journey to ~ 15
ikiiki いきいき alive 15
ikikata 行き方 way description 7

ikinuki 息ぬき relaxation 9
iku 行く walking, driving 4
ikutsu いくつ how much, how many pieces (countable) 3
ikura いくら how much, how expensive (quantity, volume) 7
ima 今 now 3
ima 居間 living room 11
imi 意味 meaning 15
imooto 妹 younger sister 3
inrain-sukeeto インライン・スケート inline skate 10
inshooteki-na 印象的な impressive 15
inu 犬 dog 3
irasshaimase いらっしゃいませ Welcome! 13
ireru 入れる enter 8
iriguchi 入(り)口 input 7
iro 色 colour
iroiro(na) いろいろ(な) different 15
iru いる are located (for humans and animals) 3
iru 要る need
isha 医者 doctor 8
isogashii 忙しい busy 6
isogu 急ぐ hurry up
issho ni いっしょに together 5
isshookenmei 一生懸命 with full power
isu いす chair 3
itadakimasu いただきます Enjoy your meal! 13
itariago イタリア語 Italian 10
itte mairimasu 行ってまいります greeting from the person leaving the house
itte rasshai 行ってらっしゃい greeting from the person staying in the house
itsu いつ when 5
itsuka いつか sometime
itsumo いつも always 4
itte mairimasu いってまいります greeting the person leaving home 13
iu 言う say 8
iya(na) いやな unpleasant
iya いや no (CF) 9

J

jaa じゃあ well then 5
ji ～時 ～ clock 4
jibiki 字引き dictionary 11
jibun 自分 yourself, yourself
jidai 時代 time, age 14
jidoosha 自動車 car = kuruma 車 2
jikan 時間 time, hour 4
jikka 実家 parent's house 12
jimusho 事務所 office 15
jinja 神社 shrine
jishin 地震 earthquake
jisho 辞書 dictionary 3
jissai ni 実際に in fact, really 14
jisshi 実施(する) perform, carry out 14
jitensha 自転車 bicycle 4
jiyuu(na) 自由(な) free
jogingu ジョギング jogging 10
joodan 冗談 joke 12

joobu(na) 丈夫(な) stable
joozu(na) 上手(な) be good at, skillful 10
juudoo 柔道 judo 10
juusho 住所 address
juusu ジュース juice 4

K

ka か AP for the question, question mark
ka na / kai ～かな・～かい question mark 12
kaban かばん pocket 3
kabe 壁 wall
kabin 花びん vase
kabuki 歌舞伎 kabuki/theater
kaburu かぶる put on a hat 13
kachoo 課長 head of the small department 9
kado 角 corner
kaeru 帰る return 4
kaeru 変える change 14
kaesu 返す return 10
kagetsu ～か月 months 3
kagi 鍵 key 7
kagi o kakeru 鍵を掛ける lock 8
kago かご basket 12
kai ～回 ～ time 11
kaidan 階段 stairs
kaigi 会議 conference, session 12
kaimono(suru) 買い物(する) purchase, shopping 4
kaisha 会社 company 1
kaishain 会社員 company employee 1
kaiwa 会話 conversation, dialog 12
kaji 火事 fire, conflagration
kakaru かかる it takes 4
kakeru かける hang up, carry 15
kaku 書く write 5
kaku / egaku 描く drawing, labeling 15
camera カメラ camera 1
kami 紙 paper 3
kami 髪 hair 11
kana 仮名 kana (hiragana and katakana) 5
kanari かなり quite 9
kangae 考え idea, thought 11
kangaeru 考える think, consider 15
kangoshi 看護士 nurse10
kanji 漢字 kanji (Chinese characters) 5
kankei 関係 relationship
kanojo 彼女 she (singular), kanojotachi 彼女たち,
kanojora 彼女ら they 1
kantan-na 簡単な simple 6
kao 顔 face 11
kara から from 4
kara ～から because ～ 7
karada 体 body
karai 辛い sharp
kare 彼 he 1
karera 彼ら, karetachi 彼たち they 1
karendaa カレンダー calendar
kariru 借りる borrow something from someone 5
karui 軽い light 6
kasa 傘 umbrella 7
kasu 貸す borrow something 10

kata 方 person, person
katazukeru 片付ける tidy up 10
katsu 勝つ win
kau 買う ~ buy 4
kawa 川 river 1
kawaii かわいい cute, sweet 9
kawaru 変わる change
kayoobi 火曜日 Tuesday 3
kaze 風 wind 12
kaze o hiku 風邪を引く catching a cold 12
kazoku 家族 family 3
ke(re)do け(れ)ど although, preliminary word 9
keeki ケーキ cake 7
keikaku 計画 plan 14
keisan 計算(する) calculate 10
keisatsu 警察 police, policeman 12
keitai-denwa 携帯電話 mobile phone 12
keizai 経済 economy 10
kekkon(suru) 結婚(する) marriage, marry 7
kekkoo けっこう quite, good 9
kenbutsu(suru) 見物(する) visit 12
kengaku(suru) 見学(する) visit 12
kesa 今朝 this morning
keshiki 景色 landscape 12
kesu 消す turn off, extinguish 7
ki 木 tree 1
kiboo 希望 wish, hope 11
kieru 消える go out (light, fire), disappear 7
kiiroi 黄色い yellow
kikai 機械 machine 7
kiken-na 危険な dangerous 12
kiku 聞く listen, ask 4
kimaru 決まる be determined
kimeru 決める decide
kimi 君 you
kimono 着物 kimono (traditional Japanese dress) 6
kin 金 gold 6
kinoo / sakujitsu 昨日 yesterday 5
kin'yoobi 金曜日 Friday 3
kippu 切符 ticket 7
kirai(na) 嫌い(な) do not like 10
kirei(na) きれい(な) beautiful, clean 2
kiru 着る dress 8
kiru 切る cut
kisetsu 季節 seasons 6
kissaten 喫茶店 cafè 5
kita 北 northern 6
kitai(suru) 期待(する) expectation, expect 14
kitanai きたない dirty 9
kitte 切手 stamp 5
kitto きっと determined
ko 子 child 15
koara コアラ koala bear 11
kobune 小船 small boat 15
kochira こちら here, this person 1
kochira koso こちらこそ Same here! 1
kodomo 子供 child 3
koe 声 voice
koibito 恋人 lover 11

koko ここ here 1
kokyoo 故郷 home town 11
kome 米 rice
komu 混む be full
konban 今晩 this evening 13
kondo 今度 this time, in the near future 5
kongetsu 今月 this month 15
kon'na こんな such
Kon'nichiwa! こんにちは Good day! 2
kono この this＋noun 1
kono aida この間 a few days ago 9
konpyuuta コンピュータ computer 1
konsaato コンサート concert 5
konshuu 今週 this week 6
kooban 交番 police station
kooen 公園 park 3
koogyoo 工業 industry
koocha 紅茶 black tea 4
koohii コーヒー coffee 4
koojoo 工場 factory 14
koora コーラ cola 10
koori 氷 ice 6
koosaten 交差点 crossing 5
koosu コース course 14
kooto コート coat 12
koppu コップ glass, cup 7
kore これ this 1
korekara これから from now on15
kotae 答 answer 8
kotaeru 答える answer 8
kotoba ことば word, language
kotoshi 今年 this year
kowai こわい be afraid
kowareru 壊れる break / be broken
kuchi 口 mouth
kudamono 果物 fruit 4
kudasai ください Please give me ~! 7
kumo 雲 cloud
kumori 曇 be cloudy 11
kuni 国 land 6
kurai 暗い dark 7
kurasikku クラシック classical music 10
kurasu クラス class 6
kurasu-meeto クラスメート classmates 11
kureru くれる ~ give to me/us
kuroi 黒い black 11
kuru 来る come 4
kuruma 車 car 1
kusuri 薬 medicine 8
kutsu 靴 shoes 5
kutsushita 靴下 socks 5
kuuraa, ~ o tsukeru クーラー、~をつける air
conditioning, ~ turn on 12
kyanpu キャンプ camping 11
kyonen 去年 last year
kyoo 今日 today 3
kyoodai 兄弟 brothers, siblings 9
kyooju 教授 professor 9
kyookasho 教科書 textbook 5
kyoomi, ~ni kyoomi ga aru 興味、～に興味がある

interest, be interested in ~ 14
kyoomi-bukai 興味深い interesting 14
kyooshitsu 教室 classroom 3
kyooto 京都 Kyoto (city) 6

M

machi 町 city 2
machigaeru 間違える make mistakes, be wrong
mada まだ still 5
made まで to 4
mado 窓 window 8
mae 前 before 3
mae ni ～前に before ~ 12
magaru 曲がる turn 7
maguro まぐろ tuna 13
mai 枚 counting word for flat things
maiban 毎晩 every evening
mainichi 毎日 every day 8
maitoshi 毎年 every year
maitsuki 毎月 every month
Maisen マイセン Meissen 14
maishuu 毎週 every week
makeru 負ける lose (game, competition)
mama ～まま so leaving 12
mamoru 守る protect, defend
man 万 ten thousand
man'naka まん中 whole center
man'nenhitsu 万年筆 fountain pen 8
marui 丸い round
masaka まさか my goodness! 12
massugu まっすぐ straight 7
mata また again
matsu 待つ wait 7
matsuri 祭 firm
mazu まず first 7
mazui まずい taste bad, not good 9
me 目 eye 11
megane めがね glasses 15
meishi 名刺 business card 1
mettani ~ nai めったに～ない seldom 11
mezurashii 珍しい rare
michi 道 street 5
midokoro 見所 sightseeing 11
midori 緑 green
mieru 見える be visible, be able to see
migaku 磨く polish 12
migi 右 right 3
mihonichi 見本市 fair 13
mijikai 短い short 11
mikan みかん tangerine 4
mimi 耳 ear 11
minami 南 south 6
minasan 皆さん everyone / ladies and gentlemen
min'na みんな all 4
miru 見る see 4
miruku ミルク milk 4
mise 店 business 14
show miseru 見せる
miso 味噌 miso paste 11
miso-shiru 味噌汁 miso soup 4

mittsu 三つ three, three pieces 3
mitsukeru 見つける find
miyako 都 capital (old name) 6
mizu 水 water 4
mizu'umi 湖 lake
mo も also 1
mochiron もちろん of course 10
mokuyoobi 木曜日 Thursday 3
mon 門 gate
mondai 問題 question, task, problem 9
mono / no もの・～の thing 15
moo もう already 5
moo hitotsu もう一つ one more 1
moo ichido もう一度 one more time
morau もらう get 9
mori 森 forest, here: family name 1
moshi moshi もしもし Hello? (on the phone)
motomoto もともと originally 15
motsu 持つ carry, have 7
motteiku 持って行く take along (items) 7
mottekuru 持って来る bring along (items) 7
motto もっと more 6
mukai むかい opposite 3
mukae ni iku 迎えに行く go to pick up 9
mukoo 向こう over there
mura 村 village 6
musuko 息子 son 10
musume 娘 daughter 10
muzukashii 難しい difficult 6
mynhen ミュンヘン Munich 9

N

na な AP for desire and emotion 10
nado 等 etc. 10
nagai 長い long 3
nagai aida 長い間 long time 15
nagano-shi, -ken 長野市・県 Nagano city, Nagano prefecture 11
nagara ～ながら during ~ 12
naifu ナイフ knife
naka 中 in, inside 3
naka demo 中でも underneath 15
naku 泣く cry, weep
naku 鳴く the verb of animal voices
namae 名前 name 1
nan / nani 何 what 1
Nan datte? 何だって？ what? 12
nan demo 何でも everything, whatever 14
nan no 何の what kind of (question about the variety) 1
nan-ji 何時 what time 4
nani ka 何か something 13
nabi mo ~ maseen (nai) 何も～ない nothing ~ 3
nan-kai 何回 how often ~? 7
nara 奈良 Nara (city) 6
naraberu 並べる put next to each other
narabu 並ぶ stand next to each other
narau 習う learn (from a teacher) 7
nareru 慣れる get used to
naru なる become 6
narubeku なるべく as possible

natsu 夏 summer 6
natsuyasumi 夏休み summer vacation
naze なぜ why
ne ね isn't it? 2
nedan 値段 price 8
neko 猫 cat 3
nekutai ネクタイ tie 8
nemui 眠い tired, sleepy 12
nen 年 year(s) 3
neru 寝る sleep, go to bed 4
netsu 熱 fever
ni に AP for place, time and destination 3, 4
nichi-doku 日独 Japanese-German 14
nichiyoobi 日曜日 Sunday 3
nigate(na) 苦手(な) weakness 10
nigiyaka-na にぎやかな animated, active 6
nihon 日本 Japan 6
nihongo 日本語 Japanese person1
nihon-jin 日本人 Japanese people 1
nihon-ryoori 日本料理 Japanese food 5
nihonsei 日本製 made in Japan
niku 肉 meat 10
nimotsu 荷物 luggage, package 12
ningyoo 人形 doll 10
ninki 人気 popularity, be popular 9
nishi 西 west 6
niwa 庭 garden 3
noboru 登る climb 11
node ～ので because ~ 7
nomimono 飲み物 drinks 4
nomu 飲む drink 4
nonbiri-suru のんびりする live quietly 14
nooto ノート issue 3
norikaeru 乗り変える change 7
norimono 乗り物 means of transportation 6
noru 乗る get on, take a means of transportation 7
nugu 脱ぐ take off clothes
nyuugaku(suru) 入学(する) enter the school
nyuusu ニュース news

O

o を AP for the direct object 4
o- お polite prefix for nouns 2
oba, obasan おばさん aunt, somewhat older woman 13
obaasan おばあさん grandmother, old woman 13
oboeru 覚える memorize, learn by heart 9
o-bon お盆 Bon festival in August 11
ocha お茶 tea 4
o-cha o ireru お茶を入れる serving tea 10
ochiru 落ちる fall
odoru 踊る dance 5
ohayoo おはよう Good morning! 13
oishii おいしい delicious, tasty 6
oji, ojisan おじさん uncle, somewhat older man 13
ojiisan おじいいさん grandfather, old man 13
okaasan お母さん mother 3
okaerinasai お帰りなさい greeting of the person who receives those who have returned
o-kane お金 money 7
okashi お菓子 sweets 4

okashii おかしい funny, comical
okiru 起きる get up (out of bed) 4
oku 置く lay down, place
okuru 送る send
oku 奥 behind in a room, inside, depth 3
okusan 奥さん wife of the other man 6
o-kyaku(san) お客(さん) guest, customer 13
omedetoo おめでとう Congratulations! 9
omocha おもちゃ toy 10
omoi 重い heavy (weight) 6
omoshiroi おもしろい interesting 6
omou 思う mean, think, believe 13
onaji 同じ same 6
onaji gurai ～と同じぐらい just as ~ as 6
onaka ga suku お腹がすく be hungry
oneesan お姉さん older sister of other 3
o-negai-shimasu お願いします I kindly ask you. 10
ongaku 音楽 music 4
oniisan お兄さん older brother of others 3
on'na 女 woman 1
on'na no hito 女の人 woman (polite)1
ooi 多い a lot 6
ookii 大きい big 2
orinpikku オリンピック Olympics 14
oriru 降りる get out 7
osake お酒 sake, rice wine 4
oshieru 教える teach, instruct 7
osoi 遅い late, slow 13
osu 押す push, shove
o-tanjoobi omedetoo お誕生日おめでとう Happy birthday! 13
otearai お手洗い toilet / washroom
o-tera (お)寺 temple 11
oto 音 noise 12
otoko 男 man 1
otoko no hito 男の人 man (polite) 1
otona 大人 adult
otoosan お父さん father of others, call name 3
otooto 弟 younger brother 3
ototoi おととい the day before yesterday
ototoshi 一昨年 year before last
otozureru 訪れる visit 11
otsuri お釣り change 7
owari 終り end 15
owaru 終わる to end 9
oyasumi(nasai) おやすみ(なさい) Good night! 13
oyogu 泳ぐ swim 5

P

paatii パーティー party 6
pan パン bread 4
pekin 北京 ペキン Peking 15
pen ペン fountain pen, pen 7
pinpon ピンポン table tennis 10
pittsa ピッツァ pizza 9
poketto ポケット pocket
puuru プール swimming pool 11

R

raigetsu 来月 next month 10
rainen 来年 next year
raishuu 来週 next week 10
rajio ラジオ radio 7
rekishi 歴史 history 10
rei 例 example
rei 零 zero
reizooko 冷蔵庫 refrigerator
renraku(suru) 連絡(する) get in touch with ~ 13
renshuu(suru) 練習(する) practice, practise 1
repooto レポート report 14
resutoran レストラン restaurant 7
ringo りんご apple 4
rippa 立派 excellent, very good 13
riyoo(suru) 利用(する) use, utilise
riyuu 理由 reason
rooka 廊下 corridor 8
rooma ローマ Rome 12
roomaji ローマ字 Latin characters 8
roshia ロシア Russia 6
ryokoo(suru) 旅行(する) journey, travelling 6
ryoohoo(tomo) 両方(とも) both
ryoori(suru) 料理(する) cooking, cook 5
ryuugaku(suru) 留学(する) study abroad, ~ do 11
ryuugakusei 留学生 student abroad 11

S

saa さあ now
sai 才 ~years old
saikin 最近 lately
saga-ken 佐賀県 Saga prefecture in Kyushu 14
sagasu 探す search , look for ~
saifu 財布 wallet
sakana 魚 fish 9
sake 酒 japanese rice wine
sakkaa サッカー football 6
saku 咲く bloom 7
sakubun 作文 essay 10
sakura 桜 cherry tree, cherry blossom 1
samui 寒い cold (only with climate) 6
san ～さん Mr ~ Mrs ~ (name suffix) 1
sanchi 産地 place of production 14
sanka(suru) 参加(する) participation, participate 14
sanpo(suru) 散歩(する) walk, go for a walk 5
sara 皿 plate
sarainen 再来年 year after next
satoo 砂糖 さとう sugar 8
satsu 冊 counting word for books
sayoonara さようなら Goodbye! 8
se 背 height 11
sebiro 背広 suit 15
seetaa セーター sweater 8
seifuku 制服 uniform 12
seiji 政治 politics 10
seikatsu 生活 life 15
sekken せっけん soap
seikoo 成功(する) success, ~ have 14
seiseki 成績 achievement, censorship 9
seito 生徒 student 1

sekai 世界 world 6
seki 席 table, place, seat 8
semai 狭い narrow
sengetsu 先月 last month 13
sensei 先生 teacher 1
senshuu 先週 last week 6
sensoo 戦争 war
sentaku(suru) 洗濯(する) washing clothes 7
setsumei(suru) 説明(する) explanation, explain 7
shachoo 社長 company director 9
shain 社員 employee 9
sharaku 写楽 Sharaku, an Ukiyoe master 15
shashin 写真 photo
shashin o toru 写真を撮る take a photo 10
shawaa シャワー shower 3, ~ o abiru ～を浴びる take a shower
shi 詩 poem 10
shigoto 仕事 work 5
shii-dii CD 5
shika しか only 3
shikashi しかし but
shiken 試験 examination 6
shima 島 island
shimaru 閉まる close, shut 7
shimeru 閉める close, shut 8
shinbun 新聞 newspaper 1
shingoo 信号 traffic light 13
shinjuku 新宿 Shinjuku: district of Tokyo 13
shinkansen 新幹線 Shinkansen (jap. bullet train) 13
shinsen-na 新鮮な fresh 12
shinsetsu-na 親切な nice 6
shinshuu 信州 Shinshuu (central area of Japan) 11
shinu 死ぬ die 7
shio 塩 salt 9
shiraberu 調べる examine, look up 14
shiriau 知り合う get to know 1
shiroi 白い white 11
shiru 知る know, know 7
shita 下 under, below 3
shitsumon(suru) 質問(する) question, ask 8
shizuka-na 静かな calm 2
shokudoo 食堂 dining room, restaurant 14
shokuji 食事 food, meal 12
shoogakkoo 小学校 primary school 2
shoogatsu 正月 New Year 11
shoorai 将来 future
shoosetsu 小説 novel 12
shooyu しょうゆ soy sauce
shujin 主人 husband
shukudai 宿題 homework 5
shumi 趣味 hobby
shuu 週 week 3
shuumatsu 週末 weekend 5
shuuri(suru) 修理(する) repair, fix 10
soba 蕎麦 buckwheat noodles 9
soba そば in the near neighbourhood
sobo 祖母 grandmother (own) 13
sochira そちら the person with you 1
sofaa ソファー sofa 3
sofu 祖父 grandfather (own) 13

soko そこ da (with you) 1
son'na そんな such
sono その the＋noun with you 1
soo そう so 1
soo desu ka そうですか That's right! 3
soo shimasu そうします I will do that. 7
soodan(suru) 相談(する) discuss, talk about 8
sooji(suru) 掃除(する) clean up 7
sora 空 sky 5
sore それ it 1
sorede それで and, and then 11
soredewa それでは so 8
sorekara それから and, then 3
sorosoro そろそろ slowly
soshite そして and (for two sentences) 2
soto 外 outside, outside 12
subarashii すばらしい wonderful 15
sugi 〜過ぎ shortly after 〜 (time) 4
sugoi すごい great, super 13
sugu すぐ immediately 12
suiei 水泳 swimming 10
suiyoobi 水曜日 Wednesday 3
suki(na) 好き(な) like, favorite 10
sukii スキー ski 10
sukiyaki すきやき sukiyaki, one-pot dish 15
sukoshi 少し a little 6
sukunai 少ない a little 6
sumaseru すませる finish 14
sumi 角 inside corner
sumimasen すみません Excuse me! 7
sumu 住む live 7
supagettii スパゲティー spaghetti 9
supootsu スポーツ sports 7
supootsu-man スポーツマン sportsman 10
suppai すっぱい sour
surippa スリッパ slippers
suru する to make, to do 4
supuun スプーン spoon
sushi 寿司 sushi 5
sutereo ステレオ stereo system 1
suteru 捨てる throw away 8
suugaku 数学 mathematics arithmetic 10
suupaa スーパー supermarket 2
suwaru 座る sit down 8
suzushii 涼しい (pleasant) cool 12

T

ta 田 rice paddy 1
tabako o suu たばこを吸う smoke a cigarette 8
tabemono 食べ物 food 11
taberu 食べる eat 4
tabun たぶん probably
tadaima ただいま Hello (greeting those returning home) 13
tadashii 正しい correct 9
taihen たいへん very 2, strenuous, serious 9
taisetsu(na) 大切(な) important
taishikan 大使館 embassy 12
taitei たいてい mostly 10
taizai 滞在(する) stay, stay 14

takai 高い expensive, high 2
takusan たくさん a lot (with verbs) 9
takushii タクシー taxi, cab 8
tamago 卵 egg 4
tanjoobi 誕生日 birthday 13
tana 棚 shelf
tanoshii 楽しい funny, cheerful 6
tanoshimi desu 楽しみです look forward to 14
tatemono 建物 building 9
tateru 建てる build 14
tatoeba たとえば for example 15
tatsu 立つ stand, get up (e.g. from a chair) 8
te 手 hand
techoo 手帳 notebook 7
teeburu テーブル table
teema テーマ theme 14
tegami 手紙 letter 7
ten'in 店員 salesperson 6
tenisu テニス tennis 7
tenken(suru) 点検(する) check, examine 12
tenki 天気 weather 6
tenki-yohoo 天気予報 weather report 15
tenpura 天ぷら tempura: delicately deep-fried vegetables and seafood 10
tenrankai 展覧会 exhibition 15
terebi テレビ television 1
terebi o miru テレビを見る watch TV 4
tesuto テスト test, examination 6
tetsudau 手伝う help 10
to と and (for nouns, complete) 3, with sbd 5
to 戸 door
tobu 飛ぶ fly, jump 5
toire トイレ toilet 12
tokei 時計 clock 1
toki 時 time when (temporal) 12
tokidoki ときどき sometimes 4
tokoro 所 place 3
tokorode ところで by the way 7
tokui(na) とくい(な) strength 10
tomaru 止まる hold 7
tomaru 泊まる stay overnight 13
tomeru 止める stop 7
tomodachi 友達 friend(s) 5
tonari となり next to 3
toodaiji 東大寺 Todaiji temple in Nara 6
tooi 遠い far, distant 2
tookaidoo 東海道 route from Edo to Kyoto or Osaka 15
tooki 陶器 porcelain 14
tooru 通る drive past, walk through 5
toori 通り street
tori 鳥 bird
toriniku 鶏肉 chicken
toru 取る take
toshi 年 year
toshite として as
toshokan 図書館 library 2
totemo とても very 2
tsugi 次 next 15
tsugoo 都合 opportunity, circumstance 13
tsuite (に)ついて about 〜 13

tsukau 使う use 7
tsukeru 点ける turn on, switch on 7
tsuku 点く turn on (light) 7
tsuku 着く arrive 12
tsukue 机 table 3
tsukuru 作る make, cook 7
tsumetai 冷たい cold (objects) 12
tsumori つもり plan 14
tsureteiku 連れて行く take along (people, animals) 7
tsuretekuru 連れて来る bring along (people, animals) 7
tsuri 釣り fishing 14
tsutomeru 勤める work
tsuuyaku 通訳 interpreting 13
tsuyoi 強い strong 6
tsuzuku (～が)続く continue 4

U

uchiawase 打ち合わせ previous discussion 13
udedokei 腕時計 watch 10
ue 上 up, above, over 3
ueno 上野 Ueno (district of Tokyo) 7
ugoku 動く move
ukiyoe-shi 浮世絵師 Ukiyoe master 15
ukiyoe-ten 浮世絵展 Ukiyoe exhibition 15
uma 馬 horse 3
umai うまい good, delicious
umareru 生まれる be born 15
umi 海 sea 5
un, うん, ja (around) 9
unchin 運賃 travel costs 7
down(suru) 運転(する) driving a car 10
untenshu 運転手 driver
ureshii うれしい cheerful, happy, rejoice 12
uru 売る sell 7
urusai うるさい loud in a negative sense 9
ushiro 後ろ behind, behind 3
usui 薄い thin
uta o utau 歌を歌う sing songs 10
Utamaro 歌麿 Utamaro: an Ukiyoe master 15
utsukushii 美しい beautiful (appearance) 6
utsurikawaru 移り変わる change, transform 15
uun ううん no (CF) 9
uwagi 上着 jacket 9

W

wa 羽 counting word for bird
wain ワイン wine 6
waishatsu ワイシャツ shirt 8
wakai 若い young 2
wakakusayama 若草山 Wakakusayama hill in Nara 6
wakarimashita わかりました Agreed, all right! 7
wakaru わかる understand 10
warau 笑う laugh, smile
wareware 我々 we 1
warui 悪い bad 6
washitsu 和室 Japanese room 3
wasureru 忘れる forget 15
wataru 渡る cross 5
watashi tachi 私たち we 1
watasu 渡す one-handed

watashi 私 I, me 1

Y

ya や and (for nouns, incomplete) 3
yakikata 焼き方 way of baking 10
yakimono 焼き物 porcelain 14
yaku 焼く bake, roast, fry 10
yakusoku 約束 promise, appointment
yakusha 役者 actor 15
yakyuu 野球 baseball 6
yama 山 mountain 1
yamanote-sen 山手線 Yamanote line in Tokyo 7
yameru 止める stop
yappari やっぱり after all 11
yaru やる make (CF) 8
yasai 野菜 vegetable 4
yasashii 易しい simple, 優しい kind 6
yasui 安い cheap 2
yasumi 休み break, vacation 11
yasumu 休む take a break 8
yatto やっと finally 9
yawarakai 柔らかい soft 9
yo よ ending particle for emphasis 2
yoko 横 next to, horizontal 3
yoku よく often, a lot 4
yomu 読む read 4
yononaka 世の中 world 15
yoofuku 洋服 European clothes 10
yooshitsu 洋室 European room 3
yori ～より as ～ 6
yorokobu 喜ぶ be pleased about ～
yorokonde よろこんで like 5
yoru 夜 night 13
yotei 予定 plan, intention, appointment 13
yowai 弱い weak
yoyaku(suru) 予約(する) reservation, reserve 8
yuki 雪 snow 11
yume 夢 dream, yume o miru 夢を見る dream
yuube 夕べ last night, evening
yuubinkyoku 郵便局 post 3
yuugata 夕方 early evening
yuumei-na 有名な famous 2

Z

zan'nen(na) 残念(な) unfortunately, too bad 11
zasshi 雑誌 magazine 4
zehi ぜひ absolutely 5
zenbu 全部 everything 8
zenkoku 全国 whole country 11
zenkooji 善光寺 Zenkooji temple 11
zenzen ぜんぜん not at all
zubon ずぼん trousers 9

Vocaburary Index (English – Japanese)

English / Vocabulary (Roomaji) / Japanese / Lession

A

a little / sukoshi 少し 6
a little bit / chotto ちょっと 4
A warm welcome! / irasshaimase いらっしゃいませ 13
about / ~ gurai, ～ぐらい 4, goro ごろ (for time) 4
about / ~ni tsuite (に)ついて 13
above / ue 上 3
abroad / gaikoku 外国 5
ach / aa ああ 2
acquaintance / chijin 知人 11
actor / yakusha 役者, haiyuu 俳優 15
additionally / hoka ni 他に 13
address / juusho 住所
adult / otona 大人
aerobics / earobikusu エアロビクス 10
aeroplane / hikooki 飛行機 5
after ~ / ~ ato de ～後で 12
after a long time / hisashiburi ひさしぶり(に)
afternoon / gogo 午後 4
again / mata また
age / jidai 時代 14
air conditioner, ~ turn on / kuuraa, ~ o tsukeru クーラー～をつける 12
airport / hikoojoo 飛行場
all / min'na みんな 4, zenbu 全部 8
All for my part! / kochira koso こちらこそ 1
All right / wakarimashita わかりました 7
almost / hotondo ほとんど, daitai だいたい
alone / hitori de 一人で 5
already / moo もう 5
also / mo も 1
although / ke(re)do け(れ)ど 9
always / itsumo いつも 4
American / amerika-jin アメリカ人 1
and (for two sentences) / soshite そして 2
and / to と (for nouns, complete) 3, ya や for nouns, incomplete) 3
and then / sorede それで 11
animal / doobutsu 動物 6
animal voice (verb) / naku 鳴く
answer / kotae 答 8
answer / kotaeru 答える 8
anyone / dareka だれか 5
AP for emotion, wish / na な 10
AP for place, time and destination / ni に 3, 4
AP for the direct object / o を 4
AP for the means, AP for the place of action / de で 4
AP for the question, question mark / ka か 1
AP for the subject / ga が 3
AP of question / ka か 1, ka na / ka i ～かな (CF) 12
apartment / apaato アパート 2
appear / ~ ni deru ～に出る
appear / ~ ni deru ～に出る 15
apple / ringo りんご 4
appointment / yoteibi 予定日 13, 約束 appointment
approach / tsuku 点く 7

approximately / gurai ～ぐらい 10
arrive / tsuku 着く 12
art museum / bijutsukan 美術館 7
as / ~ yori ～より 6, ～として
as I thought / yappari やっぱり 11
as it is (i.e. now) / V-ta mama ～まま 12
as much as possible / narubeku なるべく
as well ~ as / onaji gurai ～と同じぐらい 6
ask / kiku 聞く, shitsumon(suru) 質問(する) 8
attraction / midokoro 見所 11
August / hachi-gatsu 8月 6
aunt, slightly older woman / oba, obasan おばさん 13
autumn / aki 秋 6
away / tooi 遠い 2

B

baby / akachan 赤ちゃん 11
bad / warui 悪い 6
badly able / heta(na) 下手(な) 10
bag / kaban かばん 3
bake / yaku 焼く 10
ballpoint pen / boorupen ボールペン 1
bank / ginkoo 銀行 9
Baseball / yakyuu 野球 6
basket / kago かご 12
bath, bathroom / furo ふろ 3
be born / umareru 生まれる 15
be completed / kagi ga kakatteiru 鍵がかかっている 7
be located (for objects) / aru ある 3
be located (for people and animals) / iru いる 3
be reassured / hotto suru ほっとする 9
beautiful / kirei-na きれいな 2, utsukushii 美しい 6
because / ~ kara ～から, node、～ので 7
become / ~ ni naru ～ になる 6
beef / gyuuniku 牛肉 7
beer / biiru ビール 4
before ~ / mae ni ～前に 12
begin / hajimaru 始まる, hajimeru 始める
begin / hajimeru 始める 8
behind / ushiro 後ろ 3
Beijing / pekin 北京 ペキン 15
believe / shinjiru 信じる, omou 思う おもう 13
between / aida 間 3
bicycle / jitensha 自転車 4
bird / tori 鳥
birthday / tanjoobi 誕生日 13
black / kuroi 黒い 11
black tea / koocha 紅茶 4
blossom / saku 咲く 7
blow / fuku 吹く
blue / aoi 青い 11
body / karada 体
body size / se 背 11
Bon festival in August / o-bon お盆 11
book / hon 本 1
bookshelf / hondana 本棚 3
bookshop / hon'ya 本屋 5

borrow / kariru 借りる 5
both / ryoohoo(tomo) 両方(とも)
box / hako 箱
bread / pan パン 4
break / kowasu 壊す, kowareru 壊れる
breakfast / asagohan 朝ご飯 4
breathe a sigh of relief / hotto suru ほっとする 9
bridge / hashi 橋 5
bright / akarui 明るい 7
bring (objects) / mottekuru 持って来る 7
bring along (people, animals) / tsuretekuru 連れて来る 7
brothers and sisters / kyoodai 兄弟 9
brown / chairo 茶色
buckwheat noodles / soba そば 9
build / tateru 建てる 14
building / tatemono 建物 9, biru ビル 15
bus / basu バス 4
bus stop / basu-tei バス停 7
business card / meishi 名刺 1
busy / isogashii 忙しい 6
but (for two sentences) demo でも 2, shikashi しかし
but / ga が 2
butter / bataa バター
button / botan ボタン
buy / kau 買う 4
by (passive) / ~ ni (yotte) ～に(よって)
by the way / tokorode ところで 7

C

Cafè, coffee shop / kissaten 喫茶店 5
cake / keeki ケーキ 7
calculate / keisan 計算(する) 10
calendar / karendaa カレンダー
call / denwa o suru / kakeru 電話をする・かける 12
calm / shizuka-na 静かな 2
camera / kamera カメラ 1
camping / kyanpu camping 11
can / dekiru できる 10
can do well / joozu(na) 上手(な) 10
cap / booshi 帽子, ~ to put on / ~ o kaburu ～を被る 13
capital / shuto 首都, miyako 都 6
car / kuruma 車, jidoosha 自動車 1
carry / hakobu 運ぶ 12,
carry out/ jisshi 実施(する) 14
cat / neko 猫 3
catch a cold / kaze o hiku 風邪を引く 12
CD / shii-dii CD シー・ディー 5
center / chuushin 中心 11
central station / chuuoo-eki 中央駅 7
certain / kitto きっと
certainly / zehi ぜひ 5
chair / isu いす 3
change / kawaru 変わる, kaeru 変える 14
change (bus, train) / norikaeru 乗り変える 7
change (money) / o-tsuri お釣り 7
cheap / yasui 安い 2
cheerful tanoshii 楽しい 6, ureshii うれしい 12
cherry tree, cherry blossom / sakura 桜 1
chicken / toriniku 鶏肉
child / kodomo 子供 3, ko 子 15

chilled / reizooko 冷蔵庫
chinese / chuugoku-jin 中国人 1
chopstick / hashi 箸 12
circle / en 円 7
circular / marui 丸い
city / machi 町 2
city map / chizu 地図 12
class (during lessons) / kurasu クラス 6
classical music / kurasikku クラシック 10
classmate / kurasu-meeto クラスメート 11
classroom / kyooshitsu 教室 3
clean / kirei-na きれいな 2
clean / sooji(suru) 掃除(する)7
clear / hakkiri はっきり CD / shii-dii CD 5
clear up / hareru 晴れる 7
clear up / hareru 晴れる 7
climb / noboru 登る 11
clock / tokei 時計 とけい, ~ji ～時 (time) 4
close / shimaru 閉まる 7
close / shimaru 閉まる 7, ~ o shimeru ～を閉める 8
close / shimeru 閉める 8
clothes / fuku 服 9
cloud / kumo 雲
cloudy / kumori 曇り 11
coat / kooto コート 12
coffee / koohii コーヒー 4
cola / koora コーラ 10
cold (weather) / samui 寒い 6 (items) / tsumetai 冷たい 12
colleague / dooryoo 同僚 11
colour / iro 色
come / kuru 来る 4
company / kaisha 会社 1
company director / shachoo 社長 9
company employee / kaishain 会社員 1
computer / konpyuuta コンピュータ 1
concert / konsaato コンサート 5
conference / kaigi 会議 12
consider / kangaeru 考える 15
consult with / soodan(suru) 相談(する)8
continue / tsuzuku (～が) 続く つづく 4
control / tenken(suru) 点検(する) 12
conversation / kaiwa 会話 12
cooking, dish, cook / ryoori(suru) 料理(する) 5
cool (pleasant) / suzushii 涼しい 12
corner / kado 角
correct / tadashii 正しい ただしい 9, ちゃんと chanto
corridor / rooka 廊下 8
counting word for animals / hiki 匹
counting word for books / satsu 冊
counting word for flat things / mai 枚
counting word for birds / wa 羽
counting word for cup with contents / hai 杯 3
counting word for machine, device, car / dai 台
country / kuni 国 6
course / koosu コース 14
cow's milk / gyuunyuu 牛乳 4
cross over / wataru 渡る 5
crossing / koosaten 交差点 5
cry / naku 泣く

cultural exchange / bunka-kooryuu 文化交流 14
culture / bunka 文化 14
custom / fuuzoku 風俗 15
custom / shuukan 習慣, fuuzoku 風俗 15
customer / o-kyaku(san) お客(さん) 13
cut / kiru 切る
cute / kawaii かわいい 9

D

dance / odoru 踊る, dansu o suru, ダンスをする 5
dangerous / abunai 危ない, kiken-na 危険な 12
dark / kurai 暗い 7
daughter / musume 娘 10
day / hi 日 15
decide / kimeru 決める, decided / kimaru 決まる
deep / fukai 深い
defend / mamoru 守る
delicious / oishii おいしい 6, umai うまい
dentist / haisha 歯医者 はいしゃ 9
department store / depaato デパート 3
desire / negai 願い, nozomu 望む
desk / tsukue 机 3, teeburu テーブル 4
dialogue / kaiwa 会話 かいわ 12
dictionary / jisho, jibiki 辞書、字引き 3
die / shinu 死ぬ 7
different / chigau 違う
different / iroiro(na) 15
difficult / muzukashii 難しい 6
dining room / shokudoo 食堂 14
dinner / bangohan 晩ご飯 4
direction / hoo 方 6, hoogaku 方角
dirty / kitanai きたない 9
disagree / hantai(suru) 反対(する)
dish / shokuji 食事 12
do / suru する 4, yaru やる (CF) 8
do a job / arubaito(suru) アルバイト(する)12
doctor / isha 医者 8
dog / inu 犬 3
doll / ningyoo 人形 10
door / to 戸, doaa ドアー
draw / e o kaku / egaku 絵を描く 15
drawer / hikidashi 引き出し
dream / yume 夢, yume o miru を見る (verb)
drink / nomu 飲む 4
drinks / nomimono 飲み物 4
driver / bottom shu 運転手
during the day / hiruma 昼間

E

ear / mimi 耳 11
early / hayai 早い 6
early evening / yuugata 夕方
earthquake / jishin 地震
east / higashi 東 6
eat / taberu 食べる 4
economy / keizai 経済 10
edo period / edojidai 江戸時代 15
egg / tamago 卵 4
electricity / denki 電気 7
elementary school / shoogakoo 小学校 2

embassy / taishikan 大使館 12
employee / kaishain 会社員 9
end / owaru 終わる 9, owari 終り 15
ending particle for emphasis / yo よ 2
engine, ~ start enjin / ~ o kakeru エンジン, ～をかける 12
English / eigo 英語 1,
English person / igirisu-jin イギリス人 1
Enjoy your meal! / itadakimasu いただきます 13
enter the school / nyuugaku(suru) 入学(する)
entrance / iriguchi 入(り)口 7
entrance hall / genkan 玄関
envelope / fuutoo 封筒
essay / sakubun 作文 10
etc. / nado 等 10
European clothes / yoofuku 洋服 10
European style room / yooshitsu 洋室
evening / ban 晩, yuube 夕べ
evening, in the evening / ban 晩 4, yuube 夕べ
every day / mainichi 毎日 8
every evening / maiban 毎晩
every month / maitsuki 毎月
every week / maishuu 毎週
every year / maitoshi 毎年
everything / zenbu 全部 8, nan demo 何でも 14
exact / choodo ちょうど
exam / shiken 試験 6, tesuto テスト 6
example / rei 例
excellent / rippa 立派 13
Excuse me, please! / sumimasen すみません 7
exercise / renshuu 練習 1
exhibition / tenrankai 展覧会 15
exit / deguchi 出口 7
expect, expectation / kitai(suru) 期待(する) 14
expensive / takai 高い 2
explain / setsumei(suru) 説明(する) 7
extinguish / kesu 消す 7
eye / me 目 11

F

face / kao 顔 11
factory / koojoo 工場 14
fair / mihonichi 見本市 13
fall / ochiru 落ちる
family / kazoku 家族 3
famous / yuumei-na 有名な 2
far / tooi 遠い 2
fast / hayai 速い 2
father / chichi 父 3, otoosan お父さん
favorite / sukina ~ 好きな～ 10
fax / fakkusu ファックス 1
festival / matsuri 祭
fever / netsu 熱
field / hatake 畑, ta 田 (paddy field)1
film / fuirumu フイルム
finalise / kagi o kakeru 鍵を掛ける 8
finally / yatto やっと 9
find / mitsukeru 見つける
finish / owaru 終わる, sumaseru すませる 14, dekiru できる 12
fire / hi 火, kaji 火事 (fire)
first of all / mazu まず 7

fish / sakana 魚 9
fishing / tsuri 釣り 14
flower / hana 花 1
fly / tobu 飛ぶ 5
food / tabemono 食べ物 11
foot / ashi 足
football / sakkaa サッカー 6
for example / tatoeba たとえば 15
for the first time / hajimete 初めて
foreign language / gaikokugo 外国語 10
forest / mori 森 1
forget / wasureru 忘れる 15
fork / fooku フォーク
fountain pen / man'nenhitsu 万年筆 8
France / furansu フランス 6
free / jiyuu(na) 自由(な) , have free / hima 暇 9
French / furansujin フランス人, furansugo フランス語 6
fresh / shinsen-na 新鮮な 12
Friday / kin'yoobi 金曜日 3
friend(s) / tomodachi 友達 5
friendly / shinsetsu-na 親切な 6
from / kara から 4,
from now on / korekara これから 15
from now on / korekara これから 15
fruit / kudamono 果物 4
full / ippai いっぱい, komu 混む
funny / tanoshii 楽しい 6
future / shoorai 将来, mirai 未来

G

game / geemu ゲーム 8
garbage / gomi ごみ 8
garden / niwa 庭 3
gasoline / gasorin ガソリン 12
gate / mon 門
German / doitsugo ドイツ語 1
Germany-person / doitsujin ドイツ人 1
Germany / doitsu ドイツ 1
get / morau もらう 9
get in touch with ~ / renraku(suru) 連絡(する) 13
get on, take a means of transport / noru 乗る 7
get out / oriru 降りる 7
get to know / shiriau 知り合う 1
get up / okiru 起きる(out of bed) 4, tatsu 立つ(from a chair) 8
get used to / nareru 慣れる
give (I, we) ageru あげる, (to me, to us) kureru くれる
glass / cup koppu コップ 7
glasses / megane めがね 15
go / iku 行く 4
go back / kaeru 帰る 4
go enter / ireru 入れる 8
go for a drive / doraibu(suru) ドライブ(する) 9
go for a walk / sanpo(suru) 散歩(する) 5
go home / ie ni kaeru 家にかえる 4
go in / hairu 入る 7
go out / dekakeru 出かける 5, gaishutsu(suru) 外出 (する) 8, kieru 消える (light, fire) 7
go out /deru 出る 4. dete-iku 出て行く 12
go through / tooru 通る 5
go to ~ / ~iki ~行き 15

go to pick up / mukae ni iku 迎えに行く 9
gold / kin 金 6
good / ii いい 2
Good afternoon! / Kon'nichiwa! こんにちは 2
Good morning! / Ohayoo おはよう 13
Good night! / oyasumi(nasai) おやすみ(なさい) 13
Goodbye! / Sayoonara さようなら 8
gradually / dandan だんだん
grammar / bunpoo 文法 9
grandfather / sofu 祖父 13, ojiisan おじいさん 13
grandmother / sobo 祖母 13, obaasan おばあさん 13
green / midori 緑
greeting / aisatsu(suru) 挨拶(する) 1
grove / hayashi 林 1
guest / customer / o-kyaku(san) お客(さん) 13
guide / an'nai(suru) 案内(する)10, an'nai 案内 13
guitar / gitaa ギター 12, play ~ / ~ o hiku ~を弾く 10

H

hair / kami 髪 11
half / hanbun 半分 half , han 半 (time) 4
hand / te 手
hand over / dasu 出す
handed / watasu 渡す
hang up / kakeru かける 15
happy / ureshii うれしい 12, shiawase 幸せ
happy about ~ / yorokobu 喜ぶ
Happy birthday to you! / o-tanjoobi omedetoo お誕生日おめでとうございます 13
hat / booshi 帽子, ~ put on / ~ o kaburu ~を被る 13
he / kare 彼 1
head / atama 頭 11
head of department / buchoo 部長 8
head of the small department / kachoo 課長 9
healthy / genki-na 元気な 2
heating / hiitaa ヒーター 12
heavy (weight) / omoi 重い 6
Hello (on the phone) moshi moshi もしもし / tadaima ただいま greeting those returning home 13
help / tetsudau 手伝う 10
here / koko ここ 1
Here you go! / doo itashimashite どういたしまして 7
high / takai 高い 2
high and wild wave / aranami 荒波 15
history / rekishi 歴史 10
hobby / shumi 趣味
hold / motsu 持つ 7
hold / tomaru 止まる 7
holiday / yasumi 休み 11, kyuuka 休暇
hometown / kokyoo 故郷 11
homework / shukudai 宿題 5
hope / kiboo 希望 きぼう 11, negai 願い
horizontal / yoko 横 3
horse / uma 馬 3
hospital / byooin 病院 3
hot / karai 辛い
hot /atsui 暑い 6
hotel / hoteru ホテル 9
hour / jikan 時間 じかん 4
house / ie, uchi 家 4

How do you do? / hajimemashite はじめまして 1
how / doo どう, ikaga いかが 2
how expensive / ikura いくら 7
how much / ikutsu, donogurai いくつ、どのぐらい 3
how often / nan-kai 何回 7, nan'do 何度
human / hito 人 1, kata 方
hungry / onaka ga suku お腹がすく
hurry / isogu 急ぐ
husband / (go)shujin ご主人 6

I

I / watashi 私 1, boku ぼく (männlich) 2
I agree! / wakarimashita わかりました 7
I kind request... / o-negai-shimasu お願いします 10
I see. / soo desu ka そうですか 3
ice / koori 氷 6
idea / kangae 考え 11
immediately / sugu すぐ 12
immer / itsumo いつも 4
important / taisetsu(na) 大切(な)
impractical / fuben-na 不便な 2
impressive / inshooteki-na 印象的な 15
in / naka 中 3
in, inside / naka(ni) 中(に) 3、uchi(ni) 内(に)
in der letzten Zeit / saikin 最近
in der Nähe / chikai 近い 2, chikaku ni 近くに 3
indeed / jissai ni 実際に 14
in front of / mae 前 3, in front of the station / eki-mae 駅前 5
in the back of a room / oku 奥 3
in the morning / gozen 午前 4
increase / fueru 増える
industry / koogyoo 工業
influence, ~ exert / eikyoo, ~ o ataeru 影響, ~をあたえる 14
inline-skate / inrain-sukeeto インライン・スケート 10
innen / naka(ni) 中(に) 3、uchi(ni) 内(に)
inner corner / sumi 角
instrument / gakki 楽器, play ~ / ~ o hiku 弾く 12
interest, to be interested / kyoomi, ~ ga aru 興味、~があ る 14
interesting / omoshiroi おもしろい 6, kyoomi-bukai, 味深 い 14
interpreting / tsuuyaku 通訳 13
investigate / shiraberu 調べる 14
island / shima 島
isn't it? / ~ ne ~ね 2
it takes / kakaru かかる 4
It tasted good / gochisoosama ごちそうさま 13
Italian / itariago イタリア語 10
It's not allowed / ikemasen いけません 8, だめです 13

J

jacket / uwagi 上着 9
Japan / nihon 日本 6
Japanese / nihon-jin 日本人 1, nihongo 日本語 1
Japanese food / nihon-ryoori 日本料理 5
Japanese room / washitsu 和室 3
Japanese-German / nichi-doku 日独 14
jogging / jogingu ジョギング 10
joke / joodan 冗談 12
judo / juudoo 柔道 10

juice / juusu ジュース 4
jump / tobu 飛ぶ 5, janpu-suru ジャンプする
just / choodo ちょうど

K

kabuki theater / kabuki 歌舞伎 15
kana (hiragana and katakana) / kana かな 5
kanji (Chinese characters) / kanji 漢字 5
key / kagi 鍵 7
kimono (traditional Japanese clothes) / kimono 着物 6
kiosk / baiten 売店 7
kitchen / daidokoro 台所 3
knife / naifu ナイフ
know / shiru 知る 7
koala bear / koara コアラ 11
Kyoto (city) / kyooto 京都 6

L

ladies and gentlemen / minasan 皆さん
lake / mizu'umi 湖
landscape / keshiki 景色 12, fuukei 風景 15
lang / nagai 長い 3
language / kotoba ことば, gengo 言語
large / ookii 大きい 2
large Buddha statue / daibutsu 仏 6
large family / dai-kazoku 大家族 3
last month / sengetsu 先月 13
last week / senshuu 先週 6
last year / kyonen 去年
late / osoi 遅い 13
lately / saikin 最近
later / ato de 後で 6
Latin characters / roomaji ローマ字 8
laugh / warau 笑う
law / hooritsu 法律 10
lay / oku 置く
learn / benkyoo(suru) 勉強(する) 4, narau 習う (from a teacher) 7
leave / saru 去る, deru 出る 4
left / hidari 左 3
leg / ashi 足
lend / kasu 貸す 10
letter / tegami 手紙 7
library / toshokan 図書館 2
life / seikatsu 生活 15
lift up / ageru 上げる
light (weight) karui 軽い 6
light / denki 電気 7, akari あかり
like / suki 好き 10
like very much / dai-suki(na) 10
listen / kiku 聞く 4
little / sukunai 少ない 6
live / sumu 住む 7
live quietly / nonbiri-suru のんびりする 14
lively / ikiiki いきいき 15
living room / ima 居間 11
long / nagai 長い 3
long time / nagai aida 長い間 15
long time no see. / hisashiburi desu ひさしぶりです
look up / shiraberu 調べる 14

lose (game) / makeru 負ける
loud in a negative sense / urusai うるさい 9
lover / my friend / koibito 恋人 11
low / hikui 低い
luggage / nimotsu 荷物 12
lunch / hirugohan 昼ご飯 4

M
machine / kikai 機械 7
magazine / zasshi 雑誌 4
make / suru する 4, yaru やる 8
make / tsukuru 作る 7
make a mistake / machigaeru 間違える
make a phone call / denwa o kakeru 電話をかける 12
make an effort / ganbaru がんばる 9
man / otoko 男, otoko no hito 男の人 1
map / city map chizu 地図 12
marry / kekkon(suru) 結婚(する) 7
mathematics / suugaku 数学 10
meaning / imi 意味 15
means of transportation / norimono 乗り物 6
meat / niku 肉 10
medicine / kusuri 薬 8
meet / ~ ni au ~に会う 5
meeting / kaigi 会議 12
memorise / oboeru 覚える 9
middle school / chuugakkoo 中学校 3
milk / miruku ミルク 4, gyuu'nyuu 牛乳
mine / omou 思う 13
minute / fun 分 4
miso paste / miso みそ 11
miso soup / miso-shiru みそしる 4
mobile phone / keitai-denwa 携帯電話 12
Monday / getsuyoobi 月曜日 3
money / o-kane お金 7
month name / gatsu ～月
months / kagetsu ～か月 3
morning, in the morning / asa 朝 4
mostly / taitei たいてい 10
mother / haha 母, okaasan お母さん 3
Mount Everest / eberesuto-san エベレスト山 6
Mount Fuji / fuji-san 富士山 1
mountain / yama 山 1
mouth / kuchi 口
move / ugoku 動く
move (house) / hikkosu 引っ越す
movie / eiga 映画 5
Mr. ~, Mrs. ~ (name suffix) / san ～さん 1
much / ooi 多い 6, takusan たくさん 9
museum / hakubutsukan 博物館
music / ongaku 音楽 4

N
name / namae 名前 1
Nara (city) / nara 奈良 6
narrow / semai 狭い
naturally / mochiron もちろん 10, shizen(na) 自然(な)
near / chikai 近い 2
nearby / chikai 近い 2, chikaku ni 近くに 3
necessary / hitsuyoo(na) 必要(な)

need / iru 要る
new / atarashii 新しい 2
new year / shoogatsu 正月 11
news / nyuusu ニュース
newspaper / shinbun 新聞 1
next / tsugi 次 15
next month / raigetsu 来月 10
next time / kondo 今度 5
next to / tonari となり, yoko 横 33
next week / raishuu 来週 10
next year / rainen 来年
nice weather / hare 晴 11
night / yoru 夜 13
no / iie いいえ L1, uun, iya (CF) L.9
no problem / daijoobu だいじょうぶ 9
No thanks! / iie, kekkoudesu. いいえ、けっうです。
No, not yet / iie, mada desu いいえ、まだです 5
nobody ~ / daremo ~ だれも～ません 3
nobody is there / dare mo imasen だれもいません 3
noon, midday / hiru 昼 4
normal / futsuu 普通
north / kita 北 6
nose / hana 鼻 11
not as ~ as / hodo ~ nai ほど～ない 6
not at all / zenzen ~ nai ぜんぜん～ない
not like / kirai(na) 嫌い(な)10
not so much / amari ~ masen あまり～ません 2
notebook / nooto ノート 3, techoo 手帳 7
nothing / nani mo ~nai 何も～ません(ない) 3
novel / shoosetsu 小説 12
now / ima 今 3
now ~ / saa さあ
nowhere / doko nimo ~nai どこにも～ない 5
number / bangoo 番号, ~ ban ～番 6
number 1, here: Word for superlative / ichiban 一番 6
nurse / kangofhi 看護士 10

O
of course / mochiron もちろん 10
office / jimusho 事務所 15
often / yoku よく 4
oh! / hee へえ 13
old / furui 古い 2
older brother / ani 兄, oniisan お兄さん 3
older sister (own) / ane 姉, oneesan お姉さん 3
olympics / orinpikku オリンピック 14
on / ue 上 うえ 3
on foot / aruite 歩いて 4
once again / moo ichido もう一度
one more / moo hitotsu もう一つ 12
one year / ichi-nen 一年 6
oneself/ jibun 自分
only / dake だけ, shika しか 3
open / aku, hiraku 開く 7, akeru 開ける 8
opportunity / circumstance tsugoo 都合 13
opposite / mukai 向かい 3
ordinary / kichinto きちんと, ちゃんと 12
originally / motomoto もともと 15
other side / mukoo-gawa 向こう側
outside / soto 外 そと 12

over there / asoko あそこ 1, mukoo 向こう

P

packed lunch / bentoo 弁当 10
page / peeji ページ
paint a picture / e o kaku / egaku 絵を描く 10
paper / kami 紙 3
parcel, package / nimotsu 荷物 12
parents' house / jikka 実家 12
park / kooen 公園 3
participate / sanka-suru 参加する 14
party / paatii パーティー 6
pass by / tooru 通る 5
pause / yasumi 休み 11
pay / okane o ~ 払う、お金をはらう 8
pay money / okane o harau お金を払らう 8
pen / pen ペン 7
pencil / enpitsu 鉛筆 1
people / hitobito 人々 15
performance / seiseki 成績 9
person / hito 人 1, kata 方
photo / shashin 写真
pictures of beautiful women / bijinga 美人画 15
ping pong / pinpon ピンポン 10
pity / zan'nen(na) 残念(な)11
pizza / pittsa ピッツァ 9
place / tokoro ところ 3
place next to each other / naraberu 並べる
place of production / sanchi 産地 14
plan / yotei 予定, keikaku 計画, V-tsumori つもり 14
plate / sara 皿
play / asobu 遊ぶ 12
Please give me ~! / ~ o kudasai ～をください 7
Pleased to meet you / doozo yoroshiku どうぞよろしく 1
poem / shi 詩 10
police / keisatsu 警察 12
police station / kooban 交番
policeman / keikan 警官
polish / migaku 磨く 12
polite prefix for nouns / o- お 2
politics / seiji 政治 10
pond / ike 池 14
popularity, to be popular / ninki 人気 9
porcelain / tooki 陶器 とうき, yakimono 焼き物 14
pork / butaniku 豚肉 7
post / yuubinkyoku 郵便局 3
postcard / hagaki はがき 7
power / chikara 力 11
practical / benri-na 便利な 2
pre-meeting / uchiawase 打ち合わせ 13
press / osu 押す
pretty / good kekkoo けっこう, かなり 9
price / nedan 値段 8
probably / tabun たぶん
professor / kyooju 教授 9
promise / yakusoku(suru) 約束(する）
protect / mamoru 守る
pull / hiku 引く
pupil / seito 生徒 1
purse, wallet / saifu 財布

put / oku 置く
put on / kiru 着る(clothes) 8, haku はく(trousers, shoes), かぶる 1 (hat, cap) 3
question / shitsumon 質問, mondai 問題 9

R

radio / rajio ラジオ 7
railroad employee / eki'in 駅員 7
railroad station / eki 駅 2
rain, raining / ame, - ga furu 雨、～が降る 7
rare / mezurashii 珍しい, mettani V- nai めったに～ない 11
read / yomu 読む 4
reading books / dokusho(suru) 読書(する)12
really / hontoo 本当 12, really jissai (ni) 実際(に) 14
reason / riyuu 理由
red / akai 赤い 13
refridgerator / reizooko 冷蔵庫
relationship / kankei 関係
relaxation / ikinuki 息ぬき 9
repair / shuuri(suru) 修理(する) 10
report / repooto レポート 14
reserve / yoyaku(suru) 予約(する) 8
restaurant / resutoran レストラン 7, shokudoo 食堂 14
return / kaesu 返す 10
revived / nigiyaka-na にぎやかな 6
rice rice (cooked) / gohan ご飯 4
rice rice (uncooked) / kome 米
rice bowl / chawan 茶碗
right / migi 右 3
river / kawa 川 1
roast / yaku 焼く 10
Rome / rooma ローマ 12
room / heya 部屋 3
rose / bara ばら 1
route description / ikikata 行き方 7
run / hashiru 走る 5
Russia / roshia ロシア 6

S

sake (rice wine) / osake お酒 4
salesperson / ten'in 店員 6
salt / shio 塩 9
same / onaji 同じ 6
Saturday / doyoobi 土曜日 3
say / iu 言う 8
school / gakkoo 学校 2
sea / umi 海 5
search / sagasu 探す
seasons / kisetsu 季節 6
seat / seki 席 せき 8, saseki 座席
see / miru 見る 4
sell / uru 売る 7
send / okuru 送る
serve tea / o-cha o ireru お茶を入れる 10
shamed / hazukashii はずかしい
she / kanojo 彼女 1
shelf / tana 棚
shift, move / enki 延期(する)14
Shinkansen (jap. bullet train) / shinkansen 新幹線 13
ship / fune 船 5

shirt / waishatsu ワイシャツ 8
shoes / kutsu 靴 5
shopping / kaimono(suru) 買い物(する) 4
short / mijikai 短い 11
shortly after ~ (time) / sugi ～過ぎ 4
show / miseru 見せる
shower / shawaa シャワー 3
shrine / jinja 神社
sick, sickness, illness / byooki 病気 11
side / k(g)awa 側, right side / migigawa 右側, left side /
hidarigara 左側
silver / gin 銀 6
simple / kantan-na 簡単な, yasashii やさしい 6
sing songs / uta o utau 歌を歌う 10
sit down / suwaru 座る 8
ski / sukii スキー 10
skillful / joozu(na) 上手(な) 10
sky / sora 空 5
sleep / neru 寝る 4
sleepy / nemui 眠い 12
slippers / surippa スリッパ
slowly / osoi 遅い 13, sorosoro そろそろ
small / chiisai 小さい 2
small boat / kobune 小船 15
smoking / tabako o suu たばこを吸う 8
snow / yuki 雪 11
so / jaa じゃあ 5, dewa では, soredewa それでは 8
so / soo そう 1
so was / gurai ～ぐらい 10
soap / sekken せっけん
socks / kutsushita 靴下 5
sofa / sofaa ソファー 3
soft / yawarakai 柔らかい 9
something / nanika 何か 13
sometime / itsuka いつか
sometimes / tokidoki 時々 ときどき 4
somewhere / dokoka どこか 5
son / musuko 息子 10
sound / oto 音 12
with pleasure / yorokonde 喜んで 5
sour / suppai すっぱい
south / minami 南 6
soy sauce / shooyu しょうゆ
spaghetti / supagettii スパゲティー 9
speak / hanasu 話す 5
spend the night / tomaru 泊まる 13
spoon / supuun スプーン
sports / supootsu スポーツ 7
spring / haru 春 6
square / basho 場所, seki 席 せき 8
stable / joobu(na) 丈夫(な)
stairs / kaidan 階段
stamp / kitte 切手 5
stand / tatsu 立つ 8
stand next to each other / narabu 並ぶ
start / hajime 始め 6
stay, stay / taizai 滞在(する) 14
stereo system / sutereo ステレオ 1
still bigger / motto ookii もっと大きい 6

stop / chuushi(suru) 中止(する)14, tomaru 止まる
stop / tomeru 止める 7
store / mise 店 14
straight / massugu まっすぐ 7
strange / hen-na 変な, okashii おかしい 12
street / michi 道 5, toori 通り
strength / tokui(na) とくい(な) 10
strenuous / taihen(na) 9
strong / chikara-zuyoi 力強い 15
strong / tsuyoi 強い 6
student / gakusei 学生 1
student abroad / ryuugakusei 留学生 11
study abroad / ryuugaku(suru) 留学(する) 11
subway / chikatetsu 地下鉄 ちかてつ 7
success, ~ have / seikoo 成功(する) 14
such / kon'na こんな, son'na そんな
sugar / satoo 砂糖 8
suit / sebiro 背広 15
sukiyaki, one-pot dish / sukiyaki すきやき 15
summer / natsu 夏 6
summer vacation / natsuyasumi 夏休み
sun / hi 日, taiyoo 太陽 15
Sunday / nichiyoobi 日曜日 3
super / sugoi すごい 13
supermarket / suupaa スーパー 2
sushi / sushi 寿司 5
sweater / seetaa セーター 8
sweet / amai 甘い
sweets / okashi お菓子 4, amaimono 甘いもの 10
swim / oyogu 泳ぐ 5, swim / suiei 水泳 10
swimming pool / puuru プール 11
switch on / tsukeru 点ける 7

T
table / tsukue 机 3, teeburu テーブル 4
take / toru 取る
take a break / yasumu 休む 8
take a photo / shashin o toru 写真を撮る 10
take along (objects) / motteiku 持って行く 7
take along (people, animals) / tsureteiku 連れて行く 7
take care / chuui(suru) 注意(する)
take out / dasu 出す 12
tangerine / mikan みかん 4
taste / aji 味
taste bad / mazui まずい 9
tasty / oishii おいしい 6
taxi / takushii タクシー 8
tea / ocha お茶 4
teach / oshieru 教える 7
teacher / sensei 先生 1
technique / gijutsu 技術
telephone / denwa 電話 3
telephone number / denwa-bangoo 電話番号 3
television / terebi テレビ 1
temple / (o)tera (お)寺 11
ten thousand / man 万
tennis / tenisu テニス 7
test / tesuto テスト 6
test scores / seiseki 成績 9
textbook / kyookasho 教科書 5

Thank you very much! / arigatoo gozaimasu ありがとうございます 1
that with me / kore これ 1
that with you / sore それ 1
that over there / are あれ 1
the day after tomorrow / asatte 明後日
the day before yesterday /- ototoi おととい
The light goes on /denki ga tsuku 電気が点く 7
the other day / kono aida この間 9
the person over there / achira 1
the person with you / sochira 1
the year after next / sarainen 再来年
theme / teema テーマ 14
then / sorekara それから 3
there (with you) / soko そこ 3
there (ober there) / asoko あそこ 1
therefore / desukara ですから 4, dakara だから
thick / futoi 太い (long things), atsui 厚い (flat things, futotte iru 肥っている (body)
thin / hosoi 細い (long thing) 6, usui 薄い (flat thing)
thing / koto こと, mono もの 15
think / omou 思う 13, kangaeru 考える 15
this evening / konban 今晩 13
this month / kongetsu 今月 15
this morning / kesa 今朝
this person / kono hito この人, kochira こちら 1
this time / kondo 今度 5
this week / konshuu 今週 6
this year / kotoshi 今年
thought / kangae 考え 11
three / san 三, mittsu 三つ 3
throw away / suteru 捨てる 8
Thursday / mokuyoobi 木曜日 3
ticket / kippu 切符 7
tidy up / katazukeru 片付ける 10
tie, necktie / nekutai ネクタイ 8
time / jikan 時間 4
time / kai ～回 11
tired / sleepy nemui 眠い 12
to ~ look forward to / tanoshimi desu 楽しみです 14
to be afraid / kowai こわい
today / kyoo 今日 3
together / issho ni いっしょに 5
toilet / o-tearai お手洗い, toire トイレ 12
tomorrow / ashita, asu 明日 5
tooth, brush teeth / ha, ~ o migaku 歯, ～をみがく 12
toy / omocha おもちゃ 10
traffic light / shingoo 信号 13
train / densha 電車 1
transform / utsurikawaru 移り変わる 15
transport hakobu 運ぶ 12
travel / ryokoo 旅行, ryokoo (suru) 旅行(する) 6
travelling cost / unchin 運賃 7
tree / ki 木 1
trousers / zubon ずぼん 9
trouser pocket / poketto ポケット
true / hontoo(no) 本当(の) 12
Tuesday / kayoobi 火曜日 3
tuna / maguro まぐろ 13
turn off / magaru 曲がる 7

turn on the light / denki o tsukeru 電気を点ける 7
twenty years old / hatachi 二十歳

U

Ukiyoe exhibition / ukiyoe-ten 浮世絵展 15
Ukiyoe master / ukiyoe-shi 浮世絵師 15
umbrella / kasa 傘 7
uncle, somewhat older man / oji, ojisan おじさん 13
under / shita 下 3
understand / wakaru わかる 10, rikai(suru) 理解(する)
undress / nugu 脱ぐ
unfortunately / zan'nen(na) 残念(な) 11, fuun(na) 不運(な)
uniform / seifuku 制服 12
university / daigaku 大学 1
unpleasant / iya(na) いや(な)
unskilful / heta(na) 下手(な) 10
upper / ue 上 3
use / tsukau 使う 7
until / made まで 4

V

vacation / kyuuka 休暇, yasumi 休み 11
vase / kabin 花瓶
vegetable / yasai 野菜 4
very / totemo とても, taihen 大変 2, hijooni 非常に
video / bideo ビデオ 1
viewing cherry blossoms / hanami 花見 9
village / mura 村 6
visible / mieru 見える
visit / kengaku(suru) 見学(する), visit / otozureru 訪れる, kenbutsu(suru) 見物(する)12
voice / koe 声
volleyball / bareebooru バレーボール 10

W

watch television / terebi o miru テレビを見る 4
wait / matsu 待つ 7
walk / aruku 歩く 4, aruite iku 歩いていく
wall / kabe 壁
want to have / ほしい hoshii 10
war / sensoo 戦争
warm / atatakai 暖かい 15
wash / arau 洗う 12
washing clothes / sentaku(suru) 洗濯(する) 7
water / mizu 水 4
way to bake ~ / yakikata 焼き方 10
we / watashitachi 私たち, wareware 我々 1
weak / yowai 弱い
weakness / nigate(na) 苦手(な) 10
wear / kiru 着る (clothes), haku はく (pants, shoes, socks)
weather / tenki 天気 6
weather report / tenki-yohoo 天気予報 15
Wednesday / suiyoobi 水曜日 3
week / shuu 週 3
weekend / shuumatsu 週末 5
west / nishi 西 6
what / nan, nani 何 1
What do you mean / Nan datte? 何だって？12
what kind of / nan no 何の 1, don'na どんな 2
What please? / Nan datte? 何だって？12

what time / nan-ji 何時 4
when / itsu いつ 5
when / toki 時 12
where / doko どこ 1, dochira どちら 1
which / dono どの, dochira どちら 1
while ~ / ~ aida ～間, ~ nagara ～ながら 12
white / shiroi 白い 11
who / dare だれ 1, donata どなた 1
whole centre / man'naka まん中
whole country / zenkoku 全国 11
whose / dare no だれの 1
why /dooshite どうして 7, naze なぜ
wide / hiroi 広い 11
wife of the other person / okusan 奥さん 6
win / katsu 勝つ
wind / kaze 風 12
window / mado 窓 8
wine / wain ワイン 6
winter / fuyu 冬 6
wish / kiboo(suru) 希望(する) 11
with / ~で means 4, ~と with someone 5
with full force / isshookenmei 一生懸命
without problem / buji 無事 15
woman / on'na no hito 女の人 1
wonderful / subarashii すばらしい 15
word (s) / kotoba ことば, tango 単語
work / shigoto 仕事 5, hataraku 働く 4, tsutomeru 勤める
work of art / geijutsu-hin 芸術品 14
world / sekai 世界 6, yononaka 世の中 15
wristwatch / udedokei 腕時計 10
write / kaku 書く 5
wrong / chigau 違う, machigau 間違う

Y
Yamanote line in Tokyo / yamanote-sen 山手線 7
year / toshi 年, ~ nen ～年 3
year before last / ototoshi 一昨年
years old / sai 才 3
yellow / kiiroi 黄色い
Yen / en 円 7
yes / hai, ee, un はい, ええ, うん (CF.) 2
yesterday / kinoo / sakujitsu 昨日 5
yet / mada まだ 5
you / anata あなた (singular), anatatachi あなたたち
(plural) 1, kimi 君
young / wakai 若い 2
younger brother / otooto 弟 3
younger sister / imooto 妹 3
You're welcome! / doo itashimashite どういたしまして 7

Z
zero / rei 零
zoo / doobutsuen 動物園 7

Important kanji writing rules

1. Write stroke from left to right.

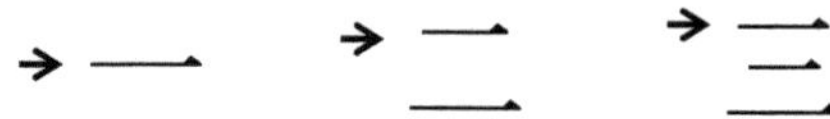

2. Write the line from left to right.

3. For the cross, first write horizontally, then vertically.

4. Write the left part first.

5. Shinnyoo ⻌ is written last.

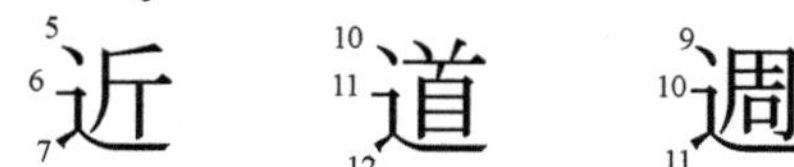

6. Write the upper part first.

7. For the top left corner, first write vertically, then horizontally.

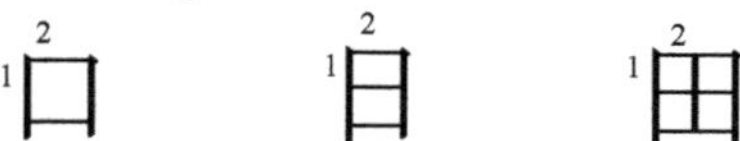

8. Write the top right corner in one stroke.

9. Write the bottom left corner in the same way in one stroke.

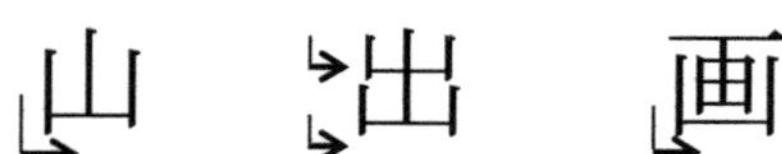

10. However, write the bottom line of the box for the bottom left corner separately and last.

11. Start at the top left if a kanji has several components.

12. If the line in the middle is continuous from top to bottom, write it last.

13. If a kanji - like point 12 - still has two slanted strokes at the bottom, after the continuous stroke, write the left stroke first, then the right stroke.

来 東 末

See the kanji list below, as there are further rules.

Kanji stroke order

L1	日	本	人	山
川	田	木	林	森
L2	大	小	高	新
古	近	元	気	有
名	前	町	学	校
花	**L3**	一	二	三
四	五	六	七	八

九	十	百	千	万
上	下	中	犬	L4
何	時	間	半	分
食	出	会	社	電
車	行	来	読	聞
L5	外	国	語	私
友	公	園	空	海

見	買	起	飲	話
書	走	L6	天	旅
東	西	南	北	寺
父	母	番	便	利
少	多	安	若	悪
L7	左	右	雨	目
円	金	今	口	駅

週	員	入	住	知
教	持	L8	先	生
水	土	病	院	毎
午	後	勉	強	休
始	乗	使	開	閉
L9	月	火	男	女
子	兄	弟	家	手

足	映	画	紙	答
長	待	作	L10	歌
音	楽	形	自	転
牛	肉	魚	料	理
方	仕	事	好	運
泳	L11	白	黒	赤
青	正	回	度	市

年	夏	冬	心	野
物	姉	妹	帰	広
L12	練	習	部	屋
窓	荷	暑	静	変
当	立	引	寝	遊
動	働	L13	朝	夜
店	客	京	都	明

親	切	言	思	合
打	着	終	L14	茶
文	化	交	流	代
歴	史	芸	術	品
参	加	止	調	計
焼	L15	力	意	味
絵	風	景	銀	座

道　船　他　雑　誌

活　美　建

Kanji Index

by stroke count

Kanji	L	On-yomi / *Kun-yomi*

1

Kanji	L	On-yomi / *Kun-yomi*
一	3	ichi / *hito-tsu*

2

Kanji	L	On-yomi / *Kun-yomi*
人	1	jin / nin / *hito*
二	3	ni / *futa-tsu*
七	3	nana, shichi / *nana-tsu*
八	3	hachi / *ya-ttsu*
九	3	kyuu / ku / *kokono-tsu*
十	3	juu / *too*
入	7	nyuu / *hai-ru, i-reru*
力	15	ryoku / *chikara*

3

Kanji	L	On-yomi / *Kun-yomi*
山	1	san / *yama*
川	1	sen / *kawa*
大	2	dai / *oo-kii*
小	2	shoo / *chii-sai*
三	3	san / *mi-ttsu*
千	3	sen
万	3	man
上	3	joo / *ue*
下	3	ge, ka / *shita*
口	7	koo / *kuchi*
土	8	do / *tsuchi*
女	9	jo / *on'na*
子	9	shi / *ko*

4

Kanji	L	On-yomi / *Kun-yomi*
日	1	nichi / ni / *hi*
木	1	moku / boku / *ki*
元	2	gen / gan / *moto*
五	3	go / *itsu-tsu*
六	3	roku / *mu-ttsu*
中	3	chuu / *naka*
犬	3	ken / *inu*
分	4	fun / *wa-keru*
友	5	yuu / *tomo*
公	5	koo / *ooyake*
天	6	ten / *ama*
父	6	fu / *chichi*
少	6	shoo, *suku-nai, suko-shi*
円	7	en / *maru-i*
今	7	kon / *ima*
水	8	sui / *mizu*
午	8	go
月	9	gatsu, getsu / *tsuki*
火	9	ka / *hi*
手	9	shu / *te*
方	10	hoo / *kata*
心	11	shin / *kokoro*
引	12	in / *hi-ku*
切	13	setsu / *ki-ru*
文	14	bun / *aya*
化	14	ka / *ba-keru*
止	14	shi / *to-maru*

5

Kanji	L	On-yomi / *Kun-yomi*
本	1	hon / pon / *moto*
田	1	den / *ta*
古	2	ko / *furu-i*
四	3	shi, yon / *yo-ttsu*
半	4	han / *naka*
出	4	shutsu / *de-ru, da-su*
外	5	gai / *soto*

6

Kanji	L	On-yomi / *Kun-yomi*
北	6	hoku / *kita*
母	6	bo / *haha*
左	7	sa / *hidari*
右	7	yuu, u / *migi*
目	7	moku / *me*
生	8	sei, shoo / *i-kiru, u-mareru*
兄	9	kei, kyoo / *ani*
仕	10	shi / *tsuka-eru*
白	11	haku / *shiro-i*
正	11	sei, shoo / *tada-shii*
冬	11	too / *fuyu*
市	11	shi / *ichi*
立	12	ritsu / *ta-tsu*
打	13	da / *u-tsu*
広	13	koo / *hiro-i*
史	14	shi
代	14	dai / *yo, shiro*
加	14	ka / *kuwa-waru*
他	15	ta / *hoka*

Kanji	L	On-yomi / *Kun-yomi*
気	2	ki
有	2	yuu / u / *a-ru*
名	2	mei, myoo / *na*
百	3	hyaku
会	4	kai / *a-u*
行	4	koo, gyoo / *i-ku*
西	6	sai, sei / *nishi*
寺	6	ji / *tera*
安	6	an / *yasu-i*
多	6	ta / *oo-i*
先	8	sen / *saki*

Kanji	L	On-yomi / *Kun-yomi*
毎	8	mai / *goto*
休	8	kyuu / *yasu-mu*
好	10	koo / *su-ki*
自	10	ji / *mizuka-ra*
肉	10	niku
回	11	kai / *mawa-ru*
年	11	nen / *toshi*
当	12	too / *a-taru, -teru*
合	13	goo, gatsu / *a-u*
交	14	koo / *maji-waru*

7

Kanji	L	On-yomi / *Kun-yomi*
近	2	kin / *chika-i*
町	2	choo / *machi*
花	2	ka / *hana*
何	4	ka, nan / *nani*
社	4	sha / *yashiro*
車	4	sha / *kuruma*
来	4	rai / *ku-ru*
私	5	shi / *watashi*
見	5	ken / *mi-ru*
走	5	soo / *hashi-ru*
利	6	ri / *toshi*
住	7	juu / *su-mu*
医	8	i
男	9	dan, nan / *otoko*
弟	9	tei / *otooto*
足	9	soku / *ashi*
作	9	saku / *tsuku-ru*
赤	11	seki / *aka-i*
言	13	gen, gon / *i-u*
芸	14	gei

8

Kanji	#	Reading
林	1	rin / *hayashi*
学	2	gaku / *mana-bu*
国	5	koku / *kuni*
空	5	kuu / *sora*
東	6	too / *higashi*
若	6	jaku, nyaku / *waka-i*
雨	7	u / *ame*
金	7	kin / *kane*
知	7	chi / *shi-ru*
使	8	shi / *tsuka-u*
始	8	shi, *haji-maru* / *haji-meru*
画	9	ga, kaku
長	9	choo / *naga-i*
泳	10	ei / *oyo-gu*
事	10	ji / *koto*
青	11	sei / *ao-i*
物	11	butsu / *mono*
姉	11	shi / *ane*
妹	11	mai / *imooto*
明	13	mei, myoo / *aka-rui*
夜	13	ya, yo / *yoru*
店	13	ten / *mise*
京	13	kyoo / *miyako*
参	14	san / *mai-ru*
味	15	mi / *ajii*
持	7	ji / *mo-tsu*
後	8	go, *ushiro, ato, nochi*
乗	8	joo / *no-ru*
映	9	ei / *utsu-ru, -su*
待	9	tai / *ma-tsu*
音	10	on / *oto*
度	11	do / *tabi*
屋	12	oku / *ya*
変	12	hen, *ka-eru, -waru*
客	13	kyaku, kaku
思	13	shi / *omo-u*
品	14	hin / *shina*
茶	14	cha, sa
計	14	kei / *haka-ru*
美	15	bi / *utsuku-shii*
風	15	fuu / *kaze*
活	15	katu / *i-kiru*
建	15	ken / *ta-teru*

9

Kanji	#	Reading
前	2	zen / *mae*
食	4	shoku / *ta-beru*
海	5	kai / *umi*
南	6	nan / *minami*
便	6	ben, bin / *tayo-ri*

10

Kanji	#	Reading
高	2	koo / *taka-i*
校	2	koo
時	4	ji / *toki*
起	5	ki / *o-kiru*
書	5	sho / *ka-ku*
旅	6	ryo / *tabi*
員	7	in
勉	8	ben / *tsuto-meru*
病	8	byoo / *yamai*
院	8	in
家	9	ka, ke / *ie*
紙	9	shi / *kami*
料	10	ryoo
夏	11	ka / *natsu*
帰	11	ki, *kae-ru*
流	14	ryuu / *naga-reru*
座	15	za / *suwa-ru*

11

Kanji	#	Reading
悪	6	aku, o / *waru-i*
教	7	kyoo / *oshi-eru*
週	7	shuu
強	8	kyoo / *tsuyo-i*
閉	8	hei / *shi-maru, shi-meru*
理	10	ri / *kotowari*
転	10	ten / *koro-bu*
魚	10	gyo / *sakana*
黒	11	koku / *kuro-i*
野	11	ya / *no*
習	12	shuu / *nara-u*
荷	12	ka / *ni*
窓	12	soo / *mado*
部	12	bu (he)
動	12	doo / *ugo-ku*
都	13	to / *miyako*
終	13	shuu / *o-waru, -eru*
術	14	jutsu
船	15	sen / *fune*

12

Kanji	#	Reading
森	1	shin / *mori*
間	4	kan, ken / *aida, ma*
買	5	bai / *ka-u*
飲	5	in / *no-mu*
番	6	ban
開	8	kai, *hira-ku, a-ku, a-keru*
答	9	too / *kotae*
運	10	un / *hako-bu*
暑	12	sho / *atsu-i*
遊	12	yuu / *aso-bu*
朝	13	choo / *asa*
着	13	chaku / *tsu-ku, ki-ru*
焼	14	shoo / *ya-ku*
絵	15	kai / *e*
景	15	kei, ke / *kage*
道	15	doo / *michi*

13

Kanji	#	Reading
新	2	shin / *atara-shii*
電	4	den
園	5	en / *sono*
話	5	wa / *hana-su*
楽	10	gaku, raku / *tano-shii*
寝	12	shin / *ne-ru*
働	12	doo / *hatara-ku*
意	15	i

14

Kanji	#	Reading
読	4	doku / *yo-mu*
聞	4	bun / *ki-ku*
語	5	go / *kata-ru*
駅	7	eki
歌	10	ka / *uta, uta-u*
練	12	ren / *ne-ru*
静	12	sei / *shizu-ka*
歴	14	reki
銀	15	gin
雑	15	zatsu, zoo
誌	15	shi

15

Kanji	#	Reading
調	14	choo / *shira-beru*

16

Kanji	#	Reading
親	13	shin / *oya, shita-shii*

日本地図　Nihon-Chizu

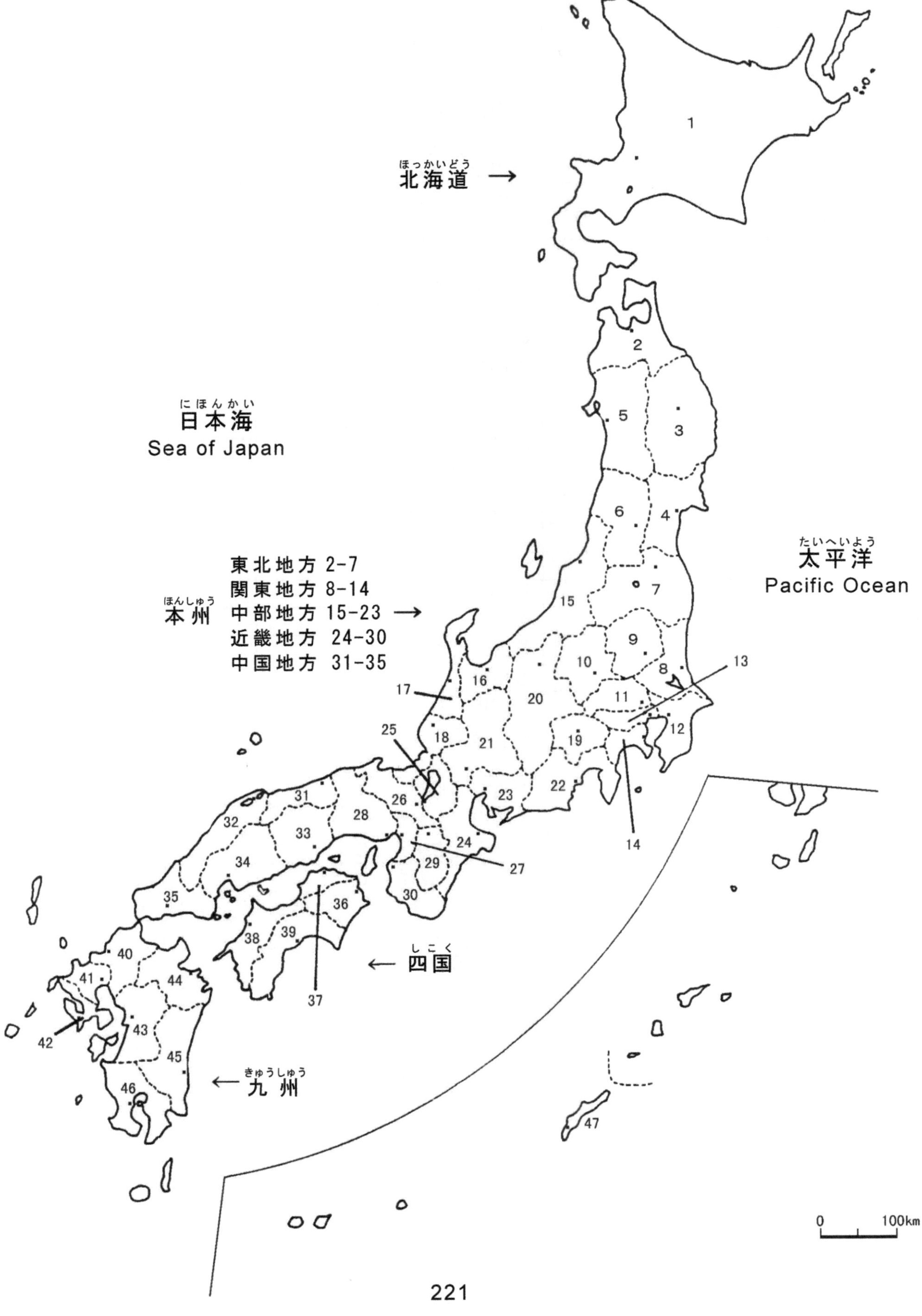

<ruby>地方<rt>ちほう</rt></ruby>、<ruby>県<rt>けん</rt></ruby>、<ruby>県庁所在地<rt>けんちょうしょざいち</rt></ruby>、<ruby>人口<rt>じんこう</rt></ruby>　country, prefecture, capital, population

	県	県庁所在地	人口（2024）
北海道地方　ほっかいどうちほう			
1	北海道　ほっかいどう	札幌市　さっぽろし	5,093,983
東北地方　とうほくちほう			
2	青森県　あおもりけん	青森市　あおもりし	1,205,578
3	岩手県　いわてけん	盛岡市　もりおかし	1,172,349
4	宮城県　みやぎけん	仙台市　せんだいし	2,242,389
5	秋田県　あきたけん	秋田市　あきたし	924,620
6	山形県　やまがたけん	山形市　やまがたし	1,027,509
7	福島県　ふくしまけん	福島市　ふくしまし	1,795,219
関東地方　かんとうちほう			
8	茨城県　いばらきけん	水戸市　みとし	2,865,690
9	栃木県　とちぎけん	宇都宮市　うつのみやし	1,916,787
10	群馬県　ぐんまけん	前橋市　まえばしし	1,919,232
11	埼玉県　さいたまけん	さいたま市　さいたまし	7,378,639
12	千葉県　ちばけん	千葉市　ちばし	6,310,158
13	東京都　とうきょうと	東京都　とうきょうと	13,911,902
14	神奈川県　かながわけん	横浜市　よこはまし	9,208,688
中部地方　ちゅうぶちほう			
15	新潟県　にいがたけん	新潟市　にいがたし	2,137,672
16	富山県　とやまけん	富山市　とやまし	1,019,004
17	石川県　いしかわけん	金沢市　かなざわし	1,109,226
18	福井県　ふくいけん	福井市　ふくいし	752,390
19	山梨県　やまなしけん	甲府市　こうふし	806,369
20	長野県　ながのけん	長野市　ながのし	2,028,135
21	岐阜県　ぎふけん	岐阜市　ぎふし	1,967,862
22	静岡県　しずおかけん	静岡市　しずおかし	3,606,469
23	愛知県　あいちけん	名古屋市　なごやし	7,500,882
近畿地方　きんきちほう			
24	三重県　みえけん	津市　つし	1,757,527
25	滋賀県　しがけん	大津市　おおつし	1,410,534
26	京都府　きょうとふ	京都市　きょうとし	2,488,075
27	大阪府　おおさかふ	大阪市　おおさかし	8,775,708
28	兵庫県　ひょうごけん	神戸市　こうべし	5,426,863
29	奈良県　ならけん	奈良市　ならし	1,315,207
30	和歌山県　わかやまけん	和歌山市　わかやまし	913,297
中国地方　ちゅうごくちほう			
31	鳥取県　とっとりけん	鳥取市　とっとりし	540,207
32	島根県　しまねけん	松江市　まつえし	650,624
33	岡山県　おかやまけん	岡山市　おかやまし	1,851,125
34	広島県　ひろしまけん	広島市　ひろしまし	2,750,540
35	山口県　やまぐちけん	山口市　やまぐちし	1,310,109
四国地方　しこくちほう			
36	徳島県　とくしまけん	徳島市　とくしまし	710,012
37	香川県　かがわけん	高松市　たかまつし	948,585

38	愛媛県　えひめけん	松山市　まつやまし	1,312,298
39	高知県　こうちけん	高知市　こうちし	675,623
九州地方　きゅうしゅうちほう			
40	福岡県　ふくおかけん	福岡市　ふくおかし	5,095,379
41	佐賀県　さがけん	佐賀市　さがし	801,051
42	長崎県　ながさきけん	長崎市　ながさきし	1,289,994
43	熊本県　くまもとけん	熊本市　くまもとし	1,728,098
44	大分県　おおいたけん	大分市　おおいたし	1,112,827
45	宮崎県　みやざきけん	宮崎市　みやざきし	1,058,710
46	鹿児島県　かごしまけん	鹿児島市　かごしまし	1,576,361
沖縄地方　おきなわちほう			
47	沖縄県　おきなわけん	那覇市　なはし	1,485,669
全国　ぜんこく			124,885,175

日本の山　Japanese mountains

	山　mountain	県　prefecture	高さ hight
1	富士山　ふじさん	山梨県　静岡県	3,775 m
2	北岳　きただけ	山梨県	3,193 m
3	奥穂高岳　おくほだかだけ	長野県　岐阜県	3,190 m
4	間ノ岳　あいのだけ	山梨県　静岡県	3,189 m
5	槍が岳　やりがだけ	長野県	3,180 m
6	悪沢岳　わるさわだけ	静岡県	3,141 m
7	赤石岳　あかいしだけ	長野県　静岡県	3,120 m
8	涸沢岳　からさわだけ	長野県　岐阜県	3,110 m
9	北穂高岳　きたほだかだけ	長野県　岐阜県	3,106 m
10	大喰岳　おおばみだけ	長野県　岐阜県	3,101 m

日本の川　Japanese rivers

	川　river	県　prefecture	長さ length
1	信濃川　しなのがわ	新潟県　長野県	367 km
2	利根川　とねがわ	千葉県　茨城県他	322 km
3	石狩川　いしかりがわ	北海道	268 km
4	天塩川　てしおがわ	北海道	256 km
5	北上川　きたかみがわ	宮城県　岩手県	249 km
6	阿武隈川　あぶくまがわ	宮城県　福島県	239 km
7	最上川　もがみがわ	山形県	229 km
8	木曽川　きそがわ	三重県　愛知県他	227 km
9	天竜川　てんりゅうがわ	静岡県　長野県他	213 km
10	阿武隈川　あぶくまがわ	新潟県　福島県	210 km